Lecture Notes in Computer Science 8328

Commenced Publication in 1973
Founding and Former Series Editors:
Gerhard Goos, Juris Hartmanis, and Jan van Leeuwen

Eric Luiijf   Pieter Hartel (Eds.)

Critical Information Infrastructures Security

8th International Workshop, CRITIS 2013
Amsterdam, The Netherlands, September 16-18, 2013
Revised Selected Papers

 Springer

Volume Editors

Eric Luiijf
TNO Defence, Safety and Security
Oude Waalsdorperweg 63, 2597 AK, The Hague, The Netherlands
E-mail: eric.luiijf@tno.nl

Pieter Hartel
University of Twente
Distributed and Embedded Security Group
P.O. Box 217, 7500 AE Enschede, The Netherlands
E-mail: pieter.hartel@utwente.nl

ISSN 0302-9743   e-ISSN 1611-3349
ISBN 978-3-319-03963-3   e-ISBN 978-3-319-03964-0
DOI 10.1007/978-3-319-03964-0
Springer Cham Heidelberg New York Dordrecht London

Library of Congress Control Number: 2013955037

CR Subject Classification (1998): K.6.5, K.4, J.7, C.2, C.4, J.1

LNCS Sublibrary: SL 4 – Security and Cryptology

Typesetting: Camera-ready by author, data conversion by Scientific Publishing Services, Chennai, India

Printed on acid-free paper

Springer is part of Springer Science+Business Media (www.springer.com)

Preface

This volume contains the revised proceedings of the 8th International Workshop on Critical Information Infrastructures Security (CRITIS 2013). The conference was held in the EYE and the Shell Technology Centre Amsterdam, The Netherlands, during September 16–18, 2013. The conference was organized by The Netherlands Organisation for Applied Scientific Research TNO.

CRITIS 2013 continued the now well-established series of successful CRITIS conferences. This conference started with an additional half-day of keynote talks that sought to provide additional perspectives by critical (information) infrastructure (C(I)I) stakeholders such a policymakers, CI operators, and researchers. The focus of the keynote talks was on *resilient smart cities,* which require resilient and reliable information and communication networks. Related notions are resilient smart grids and smart mobility, which are key enablers for smart cities.

The titles of these keynote talks were:

- "Amsterdam, A Smart City" (Ton Jonker, Amsterdam Economic Board)
- "A Hyperconnected World: EYE on the Past, Present and Future" (Henk Geveke, TNO)
- "From Requirements for Critical Industry Sectors Towards Jointly Protecting our Critical Service Chains" (Ben Krutzen, Shell)
- "Smart City, A Vision on 2030" (Max Remerie, Siemens)
- "Future Visions of Super Intelligent Transportation" (prepared by Marie-Pauline van Voorst tot Voorst, Netherlands Study Centre for Technology Trends)

During the main conference, the following keynote talks were held:

- "Future C(I)IP Challenges – A View from the Financial Sector" (Leon Strous, DNB)
- "Smart Cities, a View on Developments" (Giampiero Nanni, Symantec/EMEA)
- "European Critical Internet Infrastructure: Past, Present and Future Research" (Rossella Mattioli, ENISA)
- "From R&D to an International Operational Monitoring Centre: Monitoring the State of Critical Infrastructure(s) Using Sensor Systems" (Robert Meijer; Stichting IJkdijk, University of Amsterdam, and TNO)

All keynote speeches stimulated the debate between CI domain stakeholders and researchers in particular on the nearby and long-term organizational and R&D challenges during the remainder of the conference and hopefully thereafter. A House-of-Commons style debate, which actively involved all conference participants, took the debate another step forward while bridging the views of the CI policymakers, CI operators, and the various research communities.

As in previous years, the technical Program Committee received a large set of paper submissions. The Program Committee provided insightful reviews and comments to the submitters of 57 papers. At least three independent and blind reviews per submission took place resulting in the selection of 16 full papers, yielding an acceptance rate of 28%. Another four submissions were accepted as short papers. All these papers are published in this proceedings volume.

The selected papers and their presentations were grouped in the conference program as New Challenges, Natural Disasters, Smart Grids, Threats and Risk, SCADA/ICS and Sensors, and Short Papers. The same grouping can be found in this volume.

To stimulate international collaboration and exchange of ideas, the program chairs selected a couple of submissions not chosen for the main conference, but nevertheless of considerable value and timeliness. These contributions were discussed in an interactive parallel work-in-progress session. To stimulate collaboration even more, the conference organizers started the building of a Critical Information Infrastructures Security LinkedIn community for young (of mind) researchers: Young CRITIS. The intention is to build a virtual international community that allows junior researchers in the C(I)I domain to interact and network with peers and experienced researchers in the C(I)I domain. It is hoped this will enable researchers to reach faster and better research results and may also lead to further joint international research.

Organizing a conference like CRITIS entails an effort that is largely invisible to the participants. We, therefore, want to acknowledge the personal commitment of the local organizing team, general chairs, the contributions by the keynote speakers, as well as the support of the host organization TNO, the City of Amsterdam, The University of Twente, The Hague Security Delta (HSD), and the Shell Technology Centre Amsterdam (STCA). The Program Committee chairs express their gratitude to the Technical Program Committee members, who volunteered their services and devoted considerable time in preparing insightful reviews and comments to the authors of the papers. Together with the contributions to the discussions and interactions between all conference participants, this resulted in a very successful and stimulating CRITIS 2013.

October 2013   Pieter Hartel
                                                                 Eric Luiijf

CRITIS 2013

8th International Workshop on Critical Information Infrastructures Security

EYE and SHELL Technology Centre
Amsterdam, The Netherlands
September 16–18, 2013

Organized by

TNO Defence, Safety and Security

Executive Committee

Program Chairs

Pieter Hartel	University of Twente and TNO, The Netherlands
Eric Luiijf	TNO, The Netherlands

General Chair

Annemarie Zielstra	TNO, The Netherlands

Honorary Chair

Evangelos Ouzounis	European Network and Information Security Agency, Greece

Publicity Chairs

Cristina Alcaraz	University of Malaga, Spain
Cyril Widdershoven	TNO, The Netherlands

International Program Committee

Cristina Alcaraz	University of Malaga, Spain
Robin Bloomfield	CSR City University London, UK
Sandro Bologna	Associazione Italiana Esperti Infrastrutture Critiche (AIIC), Italy
Stefan Brem	Federal Government, Switzerland
Arslan Brömme	GI / SIG BIOSIG, Germany
Emiliano Casalicchio	Università di Roma "Tor Vergata", Italy

Local Organizing Committee CRITIS 2013

Steering Committee

Chairs

Bernhard M. Hämmerli	University of Applied Sciences Lucerne, GUC Gjøvik and CEO Acris GmbH
Javier Lopez	University of Malaga, Spain

Members

Robin Bloomfield	City University London, UK
Sandro Bologna	AIIC, Italy
Sokratis Katsikas	University of the Aegean, Greece
Reinhard Posch	Technical University Graz, Austria
Saifur Rahman	Advanced Research Institute, Virginia Tech, USA
Roberto Setola	Università CAMPUS Bio-Medico, Italy
Nils Kalstad Svendsen	Gjøvik University College, Norway
Eric Rome	Fraunhofer IAIS, Germany
Stephen Wolthusen	Gjøvik University College, Norway and Royal Holloway, University of London, UK

Table of Contents

Threats and Risk

SCADA/ICS and Sensors

Short Papers

Security Challenges for Cooperative and Interconnected Mobility Systems

Tjerk Bijlsma, Sander de Kievit, Jacco van de Sluis,
Ellen van Nunen, Igor Passchier, and Eric Luiijf

TNO, PO Box 5050, 2600 GB Delft, The Netherlands
{tjerk.bijlsma,sander.dekievit}@tno.nl

Abstract. Software is becoming an important part of the innovation for vehicles. In addition, the systems in vehicles become interconnected and also get external connections, to the internet and Vehicular Ad hoc NETworks (VANETs). These trends form a combined security and safety threat, because recent research has demonstrated a large number of security gaps for in-vehicle systems and their external connections.

This overview paper presents attacker incentives and the most important security risks that are identified for the parts that make up a cooperative mobility system. For cooperative systems, the application data integrity must be validated to determine if values can be trusted. Furthermore, secure alternatives will be required for positioning, in order to be usable by safety critical systems. To create a secure in-vehicle system, it should be secure by design. In addition to the technical challenges, overarching cyber security dilemmas are addressed, such as stimulating the economy vs. improving security. We expect that the discussed risks will be a challenge for research, industry and authorities in the coming years.

Keywords: Cooperative mobility systems, interconnected mobility systems, security, vehicular ad hoc networks, internet, in-vehicle systems.

1 Introduction

A recent trend in automotive innovation is the widespread application of software. In fact, Broy estimates that 80% of the innovation for vehicles is in the form of software [9], where for modern vehicles this software is executed by dozens of microprocessors. Among these microprocessors a variety of applications is executed, ranging from safety critical to infotainment applications. It is expected that in the near future the microprocessors and systems inside a vehicle will get even more interconnected, such that all kinds of information can be exchanged [5,9,12,35].

Another trend that we observe is the increase of connectivity. Vehicles are equipped with wireless interfaces to the internet or to Vehicular Ad Hoc Networks (VANETs) [5,12,10,23]. Examples are the telematics systems of Daimler and Kia that integrate maps, e-call and vehicle diagnostics in the dashboard. These

E. Luiijf and P. Hartel (Eds.): CRITIS 2013, LNCS 8328, pp. 1–15, 2013.
© Springer International Publishing Switzerland 2013

telematics systems use the internet to exchange vehicle status information and to perform emergency calls, resulting into interconnected mobility systems. E-call systems, which send GPS coordinates and airbag status to 112 in case of an accident, will even be mandatory throughout Europe for new vehicles as from 2015. It can be argued that telematics systems form very basic cooperative systems. In cooperative systems vehicles exchange information with each other or the infrastructure, amongst others to increase the road safety and to use the infrastructure more efficiently. It is foreseen that in the near future vehicles will include more extensive cooperative systems [28], for which vehicles will exchange information via VANETs.

These trends, however, present a combined security and safety threat. Recent studies demonstrate a large number of security gaps for current in-vehicles systems and their wireless interfaces [10,22]. These studies showed that once access to an electronic system is gained, it is fairly easy to unlock the car and control the acceleration or brakes. Such a situation is undesirable because 1) the acceptance of vehicle innovations by the society requires that, even though the external connectivity is added, guarantees must be given upon the correct functioning of safety critical systems of a vehicle and 2) exploitation of security breaches could quickly reduce mobility and bring society to a halt. Therefore security of communication and the in-vehicle systems is of utmost importance [1,30]. Insecure systems may even be a show stopper for the roll out of cooperative applications and innovations for vehicles altogether.

Previous and on-going projects have been and are addressing security problems for cooperative and interconnected mobility systems [1,10,21,22,25]. These projects focussed on either identifying risk factors for a part of the cooperative mobility system, or discussing the arising problems.

In this paper, we consider the different parts of cooperative systems and discuss the most important security risk factors for the different parts that make up a cooperative mobility system and make links to national security. In particular, we discuss how security and safety interact in the case of cooperative systems. In addition, we present some incentives an attacker might have to compromise cooperative mobility systems and the related threat in case these systems become widely adopted.

The remainder of this paper will discuss security challenges and threats as follows. Section 2 will present incentives one might have to write malware specifically targeting cooperative systems. Section 3 will relate cyber security to cooperative mobility security and discuss the corresponding risk factors. The security risk factors and challenges for VANETs will be discussed in Section 4 and subsequently Section 5 discusses them for in-vehicle systems. In Section 6 the impact of these risk factors, challenges and counter measures will be discussed. Finally, conclusions will be presented in Section 7.

2   Attack Incentives

In this section, possible incentives for attacking cooperative and in-vehicle systems are discussed. We start from the assumption that although the attacks on vehicle or cooperative systems might be different, the incentives for attackers will be similar to those for attacks on smartphones and personal computers (PCs). In the discussion, first recent trends in malware development are presented, after which these figures are extrapolated to possible incentives for writing malware for cooperative and in-vehicle systems. Our findings are summarized in table 1.

Profit. For both smartphones and PCs we observe a trend towards financially motivated crimeware. Approximately 40% of malware for smartphones generates revenues by by dialing premium numbers, using the built-in payment mechanisms like the app stores, or by cloning the mobile phone. Another 28% generates revenues by stealing personal information and user credentials. Of the former, approximately 15% is capable of intercepting and misusing the more complex two factor authentication of mobile banking. An even smaller portion of malware (less than 5%) generates revenues from ransomware and click fraud. For PCs, the numbers are thought to be somewhat different (in particular the share of premium dialing is much less), but the categories are roughly the same. [14,17]

We expect that these threats translate well to cooperative systems once they come available for two reasons. First, because in-vehicle systems will be profitable targets. These systems will probably contain personal information, banking information (e.g. to perform parking or road tolling payments) and a mobile chip that can be misused for premium services. Moreover, the cooperative system presents another possibility for profit by stealing the vehicle itself. Second, it has been shown that malware writers quickly change targets: virtually no malware existed for smartphones in 2010. Two years later the malware business turned profitable and was producing over 180.000 malware samples a month (January 2012 [11]). Based on these two reasons, it is expected that malware for cooperative systems that generates revenue for the attacker will emerge quickly, once cooperative systems are deployed at a larger scale.

Destruction or Novelty and Amusement. A third of current malware for smartphones can be categorized as destructive [14]. This type of malware is recognized by its capability to turn a smartphone or a PC into a zombie, such that it can be controlled by the attacker. Attackers can group zombies and use them together together in the form of a botnet, which can be used to inflict damage on mobile operators, call centers or internet based services. Smartphones are an especially interesting target for these attacks, due to their always on nature [6]. A related type of malware is the malware that is motivated by novelty or amusement of which the Melissa virus for the PC in 1999 [17] is an infamous example. For smartphones the examples include SMSpacem for Android, which inflicts damage by sending out text messages and Ikee.A for iOS which only changes the wallpaper and is less destructive.

We expect that for cooperative systems both incentives apply. Early in the deployment phase, it is reasonable to expect relatively harmless malware that is similar to the early malware for smartphones and PCs. Once cooperative systems are deployed, it is not difficult to imagine malware that effectively disables safety systems to do harm to the passengers or the reputation of the OEMs (Original Equipement Manufacturer). The motivation for writing such malware could be very similar to that of the Melissa worm and such malware could be the action of a single person. One step further would be malware that is written for or by foreign state bodies or terrorist groups and is aimed at causing large scale damage, social disruption or to spread fear. Due to limited data, extrapolation of this data is mere speculation and the likeliness of such malware is hard to estimate.

Eavesdropping and Espionage. Malware that is substantially less visible is malware that is used for eavesdropping and espionage. Because of its nature, it often goes unnoticed for a long period of time; for that same reason, the numbers on this type of malware are inherently unreliable. What we do know is that smartphones are a particularly interesting target because the victim carries those with him/her at any time and because they are always on.

Table 1. Incentives and likeliness of malware for cooperative systems [14,17]. The shares add up to more than 100%, because malware can have multiple incentives.

Incentive	Share for PCs and phones	Likeliness for cooperative systems
Profit: Premium services	± 40%	Serious
Profit: Information Theft	± 28%	Serious
Profit: Vehicle Theft	None	Probable
Destruction or novelty and amusement	± 33%	Probable
Profit: Ransom & click fraud	< 5%	Minor
Eavesdropping and espionage	Unknown	Minor

We expect that in-vehicle systems will be less interesting targets for eavesdropping and espionage. Mostly because compared to smartphones the window of opportunity to gain data is smaller and little additional data can be gathered from these systems. Therefore, we we expect to see only little espionage and eavesdropping malware for automotive systems.

In conclusion, Table 1 depicts an overview of the incentives. It shows the current share among PCs and smartphones for each of the discussed incentives and the expected threat at the moment cooperative systems become widely adopted. These incentives require consideration, with the abuse of premium rate services and information theft being rated as very likely for future cooperative systems.

3   Mobile Internet Communication

One of the features that has recently found its way into vehicles is a cellular network chip. Whereas, initially these components were using a plain GSM connection to make calls in cases of emergencies, today manufacturers integrate an always-on 3G, soon 4G, data connection to the internet. Such components are used for all sorts of services, such as updating the in-vehicle software, providing real-time routing information, giving the driver the possibility to browse the web and for controlling the locks and other systems of a vehicle from any remote location using e.g. a smartphone [7]. Other driving factors for this data connection could be third party applications, something which some manufacturers [7,18] already allow on their in-vehicle systems. In other words, manufacturers are opening up their closed system to connect to the internet and to third party application developers. In this section, we will discuss the challenges that they will face.

Providing internet access to the in-vehicle systems and to the users poses a number of problems and challenges for the OEMs. They will have to deal with the fact that protection against cyber security threats is a *continuous ongoing and evolving process*: on a daily basis new vulnerabilities might arise resulting in new threats. OEMs will have to develop ways to deal with aging vehicles, aging software and vulnerabilities in their systems; the life cycle management should include the in-vehicle software as well.

Moreover, OEMs will have to find a way to provide sufficient separation between the safety critical components and infotainment services.This separation should make sure that essential system parts can be relied on, even if other parts of the system are compromised. Additionally, a compromised system, should gracefully degrade, such that a reduced set of functionality stays available.

In conclusion, the addition of an internet up-link to vehicles opens up a previously closed system making it vulnerable to common attacks. The severity of the problem is aggravated by the safety critical nature of in-vehicle systems and the potential to harm national security by disabling transportation altogether. The long life cycle of a vehicle poses a challenge for designing secure in-vehicle systems, which is unrivaled in customer IT devices.

4   Vehicular Ad Hoc Networking

VANETs form an important part of the envisioned Intelligent Transport Systems (ITS) [32]. By enabling Vehicles-To-Vehicle (V2V) communication and Vehicle-To-Infrastructure (V2I) communication, VANETs can contribute to a safer and more efficient mobility system and enable a lot of applications. Authorities, road owners, and the driver can benefit from the information exchanged over VANETs. At the same time a security threat emerges, because information is shared between many parties via a wireless medium. This section will discuss problems and proposed solutions for the security of VANETs and conclude with security risk factors.

4.1   Problems and Solutions

For the communication in VANETs, a wireless technology is used, which currently is being standardized, e.g. by CEN, IEEE, and ETSI [15]. These standards govern the communication stack and within that scope also cover topics like privacy and security.

VANETs are particularly difficult to secure due to their rapidly changing topology and their inherently unorganized nature: cars that are proximate at one moment can be far apart the next [32]. Moreover road administrators are national entities by default and therefore no single authority can exist that can handle authentication and authorization for all entities in the network. Nonetheless, an ETSI working group has performed a vulnerability and risk factor analysis for communication in ITS systems in 2010 and has formulated a large list of countermeasures and improvement points for the ITS communication standard [16].

In the ETSI proposal, the challenge of the unorganized nature is overcome by stripping the existing Wi-Fi protocol of its association and authentication procedures. The network can therefore quickly change topology without any necessary procedures. The drawback is that authentication has to be solved at a higher layer. In turn, the security working group has proposed to use certificates which are issued by some Authentication Authority (AA) [15]; whereas this (partially) solves the authorization challenge, it poses a new challenge with respect to certificate revocation and validation, especially in those cases that an internet up-link is not present.

As an example, Figure 1 depicts the steps, from [15], that are required for ITS communication between a vehicle2 and a vehicle1 or a Road Side Unit (RSU). Vehicle2 starts by requesting access to ITS communication with message a), in response the Enrollment Authority (EA) authenticates vehicle2 and grants it access to the ITS communication. To send an ITS message, vehicle2 sends a message to request authoritative proof and a certificate 1), to which the AA responds by providing the proof and a certificate 2). Next vehicle2 sends a message to vehicle1 and the RSU using ITS communication 3). Vehicle1 and the RSU received the message and have to verify the attached certificate by sending it to the AA 4). Possibly the AA has to consult the EA for the verification of the certificate 5), after which it will send a verification of the certificates to vehicle1 and the RSU 6), such that they finally know if the received message can be trusted. The above illustrates the complexity and overhead of using certificates.

An approach similar to the standard in the previous paragraph is described in [22,27]. In addition to the usage of certificates, approaches to safeguard the privacy of the vehicle are described. The privacy can be safeguarded if each vehicle registers a set of key-pairs with the AA and the vehicles change the used key-pairs at predetermined time intervals. Therefore, it is proposed to use a hardware security module, which is clock synchronized with the AA, can securely generate and store key-pairs, can decrypt messages, and can encrypt messages. In addition this module can be ordered by the AA to revoke certificates.

In [22], further research challenges for VANETs are identified. Two of these challenges are data centric trust and privacy. For *data centric trust* the challenge is to determine the trustworthiness of information based on the message, rather than on the communication and sending node. The reasoning is that the topology constantly changes in a VANET, such that messages can travel via multiple vehicles and vehicles can change their identity for privacy reasons. A suggestion to determine if a message can be trusted, is by verifying it with values of local trusted sensors and cooperatively deciding upon it with nearby vehicles. The *privacy* challenge involves preventing vehicles from being tracked. Though

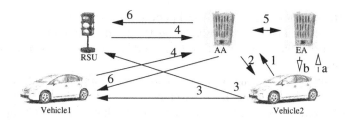

Fig. 1. Steps needed in a VANET for authenticating and sending a message by vehicle2 and verification by the recipients of that message (vehicle1 and RSU)

vehicles switch keys at a given interval, it is still possible to track them to a certain degree. Solving this could require a smaller interval for switching keys, but this increases the overhead for communicating certificates. In other words, the difficult nature of ITS systems causes a complex interplay of solutions and problems. Striking the right balance will remain a future research topic.

4.2   Security Risk Factors

The current standardization efforts on security and ITS focus on securing the data transmission. However, to build a reliable and safe system, also data integrity should be verifiable by other parties and the security of the in-vehicle systems should be considered. The remainder of this section discusses a few examples of data integrity, namely application data integrity, insecure position information, and response latency.

Since standardization focuses on communication security, the *application data integrity* cannot be solved by the security working group of ETSI. An example application for which data integrity is critical is Cooperative Adaptive Cruise Control (CACC) [29], which relies on information that is broadcast over the air. If such an application has no knowledge about the validity of received and observed data, there is little assurance that the application will work as expected; in case that another vehicle would e.g. broadcast a maximum deceleration the following car will brake as well. Kargl [22] proposed to verify received information against values from local sensors. This implies that we have to trust values from local sensors, while it is possible that these sensors are misled. Possibly a solution is described in [13], where direction and speed information retrieved from the physical radio channel are compared with information in the received message. We envision that further integrity validation techniques are a required to determine the likeliness of observed values and guarantee security of the application.

An example of data integrity is *secure position information*. ITS applications often rely on a global navigation satellite system from which insecure position information is used. Even if secured position information from a global navigation satellite system would be used there is a vulnerability for replay attacks. For safety critical applications that react based upon position information, trustworthy position information is a must. In [8] approaches are discussed to securely determine the position using IEEE802.11 communication, such an approach can be implemented by locating beacons along the road. We think that it may be necessary to fuse position information from multiple sources to get a secure and trusted position.

A third challenge is to guarantee the *response latency* for safety critical applications. These applications have strict bounds on the latency that they can accept, e.g. for reading sensor values or receiving packets. The CACC application can tolerate a latency of roughly 20ms for a communicated packet when using a time headway of 250ms. Often a tradeoff has to be made between minimizing the latency for sensor value reception and secure communication with data integrity verification. The effectiveness of cooperative safety critical applications can seriously be reduced by the additional latency of security measures, as depicted in Figure 1. For safety critical applications a careful consideration has to be made, per case, between minimizing communication latency and the degree in which security is required.

In conclusion, the complex nature of VANETs together with the contradicting requirements from the safety critical applications point-of-view and information security point-of-view poses a number of new challenges. Future research will therefore have to focus at finding optimized solutions that fulfill the contradicting requirements and without creating problems elsewhere in the system.

5   In-vehicle Systems

Internally, a modern vehicle contains dozens of microprocessors among which numerous applications are executed, for which often multiple million lines of code have been written [9,25]. For these applications, the microprocessors are interconnected via local networks and external interfaces are used, e.g. to the internet [12,18,23] or to local networks [10]. Due to these external interfaces and local networks, a security threat emerges for in-vehicle systems. It should not be the case that the whole in-vehicle system can be compromised, when one succeeds in compromising an external interface or the local network. As stated in [34], a strong but brittle security system that catastrophically fails is worse than a weaker but ductile system that degrades gradually. Therefore, this section starts by discussing security problems and solutions from literature for in-vehicle systems, subsequently the identified security risk factors are presented.

5.1   Problems and Solutions

Figure 2 provides an overview of the in-vehicle systems and security risk factors. The system parts are contained by boxes and risk factors have arrows pointing to the most relevant system parts. Please note that some security risk factors have partly been discussed in the previous section. In the following paragraphs first the vulnerabilities will be discussed, followed by solutions proposed by literature for the in-vehicle systems.

A number of examples indicate that wireless interfaces to microprocessors in a vehicle are vulnerable. Francillon et. al. [19] demonstrate that modern vehicles

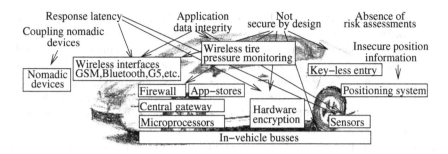

Fig. 2. Overview of in-vehicle systems and security risk factors

can be opened and started by using a so-called relay attack: by placing one antenna near the key and another near the vehicle, the key signal can be relayed to the car over large distances. For this to work, the key does not need to be in the vehicle's vicinity. Another example of a vulnerability in a tire pressure monitoring system is discussed in [31]. They show that due to a faulty authentication it is easy to send fake messages to the receiver in the vehicle for these wireless sensors. Additionally, there is a privacy problem due to the broadcasting of an ID, which makes it possible to track the vehicle. Another vulnerability with which certain vehicles can remotely be unlocked and their alarms can be disabled via GSM, was presented at the Black Hat congress [4] in 2011.

Inside a vehicle, the microprocessors communicate via wired buses or short-range wireless communication channels. Currently, the communication and the software does not include a lot of protection [10,25,35]. Amongst others, it is demonstrated that for a moving vehicle controller area network (CAN) messages can be injected, with which almost the complete vehicle can be controlled, including braking and accelerating.

It is foreseen that in the near future parts of the in-vehicle system will be software upgradable through app-stores likes the ones used by Apple and Google [18,26]. These app-store like systems will require an internet connection or other forms of communication, which makes them vulnerable to attacks over the internet. To guarantee a minimum level of safety, in-vehicle systems that can be upgraded via these app-stores should be designed in a ductile way.

In the near future, nomadic devices will couple to the in-vehicle network [22] to exchange vehicle state information, which will form another vulnerability. Currently mobile devices connect, via e.g. Bluetooth, to a vehicle for hands free calls or to play music. In the future, additional vehicle status information will be communicated to such mobile devices, e.g. to improve their position accuracy with vehicle sensor information. These nomadic devices can run an operating system like Android or iOS, which each have their vulnerabilities. For the Android security mechanisms, Shabtai et al. [33] performed a risk factor analysis, form which they conclude that these make the platform reasonable secure. However, the risk factor analysis indicates that misuse of subscriptions, communication of undesired messages and the disabling of apps or the whole system are threats that are likely to occur. To ensure that a compromised nomadic device is not a threat for the vehicle, an interface to a nomadic device needs protection as well.

Several solutions are proposed to solve vulnerability issues for the communication between microprocessors, via wired or wireless networks. In [3,35] it is proposed to insert a firewall at the CAN bus. Such a firewall can avoid undesired messages, but it has difficulties to detect whether incorrect data is communicated. An additional security measure is proposed in [35], by introducing a central gateway. This gateway distributes certificates and has protected memory to store secret keys for the microprocessors connected to the network. Alternatively, the Internet Protocol (IP), for which many secure protocols are available, could be used for the in-vehicle communication, as proposed by the Seis project [20]. Drawback of this approach is that every microprocessor and sensor interface, even the simple ones, should use the complex IP. In addition, it is questionable if the IP is suitable for the real-time communication of safety critical systems.

The Evita project proposes to use a hardware encryption module [2,21] besides each microprocessor or sensor interface. Such a module encrypts and decrypts messages, is available in a lightweight version and with different degrees of functionality. Such a module can only guarantee that no incorrect software is executed up till a certain degree, because it cannot completely control the microprocessor. In addition such modules should be located next to each microprocessor, which may hamper the coupling between in-vehicle systems and nomadic devices.

5.2   Security Risk Factors

Security measures have been proposed for in-vehicle systems, but these are not often implemented as discussed in the previous section. In addition, coupling nomadic devices or adopting an app-store like system will form a risk factor, since these systems may have a different level of security than what is required by the safety critical systems in a vehicle. This section will present the identified risk factors and their challenges.

A security risk factor that we foresee is the absence of in-vehicle systems that are *secure by design* in combination with increasing wireless connectivity. A solution that is secure by design for an in-vehicle system should provide adequate protection for the system, considering the different security requirements of the system. An in-vehicle system may have heterogeneous security requirements, where the system part that executes safety critical applications requires stringent security measures and the infotainment system can settle with less. In addition, a system that is secure by design should be *ductile*, thus if the security of a part of the system is compromised it should be shut down or *graceful degradation* should be applied in order to guarantee correct functioning of the safety critical applications. Malfunctioning software should be detected, isolated and disabled.

The previous section discussed research that demonstrated the vulnerability of current in-vehicle systems. We are not aware of OEMs developing in-vehicle systems that are secure by design for vehicles that are commercially available, e.g. most vehicles allow users full access to the CAN bus. Research suggests solutions for parts of the problem [2,20,21,22,27,35], however it is unclear if one or a combination of these solutions provide a secure system that is suitable for current in-vehicle systems. Thus, if these solutions form a ductile system that is suitable for safety critical applications. Such a system should be suitable for execution by high performance microprocessors that run app-store like applications, but also for execution by lightweight microprocessors, which are used at the sensor interface. Designing such a system that is secure by design and is suitable for the diverse in-vehicle systems, is a challenge that will have to be addressed in the near future.

A second risk factor is *coupling nomadic devices to in-vehicle systems*. These systems require a different level of security and the in-vehicle system cannot easily force stringent security measures to a nomadic device. Though, it is probable that there will be a market pull, forcing the OEMs to provide such a coupling where access should be provided to the nomadic device. We think it will be a challenge to provide a nomadic device sufficient and flexible access, also to engine management systems, and at the same time avoid that safety critical parts of the in-vehicle system can be influenced.

A third risk factor is the *lack of risk factor assessments* for the security for in-vehicle systems. As stated in [9,10] vehicles can contain a lot of vulnerable interfaces and at the same time have a lot of microprocessors executing applications. Such a vehicle requires a thorough assessment to determine its vulnerabilities. With the increasing interconnection of in-vehicle systems, such assessments will be necessary.

6   Discussion

The previous sections discussed security risks for cooperative and interconnected mobility systems. Technical risks and challenges have been identified. But these challenges cannot be solved with only technical solutions; responsible authorities, consumers and OEMs will also partly determine the solution. Finally there are also organizational challenges besides these dilemmas. This section will discuss some of the dilemmas and organizational challenges.

In [24] five dilemmas have been given for national cyber security, three of them are applicable for the security of cooperative and interconnected mobility systems. In the following paragraphs these dilemmas will briefly be discussed.

Data Protection vs. Information Sharing. Information sharing lies at the heart of cooperative applications and can be used to improve local sensor values and create a better user experience. However, from a data protection and privacy point-of-view as little information as possible should be shared. In other words, information sharing requires protection of both information and privacy. Whereas such protection imposes overhead, it is necessary to prevent that a third person can tamper with the information and that personal information becomes publicly available. Even so, applying too many security and privacy measures to such shared information makes processing this information more complex and time consuming and can degrade the quality and usability of received information. Privacy respecting technology is a must for any system that is imposed or run by any government; as seen in the past, these systems are highly vulnerable to privacy criticism and are easily cancelled by privacy lobby groups. Additionally, if a system respects privacy people are willing to share more information. We expect that per type of application a different trade-off has to be made for the security and privacy measures.

Private Sector vs. Public Sector. For many parties it can be argued that they should have a leading role in defining security for interconnected and cooperative mobility systems. It is probable that in time the leading party will change, due to the changing power balance during the life-cycle of a cooperative mobility application. One view is that the authorities should play a leading role in defining and implementing security solutions, such that they can safeguard the safety on public roads and the safety and privacy of their citizens and also keep national security in mind. Often they are also owners of the infrastructure that will be partly equipped with cooperative systems. However, it can also be argued that the private sector should have a leading role. They will build the interconnected or cooperative applications, such that they can propose an exactly matching solution. This in contrast to the probably over restricted solution that will be proposed by the authorities. Some suggest that insurance companies may lead the introduction of cooperative technologies, to increase safety and retrieve additional information. It is probable that a cooperation between private and public parties is required, which can already be seen by the standardization of the communication by ETSI and CEN to which both parties contribute.

Stimulate the Economy vs. Improve Security. The dilemma is between allowing vehicles with potentially insecure innovative (software) features or imposing strict rules for new features. It can be argued that innovation is hampered by strict rules. It may be easier and more rewarding for industry to quickly introduce new innovations. After market adaptation of such innovations, they have to be made secure and safe. For the vehicle market the OEMs have a strong history of offering safe and secure solutions, to protect their brand value. However, allowing industry to introduce innovations with limited security and safety introduces a risk for early adopters and nearby road users. Therefore, authorities will most likely try to force a minimum level of security and safety, if they are aware of potential risks. We think it is even possible that in the future the authorities introduce an in-vehicle software security test that is periodically enforced, possibly every trip, to assess the vehicle security and safety. This would be an extension of a Ministry of Transport (MOT) test.

For the near future we expect that the number of external connections in a vehicle will increase and that in-vehicle system will become interconnected. In addition, we expect software to play a significant role in innovations for vehicles. Therefore, the above mentioned dilemmas will become increasingly relevant and have to be partly, or maybe even completely, solved in the coming years.

Organizational Challenges. In addition to the discussed security challenges and dilemmas, cooperative and interconnected mobility systems also pose a set of organizational challenges. First of all, mechanics and others maintaining a vehicle should be educated in cyber security and cyber hygiene. They have to protect their ICT based maintenance tools from malware to avoid infections for the maintained vehicles. Secondly, OEMs need to prepare for either massive and fast recall actions to update software in vehicles or build an infrastructure to do this remotely, when exploits become available for vulnerabilities in their software and components. Thirdly, authorities may need to change their vehicle safety laws. The third dilemma discussed above, already mentioned the possibility of enforcing a in-vehicle software security tests. Fourthly, it is likely that 'old' and 'new' security-related algorithms and cryptographic protection mechanisms need to function in parallel for some period of time. Computer history has taught that backwards compatibility is an inroad for propagation of security weaknesses. Fifthly, security related modules should keep a log of relevant data, such that in case of an accident it can be analyzed if a software-related attack caused it. Finally, a "license revocation" ability for cooperative and interconnected mobility systems may be needed, based on security components or vehicle brands and types.

7   Conclusions

Security for cooperative and interconnected mobility systems is a topic that is likely to become more important in the coming years, with the increase of in-vehicle software and the connectivity of in-vehicle systems. We expect that security can play a crucial role for the acceptance and success of cooperative mobility systems. This paper discussed attacker incentives and presented an overview of the security risks and challenges for the different parts of such systems.

The most serious identified incentive to compromise cooperative mobility systems is profit. Security risks have been identified for the mobile internet communication, vehicular ad hoc networks and in-vehicle systems. The biggest security risk factors foreseen are application data integrity validation, the usage of insecure position information and systems that are currently not secure by design. These risk factors will have to be addressed in the coming years, to pave the road for successful introduction of cooperative and interconnected mobility systems. Application data integrity validation is a must for safety critical applications, in order to increase the trust in, and quality of, environment information used by applications in the vehicle. Besides the currently available GPS position information, secure alternatives should be provided for usage by safety or financially critical applications. In-vehicle systems should become secure by design, to reduce the risks that will be introduced by the increase of connectivity. Besides these technical problems, there are also dilemmas and organizational challenges, e.g. whether private or public parties should be leading in the search for solutions of the mentioned risks.

We expect that in the coming years authorities and industries will gradually start providing cooperative and interconnected mobility systems, which require security solutions to ensure acceptance by the customers. Therefore, the research challenge will be to address and solve the identified security risks, with initially the focus at the most important topics, which have been identified in this paper.

References

1. Almgren, M., et al.: Deliverable d6.2: Intermediate report on the security of the connected car. Technical report, SysSec (September 2012)
2. Apvrille, L., et al.: Secure automotive on-board electronics network architecture. In: World Automotive Congress (May 2010)
3. Arilou Tech. Car cyber security (December 2012), http://www.ariloutech.com/pages/carcyber.htm
4. Bailey, D.: War texting: Identifying and interacting with devices on the telephone network. Blackhat USA (2011)
5. Barton, M.: Mercedes revs mbrace2 with cloud updates (September 2012), http://www.wired.com/insights/2012/04/mercedes-mbrace2/
6. Becher, M., et al.: Mobile security catching up? revealing the nuts and bolts of the security of mobile devices. In: IEEE Symposium on Security and Privacy (SP), pp. 96–111 (May 2011)
7. BWM Group. BWM connected drive 2012: Press release (2012), https://www.press.bmwgroup.com/pressclub/p/pcgl/download.html?textId=156904&textAttachmentId=192779
8. Capkun, S., Hubaux, J-P.: Secure positioning of wireless devices with application to sensor networks. In: Joint Conference of the IEEE Computer and Communications Societies (INFOCOM), vol. 3, pp. 1917–1928. IEEE (2005)
9. Charette, R.: This car runs on code (February 2009), http://www.spectrum.ieee.org/feb09/7649
10. Checkoway, S., et al.: Comprehensive experimental analyses of automotive attack surfaces. In: Proceedings of USENIX Security (2011)
11. Commtouch. Commtouch internet threats trend report 2013 february (2013), http://www.commtouch.com/uploads/pdf/Commtouch-Internet-Threats-Trend-Report-2013-February.pdf
12. Daimler Technicity. mbrace2: The most important services of the new telematics platform in the U.S. (2012), http://www.daimler-technicity.de/en/mbrace2-services/
13. de Kievit, S., et al.: European Patent 12197138 (2012)
14. ESET Latin America's Lab. Trends for 2013: Astonishing growth of malware (2012), http://go.eset.com/us/resources/white-papers/Trends_for_2013_preview.pdf
15. ETSI. Intelligent transport systems (its); security; security services and architecture. Technical Report ETSI TS 102 731 V1.1.1, Sophia Antipolis Cedex - FRANCE, DTS/ITS-0050001 (September 2010)
16. ETSI. Intelligent transport systems (its); security; threat, vulnerability and risk analysis (tvra). Technical Report ETSI TR 102 893 V1.1.1, Sophia Antipolis Cedex - FRANCE, DTR/ITS-0050005 (March 2010)
17. Felt, A., et al.: A survey of mobile malware in the wild. In: Proc. of the Workshop on Security and Privacy in Smartphones and Mobile Devices, pp. 3–14. ACM (2011)
18. Ford Motor Company. Ford launches app developer program marking new course for customer-driven innovation and value creation (2013), http://media.ford.com/article_display.cfm?article_id=37551

19. Francillon, A., Danev, B., Capkun, S.: Relay attacks on passive keyless entry and start systems in modern cars. IACR ePrint Report 332 (2010)
20. Glass, M., et al.: Seissecurity in embedded ip-based systems. ATZelektronik Worldwide 5(1), 36–40 (2010)
21. Henniger, O., et al.: Securing vehicular on-board it systems: The evita project. In: VDI/VW Automotive Security Conference (2009)
22. Kargl, F., et al.: Secure vehicular communication systems: implementation, performance, and research challenges. IEEE Communications Magazine 46(11), 110–118 (2008)
23. Kia Motors America. Kia motors announces google maps integration to enhance in-car connectivity (2013), http://www.prnewswire.com/news-releases/kia-motors-announces-google-maps-integration-to-enhance-in-car-connectivity-185401682.html
24. Klimburg, A., et al.: National Cyber Security Framework Manual. NATO CCD COE, Tallinn (2012)
25. Koscher, K., et al.: Experimental security analysis of a modern automobile. In: IEEE Symposium on Security and Privacy (SP), pp. 447–462 (2010)
26. Mollman, S.: From cars to tvs, apps are spreading to the real world (October 2009), http://edition.cnn.com/2009/TECH/10/08/apps.realworld/index.html
27. Papadimitratos, P., et al.: Secure vehicular communication systems: design and architecture. IEEE Communications Magazine 46(11), 100–109 (2008)
28. Passchier, I., et al.: New services enabled by the connected car. Technical report, TNO, SMART 2010/0065, TNO-RPT-2011-01277 (June 2011)
29. Ploeg, J., et al.: Design and experimental evaluation of cooperative adaptive cruise control. In: Intelligent Transportation Systems (ITSC), pp. 260–265. IEEE (2011)
30. Raya, M., Hubaux, J.: The security of vehicular ad hoc networks. In: Proc. of Workshop on Security of Ad Hoc and Sensor Networks, pp. 11–21. ACM (2005)
31. Rouf, I., et al.: Security and privacy vulnerabilities of in-car wireless networks: A tire pressure monitoring system case study. In: Proceedings of USENIX Security, pp. 323–338 (2010)
32. Schoch, E., et al.: Communication patterns in vanets. IEEE Communications Magazine 46(11), 119–125 (2008)
33. Shabtai, A., et al.: Google android: A comprehensive security assessment. Security & Privacy 8(2), 35–44 (2010)
34. Simmonds, A., Sandilands, P., van Ekert, L.: An ontology for network security attacks. Applied Computing, 317–323 (2004)
35. Wolf, M., Weimerskirch, A., Paar, C.: Security in automotive bus systems. In: Workshop on Embedded IT-Security in Cars, pp. 11–12 (2004)

Study of In-Data Centre Backup Offices for Banks

Yasutake Sayanagi

Nagoya Institute of Technology, Gokiso-cho, Showa-ku, Nagoya, Aichi, 466-8555 Japan
Barclays Securities Japan Limited, 6-10-1 Roppongi, Minato-Ku, Tokyo 106-6131, Japan
web.yasu@gmail.com

Abstract. Although there were no significant physical damages in Tokyo, as a result of the Tohoku Pacific Earthquake (known as the Great East Japan Earthquake in Japan) on 11th March 2011, a couple of thousand Automated Teller Machines (ATMs) were out of service for more than a week. Most banks' critical operations were impacted due to the shortage of electrical power supply. The purpose of this study is to review those incidents from a banking operational point of view. The business continuity challenges have been analyzed and the resulting set of recommendations are discussed in this paper.

Keywords: Finance, BCM, Bank, backup office, DC.

1 Introduction

After the Tohoku Pacific Earthquake[1] on 11th March 2011, the financial industry in Tokyo experienced very severe situations due to the lack of electricity. Though the situation was quite similar to that of other industries, financial companies such as banks, securities and insurance firms have huge dependencies on Information and Communication Technology (ICT), and thus a lack of electricity has a very critical impact on their business continuity.

This study is based on the research by a global financial company to create an additional backup office in the Kansai region of Japan, which is located 500 km west of Tokyo, following the Tohoku Pacific Earthquake. The research identified a gap between actual market needs and the System Integrator (SI) and Data Center (DC) vendor side understanding on backup offices. A proposal on how to bridge this gap is presented.

2 Mission Statement of the Banks in Japan

Before discussing "What are the societal responsibilities of banks?" we review the BCM mission statements of both domestic and international financial companies in

---

[1] The Tohoku Pacific Earthquake or Great East Japan Earthquake, occurred on March 11, 2011 in the Tohoku region of Japan and had a strength of Moment Magnitude (Mw) 9.0. 18,550 people were confirmed dead or missing as of July 2013.

E. Luiijf and P. Hartel (Eds.): CRITIS 2013, LNCS 8328, pp. 16–25, 2013.
© Springer International Publishing Switzerland 2013

Japan. The Bank of Japan (the BOJ, a central bank of Japan) stated in [4] that the three critical points to be taken into account with BCM in banks were as follows:

- To continue social and public support systems, such as cash supply and money transfer;
- To continue settlements;
- To manage risk and the economic impact of bad loans, etc.

The BOJ suggests that "To continue settlements" must be given the top priority, simply because of the potential economic impact on domestic and international markets. The BOJ analyzed the importance of BCM in financial companies in [3] and pointed out that financial companies should be categorized as extremely critical infrastructure operations, together with electricity, water, gas, telecommunications, public transportations, police and fire departments, etcetera. According to [3], the BOJ-Net, the Japanese yen (domestic) settlement system to which all domestic banks and major international banks are connected and which manages a total of JPY 100 trillion per day on average, would impact the domestic and international financial markets if it were to stop after a massive disaster. The Japanese government considers the Tokyo Inland Earthquakes as the most damaging threat scenario around Tokyo: an expected Mw 7.3 level quake which has a probability of 70% to occur in the next 30 years, 850,000 damaged or destroyed houses, 210,000 injured people, 11,000 casualty, and an economic impact of JPY 112 trillion. Lifeline services will be interrupted around 15 km from the epicenter. The BOJ expects that financial companies keep their BCM solutions working properly at all times during such an event.

3   Incident Review

3.1   Business Impact of the Tohoku Pacific Earthquake

Direct Impact.
According to the Japanese Financial Services Agency, among 2,700 branch offices of the local banks in the Tohoku region (Northeast Japan) about 11% closed their offices due to the impact of the earthquake and tsunami. Most were able to reopen within three months. The main reasons for closure were physical damage to the premises and the unavailability of infrastructure such as electricity, gas and telecommunications. Together with the lessons learned from the Great Hanshin Awaji Earthquake[2] of 1995 in West Japan, the biggest BCM challenges for banks was how to continue their societal responsibilities such as settlement and money supply even when they had lost some of their branches and/or electrical power supply in their business area.

---

[2]   The Great Hanshin Awaji Earthquake: known as Hyogo-Ken Nanbu Earthquake overseas, occurred on 17th January, 1995 in Hyogo prefecture. It was Mw7.3 and 6,434 people lost their lives.

Indirect Impact.
Other serious impacts occurred around the Tokyo metropolitan area. Mainly due to the Tsunami impact at the Fukushima nuclear power plant, the capacity of electricity power generation by Tokyo Electric Power Company (TEPCO) was 40% down from 52 GW/h to 31 GW/h, resulting in a 10 GW gap between demand and supply. Soon after the earthquake, TEPCO announced a series of scheduled power shutdowns to avoid blackouts in the Tokyo metropolitan area. They split the area into five zones and cut power for two to three hours on a rotational basis. Over 57 million households were impacted in the first nine days. A total of 73 hours and 50 minutes of outage time occurred (**Table 1**). There are a number of in-branch and out of branch ATMs in the areas affected by the scheduled power downs. Although ATM service is one of the societal responsibilities of banks, the Japan Post Bank announced a shutdown of 1,100 branch ATMs as well as all out of branch ATMs in Tochigi, Gunma, Ibaraki, Saitama, Chiba, Kanagawa, Yamanashi, Shizuoka (East area only) and 220 ATMs in Tokyo's 23 wards, in total 3,000 ATMs. The Sumitomo-Mitsui Bank shut down 360 of their 660 out of branch ATMs and 240 of their 460 branch ATMs. Quite similar situations were seen with other banks, such as Mizuho Financial Group, Tokyo-Mitsubishi-UFJ Financial group, and many local banks. As that happened in the same areas that were affected by TEPCO's scheduled power downs, customers would sometimes have to take trains and buses to get to the nearest available ATM. In the event of wide area disaster, it is clear that banking services such as ATMs cannot be continued at all locations. However, banks should better plan for "Zone base service continuity plans" (see 7.2). This means banks should continue their services and business within customer walking or bicycle distance. This requires a service alliance agreement with other banks to cover each other when a disaster happens.

Table 1. Impact of the scheduled power downs in the Tokyo metropolitan area ([6])

Date	Did a scheduled shutdown take place?	Number of households affected	Total hours of outage per day	TEPCO's power generation capacity	Anticipated power demand	Demand-supply gap
14th	Y	113,000	1:30	31.0 GW	41.0 GW	-10.0 GW
15th	Y	5,020,000	12:40	33.0 GW	35.0 GW	-2.0 GW
16th	Y	10,920,000	15:40	33.0 GW	35.0 GW	-2.0 GW
17th	Y	18,160,000	15:40	33.5 GW	40.0 GW	-6.5 GW
18th	Y	13,680,000	15:40	35.0 GW	37.0 GW	-2.0 GW
19th	N	0	0	34.5 GW	31.0 GW	+3.5 GW
20th	N	0	0	34.5 GW	29.0 GW	+5.5 GW
21st	N	0	0	35.5 GW	34.0 GW	+1.5 GW
22nd	Y	9,990,000	12:40	37.0 GW	37.0 GW	0

The earthquake incident shows how important it is to have a relevant level of electricity with the BCM of the banks. Though each bank has been conducting BCM exercises every year as well as taking part in street-wide exercises that are conducted by the bankers association, no one considered a situation of lack of electrical power for such a long period. As the banking business has huge dependencies on ICT, a lack of electricity is sure to have a big impact on their BCM. This lack of power situation happened even though the Tokyo metropolitan area did not experience significant physical damage due to the earthquake.

Comparison with the September 11 Terrorist Attacks.
There are a lot of similar suggestions by the US GAO after the September 11 terrorist attacks in [1] with the Japanese government analysis of the Tokyo Inland Earthquakes scenario [2] such as: "...Many financial institutions' BCPs addressed limited-scope event..." and "...The attacks also caused major power outages in lower Manhattan.... As a result, more than 13,000 Con Edison (the local power provider) business customers lost power, which required them to either relocate operations or use alternative power source such as portable generators...".

Table 2. Comparison of recommendations by [1] and [2]

Impacts	September 11 attacks	Tokyo Inland Earthquakes
People dead	2,800 [1]	11,000 estimated
Lost power supply	More than 13,000 customers of Con Edison (the local power provider)	57,000,000 houses/offices assuming the same level as The Tohoku Pacific Earthquake
Down time for life line infrastructure	About a month for partial recovery but took years for full recovery	Considering the Great Hanshin Awaji Earthquake of 1995, the estimated recovery time is about a month
Recommended distance between the main office and the backup office	[1] recommends "hundreds of miles away"	No official recommendations but according to the Japanese government analysis it should be more than 20 km to avoid simultaneous damage

Table 3. Recovery strategy of the BOJ in the event of a malfunction of the head office and DC

Major scenario	Site		Notes
	Head office	DC	
A malfunction in the BOJ DC	working	not working	Switch to the backup DC
A malfunction in the BOJ head office	not working	working	Switch to the backup office
A malfunction in both the BOJ DC and the BOJ head office	not working	not working	Switch to the backup DC and the backup office
The BOJ's critical staff cannot come to the office	working	working	Backup staff will cover the critical business

4   A Recovery Strategy

4.1   A Recovery Strategy of the BOJ (the Bank of Japan)

In order to keep settlement and other critical operations operating anytime, the BOJ has a very clear recovery strategy (**Table 3**):

- The BOJ Osaka branch will assume the BOJ Tokyo head office function if they lose connection with the head office in the event of a disaster around Tokyo.
- When a malfunction happens in the BOJ main DC, the backup DC will take over immediately.
- If a malfunction happens in both the BOJ head office and the BOJ main DC, their critical functions/facilities will be taken over by the backup ones at the same time. Though this should be the worst scenario, target recovery time is within two hours. The BOJ exercises this every month. Critical business staff lives within a 30 minutes range by foot.
- When a financial company that is using the BOJ-Net for settlement has a malfunction and cannot connect with the BOJ DC, they must come to the BOJ supervisory office. For example, financial companies located in Tokyo should go to the BOJ head office in Nihonbashi, Tokyo. When the BOJ head office function is taken over by the BOJ Osaka branch, a financial company that has a malfunction in Tokyo should go to the BOJ Osaka branch. This is why most of financial companies have their backup office and backup DC around Osaka.

Table 4. A Near Recovery site with a typical disaster scenario and actions

Typical scenario	Actions
A building evacuation (fire, bomb alert etc.)	Business critical staff to be moved to the backup office to maintain business operations
A power outage (short to medium term)	Business critical staff to be moved to the backup site if it is a local issue, and can minimize the impact when moving to the backup site
An earthquake	

Table 5. A Far Recovery site with a typical disaster scenario and actions

Typical scenario	Actions
A Tokyo wide area evacuation (earthquake, nuclear issues etc.)	Business critical staff to be moved to the backup office to maintain business operations
A black out (medium to long term)	
The BOJ head office to move to Osaka	

4.2   A Recovery Strategy of an International Financial Company

Most of the international finance companies have a main office around Tokyo's Central Business District, and a Nearby Recovery site around Tokyo. A Nearby Recovery site (**Table 4**) is normally set up within 10 to 30 km from the main office to cover a malfunction in the main office such as a fire. This site needs to be accessed easily and quickly from the main office because this malfunction is company specific. The site is mainly used for same day (intraday) recovery. All of the international financial companies potentially have this option.

To meet with the BOJ's recovery strategy, they should have a Far Recovery site in the Kansai region. A Far Recovery site (**Table 5**) is normally set up more than 300 km away from the main office to avoid a simultaneous shutdown risk. Transportation between the main office and the Far Recovery site is sometimes an issue. In the financial companies, this site is to be consistent with the BOJ's recovery strategy. About one third of the international financial companies have this option.

Despite having only a very limited number of offices and sites in Japan, institutions have very strong backup functions in Singapore or Hong Kong, a so called on shore - off shore combination where companies use overseas office or an operations center abroad to cover critical operations. The BOJ prohibits the BOJ-Net operation from abroad. This most critical operation should be managed somewhere in Japan but considering the BOJ's recovery strategy, location of the recovery site must be around Osaka. Potentially, all of the international financial companies use this option.

5   Dependencies and Criticality Tiers

By using an example of BCM in Barclays, one of the global leading financial companies, the dependencies between business criticality and required spec of the premises to meet with the business needs have been studied.

5.1   For the Main Office

Barclays Securities Japan and Barclays Bank Tokyo branch (Barclays) have both been located in the Roppongi Hills since a few years before the Tohoku Pacific Earthquake. This is because Barclays believes that the Roppongi Hills is the most resilient building in Tokyo as it has a co-generator power plant at the lower ground level. The Roppongi Hills co-generator power plant has six sets of 6.4 MW gas turbines that have a < N+1> (install an additional power generator) spec resiliency. <N+1> is one of the solutions to keep spare capacity in case of system failure or maintenance[3]. An extra generator beyond the anticipated demand is installed, and normally one is kept switched off. It runs 24x7 to supply all the electricity, cooling and heating services for offices and residential areas in the Roppongi Hills. The primary backup of this co-generator power plant is TEPCO; the secondary backup is fuel. In line with the electrical and cooling spec, the Roppongi Hills is about the same level of a DC spec. Roppongi Hills also has one of the most advanced earthquake resistance mechanisms. Each floor has semi-active oil dampers to reduce the effect of the shakes to minimize the damage. By using those two strong facilities, the Roppongi Hills announced that

---

[3]   Actually during the period of the power supply restrictions by TEPCO after the Tohoku Pacific Earthquake, the Roppongi Hills' co-generator power plant kept providing electricity to TEPCO to minimize the demand-supply gap.

they can accept about 5,000 people in the event that a disaster happens in or around Tokyo. Compared with the premises of other banks in Tokyo, the level of resiliency of the Roppongi Hills is much higher as it has two levels (1st and 2nd backup) of backup power, it operates 24x7, and it has 400,000 liters of fuel stored.

5.2   For the Backup Office

The primary backup office of Barclays in Japan is located about 30 km away from Tokyo. It is easy to access in the event of a disaster, and can avoid simultaneous damage with Tokyo. The primary backup office is in an earthquake isolation structured DC building that has an <N+1> spec power generator to meet with the business needs of their BCM. The secondary backup office is in the Kansai region, 500 km away from Tokyo. It is also in the DC building with an <N> spec power generator. As explained, the business criticality has to be matched with the spec of the premises. Without having resilient facilities, not only of the systems/DC but also of the backup offices, banks cannot complete their societal responsibilities.

6   Case Study: Creating the Secondary Backup Office in the Kansai Region

Considering the business impact when not having a strong and resilient power supply after an incident such as Tokyo Inland earthquakes, it is important for banks to have a backup office in a building that has an <N+1> or <N> spec power generator as well as an earthquake resilient structure. Only a very limited number of office buildings have those capabilities. According to recent research in the Kansai area only 3.7% (1 office out of 27) has a power generator to support tenants and 11.1% (3 out of 27) can provide space for tenants to set up their own power generator. This figure is very serious because those 27 office buildings are the top class buildings there. Therefore assume that almost all office buildings for rent do not have BCM capability

Discussing with the top-32 SI and DC vendors in the Kansai region, almost all of them would not like customers to use a DC building with office space. Asking for a quote for 400-500 m2 without setting a limitation with the rent but 81.3% (26 SI and DC vendors out of 32) declined due to reasons of security policies, while just 6.3% (2 out of 32) of them accepted and provided quotations. Note that all of those SI and DC vendors are the leading companies in the domestic market.

7   Diagnoses and Potential Solutions

7.1   An In-Data Center (DC) Backup Office

Diagnosis.
The spec of most premises didn't meet with the business recovery needs of banks. Only a very limited number of office buildings have a power generator to support a tenant. There is a gap between the business requirements and the existing solutions in

the DC vendor market mainly due to the security policy. The security controls of the DC in Japan are mostly based on ISMS (Information Security Management System [8]).

Although it is possible to create an isolated office area from the DC area, a DC vendor does not like frequent human access to the DC building. The reason behind this is probably the preference from users such as banks whom want their DC to meet all the requirements of JIPDEC mainly for ISMS compliance reasons although ISMS does not state anything about the combined use of the DC and the backup office. Thus, once banks take a look at ISMS again in detail and understand that an in-DC (DC) backup office has an acceptable risk which gives them an advantage, the market situation should change.

Potential Solution 1:   Combined solution for the DC and the backup office.
Considering the business impact of not having a strong and resilient power supply in the event of an incident alike the Tokyo Inland Earthquakes, it is important to have a backup office in the building that has an <N+1> or <N> spec power generator as well as being in an earthquake resilient building. Only a very limited number of office buildings have those capabilities and almost all the SI and the DC vendors would not like their customers to use the DC buildings for office space. However around eight years ago, Barclays successfully agreed with the DC vendor to have a combined solution with an in-DC backup office that has more than hundred recovery desks for critical operations. This In-DC backup office is located in the DC spec building that has an earthquake isolation mechanism, <N+1> spec power generator systems, multiple backup with telecommunications, cooling systems, and plenty of stocks of water and fuel. Therefore, contracting the DC and the backup office into one might be an ideal solution.

Barclays wanted its backup office to have strong infrastructure such as electricity, telecommunications, and cooling systems. However, no company provides this type of "shared infrastructure solutions" in the market, and so Barclays started discussions as a plan B with the DC vendors to create the office space in the DC.

Almost all of the DC in Japan are designed and meet the ISMS (Information Security Management System) standard. The access management standard for physical human access to the DC building creates conflict with the business needs of the backup office.

Potential Solution 2:   Renovating the old DC of the mega bank.
In the last decade, a number of mergers happened in the banking market resulting in the establishment of three megabank groups: Tokyo-Mitsubishi UFJ Financial Group, Sumitomo-Mitsui Financial Group and Mizuho Financial Group. After those mergers, many old DCs are left unused simply because they were no longer needed. As those ex-DCs still have excellent resiliency, have power generators and telecommunications, etc., renovating them to accommodate the backup offices of local banks would be a potential solution. This solution might be a good business model for the mega-banks to make best use of their unused premises and facilities. For example, one of the ex-DC of Mizuho Financial group is located in CBD Tokyo that has sufficient DC

rooms and office space to accommodate thousands of people. As the building was designed to host computers, electricity capacity and cooling are relatively good. A total stock of fuel would last for more than a week when fully loaded. Renovating and renting it as a new backup office facility for international and domestic local banks would be a potential solution for their business continuity in the event of a disaster.

Potential Solution 3:   The activation of co-generator solutions.
Another candidate for an In-DC backup office in Japan is located in a sub-building with the backup control center of Osaka GAS, which also has co-generators in it. This solution is already in the market, and seems to be a best fit with business needs. However, co-generator power supply doesn't cover the office space. As most of the core infrastructure is already in place, extending power distribution cables to the office space to expand coverage might be a feasible solution.

7.2   ATMs

Diagnosis.
Thousands of ATMs were suspended after the Tohoku Pacific Earthquake due to the lack of electrical power supply. Currently, there are no zone based service continuity plans for ATMs. There is also no alliance program that is focused on the disaster situations to support each other. Indeed, suspending almost all ATM services in the power brownouts zones happened which had a significant impact on customers.

Potential Solution 4:   A zone based service continuity plan for ATMs.
Suspending all ATM services in the particular zone has a significant impact on customers. Therefore, the idea of "a zone based service continuity" is based on the service level not by each company but by each zone, and deciding which facilities such as ATMs should be continued or suspended. Considering the difficulty of public transportation after a disaster, service continuity should be managed every 500 m radial circle so that services are available within a 1 km walking distance for most people. Banks don't need to continue all ATM services but should selectively run ATMs to maintain their service continuity as part of the zone by zone plan. Other infrastructure such as mobile phone antennas and traffic lights also need a zone based service continuity plan. Thus essential infrastructures like a power generator can be shared between service providers. This solution requires cooperation, co-working and an alliance among the different companies across different industries. However such coordination supports a local community in the event of a disaster. From a different angle, it is also a good idea to work with the convenience stores to set up power generators and UPS for in-store ATMs. To take one more step, to make the best use of the cashier in the convenience store, banks can promote cash payment services. Such services are popular service in Europe and America but not in Japan. By using a "Debit Card" one can ask the cashier to draw cash during a shopping trip. This might be a preferable service for customers and could be very cost effective.

8   Conclusions

As discussed the banks have huge dependencies on electricity. Thus the specs of the premises need to be able to meet these requirements. In order to fulfill the social responsibility that is required by the BOJ and to meet with the business recovery needs such as the Recovery Time Objective, an <N+1> or <N> spec power generator is necessary not only for the main office and the DC, but also for the backup offices. However, of the top 27 office buildings in Kansai only 3.7% (1 office out of 27) has a power generator. Also, among the top 32 SI and DC vendors in Kansai, 81.3% (26 SI and DC vendors in 32) declined DC space for office use due to the security reason.

Three potential solutions discussed in this paper to mitigate risk are as follows:

- Contracting the DC and the backup office into one.
- Renovating unused mega bank DCs to support small, medium, and local banks.
- Enhancing to activate (the activation of) co-generator solutions.

Another proposal is for services continuity by establishing zone based service continuity plans for ATMs by creating alliances and collaborations of banks to support the local community. These are still very small steps to start with, but it is very important for us to revisit with the lessons learned from the events of the Tohoku Pacific Earthquake and improve our resiliency in preparation for future possible incidents.

References

1. GAO-03-251: Potential Terrorist Attacks: Additional Actions Needed to Better Prepare Critical Financial Market Participants, U.S. Government Accountability Office, Washington D.C., USA (2003), http://www.gpo.gov/fdsys/pkg/GAOREPORTS-GAO-03-251/pdf/GAOREPORTS-GAO-03-251.pdf
2. BCM committee report, Cabinet Office, Japan (March 2012), http://www.bousai.go.jp/3oukyutaisaku/syuto_chusu/report.pdf
3. Bank of Japan, Review of the impact of the Tohoku Pacific Earthquake on financial companies, Tokyo, Japan (June 24, 2011), http://www.boj.or.jp
4. Bank of Japan, BCM in financial companies, Japan (July 25, 2003)
5. Bank of Japan, Closed branch offices of banks in the Tohoku region, http://www.boj.or.jp/research/brp/ron_2011/data/ron110624a.pdf
6. TEPCO, Impact of the scheduled power down in Tokyo metropolitan area, http://www.tepco.co.jp/index-j.html
7. Bank of Japan, A basic recovery strategy of the BOJ in the event of a malfunction of head office and DC, http://www.boj.or.jp/
8. JIS Q (Japanese Industrial Standards) 27001:2006, ISO/IEC 27001:2005 of JIPDEC (Japan Institute for Promotion of Digital Economy and Community)

Protecting a Federated Database Infrastructure against Denial-of-Service Attacks

Arne Ansper[1,2], Ahto Buldas[1,2], Margus Freudenthal[1], and Jan Willemson[1]

[1] Cybernetica AS, Mäealuse 2/1, Tallinn, Estonia
[2] ELIKO Competence Centre in Electronics-, Info- and Communication
Technologies, Mäealuse 2/1, Tallinn, Estonia*

Abstract. The need for combining various heterogeneous data sources into a uniformly accessible infrastructure has given rise to the development of federated database systems. Security aspects of such systems have been well-studied, but they have mostly concentrated on privacy and access control issues. In this paper, we take a closer look at the availability problems caused by the network failures, Denial-of-Service attacks, etc. We take the X-Road infrastructure developed in Estonia as the basis of our studies and propose several methods to improve its resilience. We discuss the usage of alternative communication channels, replication of critical databases and replacing the present critical central services with more flexible alternatives.

Keywords: Federated database systems, X-Road, service availability, Denial-of-Service attacks.

1 Introduction

There is a growing trend to make governmental services available through the Internet and to interconnect electronic governmental databases and registers. In Estonia, the key factors for such a trend have been the large-scale use of ID-cards (about 1.2 million active cards) and the development of the X-Road infrastructure which acts as a unified access layer to the governmental registers providing state authorities and citizens with efficient lawful access to governmental information. Today, more than 600 state registers are available through the X-Road infrastructure.

The main challenge to overcome during the X-Road development was achieving a unified access mechanism for a diverse ecosystem of separate databases that had been developing since early 1990s. Building one large data warehouse to host all the state databases was not an option from neither the organizational, nor the privacy point of view. Rather it was decided to build an overlay network, keeping the amount of changes needed for the existing autonomous database components to minimum.

---

* This research has been supported by European Union through European Regional Development Fund under ELIKO Competence Center (EU30017) and EXCS Center of Excellence in Computer Science.

E. Luiijf and P. Hartel (Eds.): CRITIS 2013, LNCS 8328, pp. 26–37, 2013.

As such, X-Road can be viewed as an instance of a *federated database system*, a concept known from mid-1980s [7,13]. By mid-1990s, several of such systems had already been developed and deployed [14,15]. Originally, a lot of attention was paid to interoperability issues during the X-Road development. In the first versions, specific adapter servers were used to achieve this [2]. However, once the adapter layer was established, the X-Road development focus has mainly been on confidentiality, integrity and access control, central security issues of the federated database management systems in general [5,4].

Surprisingly, availability issues of the federated databases have not received equally extensive treatment in research community. Some results have been reported on query optimization [6,11] and dynamically configurable database networks [3,1], but none of these approaches provide full resilience against massive malicious online attacks.

So far, the X-Road infrastructure has also been positioned as a *peace-time system*, normal operation of which assumes normal functioning of the Internet. However, considering the growing importance and criticality of the X-Road system for the state to fulfil its role, cyber security threats must be taken into account. The X-Road system should at least guarantee that for some high-priority clients certain services remain accessible even in the crisis situations where the normal functioning of the Internet is affected by cyber attacks. For example, in its current implementation, the X-Road central servers are potentially subjects of Denial-of-Service (DOS) attacks, which would in turn threaten the whole infrastructure. In 2007, Estonia was hit by a massive distributed DOS attack [12]. Luckily, the X-Road infrastructure was not hit directly, but given the current state of cyber warfare, it is unreasonable to hope that we would be equally lucky next time.

In this paper, we discuss the possibility of upgrading the X-Road system to a *war-time system*. To achieve this, we propose several ways to improve the X-Road infrastructure so that in case of Internet failures or inaccessibility of central services, the network of important databases would still be operable using alternative communication channels.

The paper is organized as follows. In Section 2, we give an overview of the X-Road system. In Section 3, we set up the main new requirements to the X-Road infrastructure and analyze the achievability of the requirements. In Section 4, we outline the solutions, and finally Section 5 draws some conclusions.

2   X-Road Overview

By early 2000s the level of computerization in the Estonian state databases had reached both the level of sufficient technical maturity and a certain critical volume so that the need for a unified secure access mechanism was clear. To address that need, the development activities on the modernization of national databases started in the beginning of 2001 [10,8]. The first version of the developed X-Road infrastructure was launched on December 17th 2001. The number of queries and replies mediated through the infrastructure per year exceeded 240 million in

2011 [9]. Today, already the fifth generation of the X-Road is in operation, and the current paper describes part of the effort to produce the sixth generation.

Detailed technical descriptions of the whole system can be found in [2,16]; here we will just shortly cover the main aspects needed in the context of the current paper.

On the high level (Fig. 1), the X-Road infrastructure consists of the organizations providing and requesting data, and some central services. In order to communicate over the X-Road, each participating organization must install a dedicated *security server* that acts as a secure access gateway. Security servers are responsible for encrypting the communication between the organizations, and also for cryptographic authentication and digitally signing the information that is exchanged during the communication. To facilitate this, three central services are needed.

- **Certification Authority, CA** is responsible for providing public key certificates for authentication and signing, together with the Online Certificate Status Protocol (OCSP) responder used to distribute certificate validity information.
- **Time-stamping Authority, TSA** is responsible for providing time-stamps to the digital signatures used to validate the X-Road queries and replies.
- **X-Road Center** is responsible for distributing the service directory and service configuration information. Out of these, access to up-to-date configuration is potentially security critical, since it contains certificate chains together with trusted root certificates and the correspondences between organizations and their security servers.

In the first versions of the X-Road, the CA and TSA were also integrated into the X-Road Center, but in the more recently developed versions these services are separated to allow for better integration with external service providers.

In its present state, the X-Road security servers are, to some extent, capable of communicating with each other even if all the central servers are inaccessible. The OCSP responses and configuration information have a pre-determined life-time, which is currently set to 6 hours. If no updates are possible within this period, the subsequent communication is considered insecure and terminated. However, using potentially insecure communication can under many circumstances still be preferable to having no communication at all. This is one of the main improvement goals of the current paper.

3   Requirements

Our goal is to improve the X-Road infrastructure so that it would become a proper *war-time system*, i.e. it has to stand massive cyber-attacks (e.g. DOS attacks) from the Internet. The main requirement is that the X-Road servers must be able to securely communicate and guarantee the availability of *critical services* even if

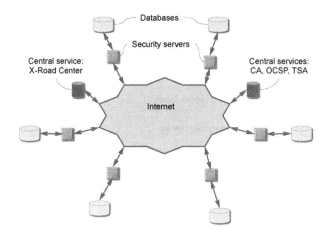

Fig. 1. The peace-time infrastructure of X-Road

- usual communication through the Internet is impossible or considerably distracted;
- central services (CA, OCSP, TSA) are inaccessible;
- (optionally) the X-Road Center is inaccessible and does not provide configuration information.

This means that the clients must have a better and service-based control over the configuration and evidence collection functions. This enables mediating the services where in certain cases (in crisis situations) the service availability is much more important than the ability of creating evidence, and it is safe to assume that the configuration has not been changed. For example, the 112 (911) services may need critical information from state registers to save human lives. Compared to such important goals, proper collection of evidence for proving the digital signatures is of secondary importance.

This means that in case of cyber-attacks or any other large-scale Internet failure, the system must be able (in time) to switch over to alternative channels (private lines, radio links, etc.) that keep the critical services alive (Fig. 2). Alternative channels are often slower, more expensive, or have some other restrictions, so their required capacity must be carefully determined.

In principle, the choice between different channels can be implemented in the network layer, but this may be awkward and hard to manage, because IP-packets originated from services of different criticality are indistinguishable. Instead, the security servers may support alternative channels on the application level and be able to automatically switch over in case of the main channel malfunction. Priority tags could be assigned to services and customers in order to guarantee a reasonable use of the alternative channels.

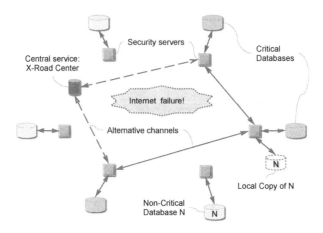

Fig. 2. The war-time infrastructure of X-Road

Today, the X-Road system supports multiple central servers, which guarantees normal work of the system during a limited period of time, even if one of the central servers of X-Road (maintained by the X-Road Center) is inaccessible. However, the continuous work of the system is not guaranteed after a destruction or a long-term downtime of the X-Road Center. There has to be a possibility of using secondary central servers that keep fresh copies of all the information held in the X-Road Center, including the configuration of the whole system.

It should also be possible to improve the availability of the services when the availability requirements set by the client exceed the availability level guaranteed by the service provider. If it is unreasonable to increase the availability level of the service provider, there is a need of using local copies of the serving database. Local copies of databases are already in use in the Estonian Police and Border Guard Board and in some other institutions, but these are *ad hoc* solutions without any unified framework. It would be desirable to develop a reliable X-Road service for making local copies of databases and for regularly keeping them updated.

In the next Section, we propose solutions to the above-mentioned availability problems.

4 Solutions

4.1 Center-Independent Work

In all the previous X-Road generations, Domain Name System Security Extensions (DNSSEC) directory service has been used to propagate the configuration of X-Road servers, and this solution has worked well this far. However, the use of DNSSEC becomes an obstacle if we require independence from the central services. If the central servers are unreachable and the buffering name servers of the security servers cannot update their data, eventually the names become non-resolving and it will become impossible to check the status of public-key certificates. There is no preventive buffering in DNSSEC and hence if after the service interruption it will be necessary to access one of the security servers, the DNS information would be unusable.

When building the broadcast mechanism for certificate validity information, it is unreasonable to add non-standard extensions to standard protocols. Hence, it is appropriate to abandon DNSSEC altogether and to use an application level solution for the configuration management. It should be ensured, however, that the availability of the system will not decrease.

Hence, to achieve the goal of center-independence, we have to design an application-level high-availability configuration management protocol that ensures an authenticated update of configurations, whereas the configuration update policy should be under control of the owners of security servers.

The requirement of the center-independent operations poses some restrictions to the ways of using the Public Key Infrastructure (PKI) services. Two online services are needed: OCSP for certificate validity information and time-stamping for ensuring the preservation of the evidentiary value of electronic evidence. A recipient of an X-Road message should first check the validity of the corresponding certificate via OCSP and then obtain a timestamp for the signed message.

Later verification of evidence consists of checking that the message is properly signed with a public key listed in the certificate and that the timestamp on the signed message together with a sufficiently fresh OCSP response confirms the validity of the certificate. The signer is responsible for obtaining the OCSP response. Receivers of signed messages determine their policies on how old OCSP responses are acceptable. In principle, in crisis situations where the X-Road center is unreachable, security servers may temporarily abandon all age restrictions to OCSP responses or may choose not to use OCSP at all. Later, if the network operation becomes normal again, OCSP responses can be obtained *post factum*. Note that a positive OCSP response that is dated much later than the signature also confirms the validity of the signature.

The receiver of the signed messages is responsible for the use of the time-stamping service and the receiver is able to define its own acceptance policy for the incoming messages.

In order to support redundant X-Road centers, a protocol must be designed for creating backup copies of the whole X-Road Center (including the Certification Authority) so that backup services can be set up promptly if needed. The copies of the keys used to sign the configuration must be held in backup devices (clones of the original Hardware Security Module (HSM)). This would enable to immediately switch over to one of the secondary X-Road centers if necessary.

4.2   Alternative Channels

A flexible use of redundant channels would extend the X-Road's scope of usability even more, because the critical services would stay accessible even in case of Internet malfunction.

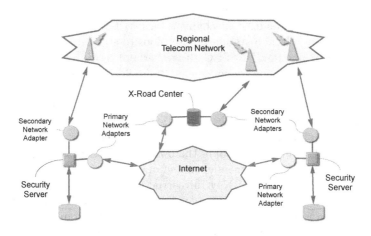

Fig. 3. An implementation of alternative channels through local telecom networks

Alternative communication networks can be used at several different layers. At the network layer, it is possible to add routers between every security server and the Internet, so that the messages can be routed through alternative network devices such as radio modems. These modems should communicate by using a common routing protocol and should ideally be maintained by a single organizational entity. The main drawback of the network-layer solutions is that since the communication between the security servers is encrypted, it would be nearly impossible for ordinary network routers to selectively direct certain services to alternative channels.

A more flexible solution is making the security servers able to differentiate between different networks. Already the presently deployed security servers have a built in mechanism for using redundant security servers. This mechanism can be extended with the support for alternative networks. In the case of the main network (Internet) malfunction and if certain services are allowed to use alternative channels, the security servers are accessed via an alternative network (using different IP addresses). The credentials for using alternative networks can be defined at the service layer, enabling thereby differentiation between critical services (that must be accessible in crisis situations) and ordinary services that, for economical reasons, will not be offered through lower-bandwidth and/or more expensive channels.

The solution we propose is the following (Fig. 3). The security servers of the databases that have been declared to be critical must be equipped with secondary network adapters that are connected to the network of a regional telecom operator. We assume that a regional telecom network can be protected against external DOS attacks by separating it from the Internet. A separate agreement for the local telecom operator is required so that the regional part of the network stays accessible even if the rest of the Internet is cut off from it. Usually, such connections are priced per transmitted bytes plus some constant monthly fee that depends on the channel capacity. From customers' point of view, such connections look just like ordinary Internet connections.

Service level applications (Fig. 4) should distinguish between the critical queries/responses and the ordinary ones. There should also be a service quality measurement system and a smart decision-making mechanism that is able to send messages through the secondary network adapter if needed. Note that the views of different security servers may lead to different decisions about the emergency situations and hence, one server may send a message through alternative channels while for the rest of the servers, the Internet seems working properly. This means that all critical servers must always be ready to receive messages through alternative channels, even if to the best of their knowledge the Internet is working properly.

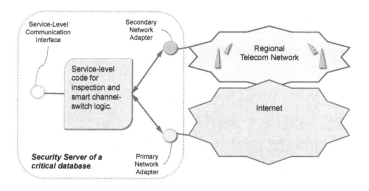

Fig. 4. A security server that supports alternative channels

Though the alternative channels are mostly (in peace time) not used, one has to be sure that they are operable when needed. This means that alternative connections cannot be entirely passive even if they are not directly needed. Constant pinging is necessary for monitoring their health (see Section 4.4 for a more detailed discussion).

The X-Road Center can also be considered as a critical on-line database and may also be equipped with alternative channels support. This would enable to overcome the need of solving the center-independent work problem.

4.3   Replication of Databases

Replication of databases is actually a controversial issue for the X-Road. On one hand, it is required to provide data availability in case of DOS attacks or other Internet malfunction scenarios. On the other hand, it contradicts the basic principle of X-Road that each data source should be kept only in one place to guarantee its freshness and have a clearly defined party responsible for its quality. For this reason, database replication has not been supported nor encouraged in the previous generations of X-Road.

Technically, however, this is possible already today. If a critical database B needs some view of database A to maintain its operations in the time of crisis, its developers can obtain this view just by performing regular X-Road queries. In case the database A is large, this may be a tedious task. It may also be the case that the entire database A is not even needed for B, but it is easier for the developers not to care about this and download entire A, putting unnecessary load to A. Also, the task of keeping the local copy of (the local view of) A up-to-date is a non-trivial task.

Hence, the least we can do to improve the situation is to define a set of templates and best practices for the developers to follow when replicating the databases. The good aspect of such a solution is that it requires minimal intervention into the existing systems. However, it is very difficult to guarantee that the developers would actually follow these best practices, so potentially this solution would not improve the current state of affairs too much.

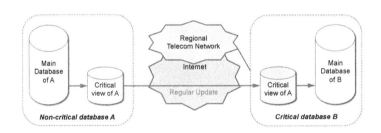

Fig. 5. A view of a non-critical database A saved at a critical database B

As a more advanced solution, a special component can be added to the security servers of the clients. This component directly implements the best practices of creating local copies of the client views of the databases (Fig. 5). This component is configured with the specifics of the database and the anticipated use patterns. Compared to the first solution, more work must be done with the X-Road system, but the result would be a much better unified and easy-to-use replication mechanism.

4.4   Channel Switching Logic

For reasonable use of alternative channels, every security server must be able to automatically determine when exactly is it necessary to use alternative connections instead of the primary ones. It would be hard for the whole infrastructure to synchronously switch to alternative connections and hence, such decisions must be made separately for every point-to-point connection. Note that the databases may be subjects to selective DOS attacks, so that server A does not necessarily know if another server B is under attack or not. It may also be the case that neither A nor B is under a direct attack, but there is just no proper Internet connection between these two servers. For example, server B might be down because of regular maintenance. In this case, it would be unreasonable for A to try to connect with B via an alternative channel. So, A must be able to distinguish between the situations where B is under attack, and where B is just down for some temporary technical reasons.

We will assume that A will recognize if there is a DOS attack against A itself and is able to shut down the regular connection in this case. We will also assume that even if the regular channel has been shut down, A would be able to recognize the end of the DOS attack. This check can be implemented by A periodically trying to re-open the regular Internet connection and shutting it down again if the attack continues.

In this Section, we propose a channel switching logic for server A that has a connection with server B (either for providing the data to or querying the data from B). This logic is applied on the service level and the transactions between the servers are in the form of query/response. The same logic must be applied by A for every B that it is connected to via an alternative channel.

The logic consists of the following main items.

- A has to regularly ping every connected server B through the alternative connection in order to determine whether the connection is healthy and whether B is up.
- A has to make regular *dummy queries* to every connected server B (answered by B with *dummy responses*), the purpose of which is to determine, whether the regular connection works between A and B.
- If A is queried by B via the alternative connection, the query must be answered via the alternative connection.
- If A is queried by B via the regular connection, the query must be answered via the regular connection.
- If A is under a DOS attack, it will shut down the regular channel and start using the alternative channel for every partner B, until the DOS attack ends.
- If certain number of (dummy) queries by A to B are not answered by B, but at the same time, B pings via the alternative channel then A decides that B is up but is unable to answer to A's queries via the regular channel. This means that the regular channel is down, and hence A starts using the alternative channel for sending requests to B. Still, A continues to send the dummy queries to B via the regular channel in order to be able to change back to the regular channel later.

– If A uses an alternative channel with B and a certain number of A's dummy requests have been successfully answered by B then A decides that the regular channel between A and B is operational again and A changes over to the regular channel with B.

5   Conclusions and Further Work

In this paper, we studied the methods for increasing availability of federated database systems in case of severe network failures (e.g. due to Denial-of-Service attacks). As the basis of our studies we chose the X-Road infrastructure, developed in Estonia to allow unified and controlled access to various governmental databases. In its core, the X-Road infrastructure is rather generic to allow generalization of our proposals to other similar infrastructures.

We analyzed the requirements for improvement under the network-failure scenario. As a result of the analysis, we proposed three main categories of measures to achieve better service availability in this scenario.

First, in order to have continuous access to certificate validity information and other secure configuration data, the current DNSSEC-based solution needs to be replaced by more flexible protocols (e.g. OCSP allowing the response caching as a standard measure).

Second, alternative communication channels between critical ervices need to be introduced. These alternative channels may be considerably more expensive, hence the security servers need to support better filtering of services based on their priority.

Third, selected views of critical databases may be replicated at the service consumer's site. Specific extra components need to be developed for security servers in order to achieve such a functionality.

Finally, we stated the main procedures and criteria to decide when to switch over to alternative channels and back. Still, it has to be noted that the way channel switching logic is presented in the current paper is just a theoretical proposal. Before practical implementation it should be validated (e.g. using some simulation framework), but this effort remains out of the scope of this paper.

All of the above-described solutions are planned to be implemented for the next generation of X-Road. After the implementation phase, a thorough analysis on the quality of service and the provided level of resilience against the network problems and Denial-of-Service attacks must be conducted. Conducting such a study will also remain a subject for future work.

Acknowledgements. Authors are grateful to Viljar Tulit and Alar Jõeste for helpful discussions.

References

1. Apache Hadoop project, http://hadoop.apache.org/
2. Ansper, A., Buldas, A., Freudenthal, M., Willemson, J.: Scalable and Efficient PKI for Inter-Organizational Communication. In: Proceedings of the 19th Annual Computer Security Applications Conference, ACSAC 2003, pp. 308–318 (2003)

3. Bent, G., Dantressangle, P., Vyvyan, D., Mowshowitz, A., Mitsou, V.: A dynamic distributed federated database. In: Proc. 2nd Ann. Conf. International Technology Alliance (2008)
4. Dawson, S., Qian, S., Samarati, P.: Providing security and interoperation of heterogeneous systems. In: Security of Data and Transaction Processing, pp. 119–145. Springer (2000)
5. De Capitani di Vimercati, S., Samarati, P.: Authorization specification and enforcement in federated database systems. Journal of Computer Security 5(2), 155–188 (1997)
6. Gardarin, G., Sha, F., Tang, Z.-H.: Calibrating the Query Optimizer Cost Model of IRO-DB, an Object-Oriented Federated Database System. In: VLDB, vol. 96, pp. 3–6 (1996)
7. Heimbigner, D., McLeod, D.: A federated architecture for information management. ACM Trans. Inf. Syst. 3(3), 253–278 (1985)
8. Kalja, A.: The X-Road Project. A Project to Modernize Estonia's National Databases. Baltic IT&T Review 24, 47–48 (2002)
9. Kalja, A.: The first ten years of X-road. In: Estonian Information Society Yearbook 2011/2012, pp. 78–80. Department of State Information System, Estonia (2012)
10. Kalja, A., Vallner, U.: Public e-Service Projects in Estonia. In: Haav, H.-M., Kalja, A. (eds.) Databases and Information Sustems, Proceedings of the Fifth International Baltic Conference, Baltic DB&IS 2002, vol. 2, pp. 143–153 (June 2002)
11. Lim, E.-P., Srivastava, J.: Query optimization and processing in federated database systems. In: Proceedings of the Second International Conference on Information and Knowledge Management, CIKM 1993, pp. 720–722. ACM, New York (1993)
12. Ottis, R.: Analysis of the 2007 Cyber Attacks Against Estonia from the Information Warfare Perspective. In: Proceedings of the 7th European Conference on Information Warfare and Security, pp. 163–168 (2008)
13. Sheth, A.P., Larson, J.A.: Federated database systems for managing distributed, heterogeneous, and autonomous databases. ACM Comput. Surv. 22(3), 183–236 (1990)
14. Templeton, M., Henley, H., Maros, E., Van Buer, D.J.: InterViso: dealing with the complexity of federated database access. The VLDB Journal 4(2), 287–318 (1995)
15. Tomasic, A., Raschid, L., Valduriez, P.: Scaling access to heterogeneous data sources with DISCO. IEEE Transactions on Knowledge and Data Engineering 10(5), 808–823 (1998)
16. Willemson, J., Ansper, A.: A Secure and Scalable Infrastructure for Inter-Organizational Data Exchange and eGovernment Applications. In: Proceedings of the Third International Conference on Availability, Reliability and Security ARES 2008, pp. 572–577. IEEE Computer Society (2008)

Minimizing the Impact of In-band Jamming Attacks in WDM Optical Networks

Konstantinos Manousakis and Georgios Ellinas

KIOS Research Center for Intelligent Systems and Networks,
Department of Electrical and Computer Engineering, University of Cyprus, Cyprus
{manousakis.konstantinos,gellinas}@ucy.ac.cy

Abstract. This work presents an algorithm for the planning phase of wavelength division multiplexing (WDM) optical networks considering the impact of physical layer attacks. Since the signals in transparent WDM networks are transmitted all-optical, these networks are vulnerable against high-power jamming attacks. Due to crosstalk induced interactions among different connections, malicious high-power signals are spread in the network. To this end, it is necessary to plan an optical network in a way that the spread of an attack is minimized. In this work an Integer Linear Programming (ILP) formulation is proposed that addresses the problem of Routing and Wavelength Assignment (RWA) with the objective to minimize the propagation of the introduced high-power malicious signals. The physical layer attack propagation is modeled as interactions among connections through in-band channel crosstalk. Additionally, Linear Programming (LP) relaxation techniques are used to handle larger network instances.

Keywords: physical layer attacks, routing and wavelength assignment, optical networks.

1 Introduction

In all-optical wavelength division multiplexing (WDM) networks data are transmitted through lightpaths, which may span multiple consecutive fibers. A lightpath is realized by determining a path between the source and the destination of a connection and allocating a free wavelength on all the links of the path. The selection of the path and the wavelength to be used by a lightpath is an important optimization problem, known as the routing and wavelength assignment (RWA) problem [1-2].

The RWA problem is usually considered under two alternative traffic models. Offline (or static) lightpath establishment addresses the case where the set of connections is known in advance, usually given in the form of a traffic matrix that describes the number of lightpaths that have to be established between each pair of nodes. Dynamic (or online) lightpath establishment considers the case where connection requests arrive at random time instants, over a prolonged period of time, and are served upon their arrival, on a one-by-one basis.

E. Luiijf and P. Hartel (Eds.): CRITIS 2013, LNCS 8328, pp. 38–49, 2013.

All-optical transparent networks, where data signals remain in the optical domain for the entire path, are vulnerable to the propagation of malicious signals through several parts of the network. Optical telecommunications networks need to be able to detect and locate failures (fault or attack) and degradations as fast and as accurately as possible, in order to restore lost traffic and repair the failure or mitigate the attack. An attack is defined as an intentional action against the ideal and secure functioning of the network [3]. An overview of possible physical layer attacks in transparent optical networks can be found in [4].

One form of an attack in transparent optical networks is a high-power jamming attack that can be classified into two categories based on the effects it inflicts on the signal: *in-band jamming* that is the result of intra-channel crosstalk and *out-of-band jamming* that includes inter-channel crosstalk and nonlinearities. Due to inter- or intra-channel crosstalk induced interactions among different connections, attacks propagate through the network affecting several connections. As a consequence the attack localization is a difficult problem. Thus, because of the high bit-rates of connections in optical networks, and the interaction of the connections, an attack can potentially cause a huge amount of information loss. Therefore, the limitation of attack propagation is a crucial consideration in designing transparent WDM networks.

There are two different methods that can be used in order to reduce jamming attack impact. One approach is to use optical wavelength-selective attenuators as power equalizers inside network nodes to limit the propagation of high-power jamming attacks [5]. The other approach is the attack awareness of routing and wavelength assignment algorithms in order to reduce the interaction among lightpaths and as a consequence the spread of the attack.

The concept of preventive, attack-aware RWA problem was proposed in [6]. The authors formulate the routing sub-problem of RWA as an Integer Linear Program (ILP) with the objective to decrease the potential damage of jamming attacks causing out-of-band crosstalk in fibers and gain competition in optical amplifiers. A tabu search heuristic was proposed to cover larger network instances. In [7], authors proposed a wavelength assignment approach to limit the potential propagation of in-band crosstalk attacks throughout the network. Authors in [8] extended upon their work in [7] by considering a more realistic case where crosstalk attacks could maximally spread in one or two steps. This means that secondary attacked signals are not strong enough for the attack to propagate further.

This work proposes an optimization approach with the objective to assign routes and wavelengths to the traffic demands so as to minimize the impact of high-power signals through in-band jamming attacks. Network prevention is considered during the network planning phase so that the number of the affected connections from an intentional attack to be minimized. An ILP formulation is proposed that solves the RWA problem jointly (Routing and Wavelength Assignment) while minimizing the propagation (due to lightpath interactions through in-band jamming) of high-power signal attacks. In particular, the ILP formulation uses constraints to minimize the impact of an attack through in-band jamming. By minimizing the channel interactions among lightpaths due to in-band crosstalk, the transition of high-power signals from one lightpath to another is also minimized. Additionally, variations of the formulation objective and Linear Programming (LP) relaxation techniques are used to address the problem in larger scale networks. The simulation results show that by considering attack-aware RWA algorithms, a significant decrease in the impact of in-band jamming attacks is achieved in transparent WDM networks, validating the need for such an approach during the planning phase of the network.

In Section 2 of this paper the network and the attack propagation models are initially described. This is followed in Section 3 by the proposed ILP formulation that accounts for the minimization of high-power signal propagation through in-band crosstalk, thus minimizing the effect of high-power jamming attacks. The same section also presents variations of the ILP objective as well as a Linear Programming relaxation technique. Simulation results are presented in Section 4 while concluding remarks are given in Section 5.

2   Network and Attack Models

This section describes the network and the attack propagation models that are used in this work.

2.1   Network Model

A network topology is represented by a connected graph $G=(V,E)$, where V denotes the set of optical cross-connects (nodes), which are assumed to not be equipped with wavelength conversion capabilities, and E denotes the set of (point-to-point) single-fiber links. Each fiber is able to support a common set $C=\{1,2,...,W\}$ of W distinct wavelengths.

2.2   Attack Propagation Model

In this work an attack is considered as a high-power signal injection in one of the cross-connects. Fig. 1 illustrates an example of such an attack in node n_1 of the network. An attacker using a high-power signal can spread the attack further in the network using lightpath (p_1,w_i), through intra-channel crosstalk (in-band jamming). Intra-channel crosstalk is related to the non-ideal switching matrix of an optical cross-connect switch. In particular, intra-channel crosstalk is the effect of power leakage between lightpaths crossing the same switch and using the same wavelength due to non-ideal isolation of the inputs/outputs of the switching fabric. Intra-channel crosstalk cannot be filtered out, since the interfering signal is on the same wavelength as the one affected. Thus, a high-power jamming signal can cause significant leakage inside the switches between lightpaths that are on the same wavelength as the attacking signal.

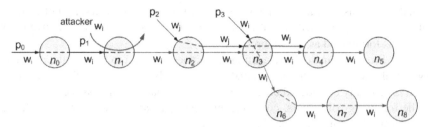

Fig. 1. High-power in-band jamming attack propagation

In Fig. 1 the high-power signal propagation through the effect of in-band jamming is depicted. As can be seen, a lightpath (p_0,w_i) from node n_0 to node n_5 is established using wavelength w_i. Also, a lightpath (p_3,w_i) from node n_3 to node n_8 is established using the same wavelength, w_i, and finally, a lightpath (p_2,w_j) from node n_2 to node n_4 is established using a different wavelength w_j. Let (p_1,w_i) be a malicious lightpath (high-power signal) using wavelength w_i. This lightpath affects the other lightpaths using the same wavelength w_i crossing the same nodes. Lightpath (p_0,w_i) is then affected by lightpath (p_1,w_i) and becomes an attacker too, called a "secondary attacker". Thus, lightpath (p_0,w_i) spreads the attack further to lightpath (p_3,w_i). Note that the malicious lightpath (p_1,w_i) does not affect lightpath (p_2,w_j) through intra-channel crosstalk despite the fact that the lightpaths cross the same node, n_2, as lightpath (p_2,w_j) uses a different wavelength than the attacking lightpath. However, lightpath (p_2,w_j) can be affected by lightpath (p_1,w_i) through out-of band jamming (inter-channel crosstalk) between nodes n_2-n_3 and n_3-n_4 in case the two lightpaths use adjacent wavelengths (that is $j=i$-1 or $j=i$+1). However, this type of attack will not be considered in this work that focuses only on intra-channel crosstalk effects.

3   Attack-Aware RWA Problem

In this section, the proposed Integer Linear Programming (ILP) formulation is presented aiming at minimizing the propagation of physical layer attacks, in terms of affected lightpaths through intra-channel crosstalk by high-power jamming attack signals. As explained above, a high-power input signal can affect a lightpath through intra-channel crosstalk and an affected lightpath can also affect other lightpaths, thus spreading the attack to other parts of the network.

In this work, the static version of RWA is considered that assumes an a-priori known traffic scenario given in the form of a matrix of non-negative integers, Λ, called the traffic matrix. Then, Λ_{sd} denotes the number of requested wavelengths from source s to destination d. Note that there may be multiple lightpath requests for a given source-destination pair (s,d) and they can be routed over different paths.

The algorithm is given a specific RWA instance; that is, a fixed network topology, the set of wavelengths that can be used, and a static traffic scenario. The Routing and Wavelength Assignment (RWA) algorithms consist of two phases. In the first phase, k candidate paths are identified for serving each requested connection. These paths are selected by employing a variation of the k-shortest path algorithm. After a subset P_{sd}

of candidate paths for each commodity pair $s-d$ is computed, the total set of computed paths, $P = \bigcup_{s-d} P_{sd}$, is inserted to the next phase. In the second phase, the given RWA instance is formulated as an ILP problem.

Linear Programming (LP) relaxation techniques are used to address the problem in larger scale networks. The corresponding LP is solved using the Simplex method, which is generally considered efficient for the great majority of possible inputs.

The following parameters, constants, and variables are used to formulate the high power in-band jamming attack RWA problem:

Parameters:

- $s,d \in V$: network nodes
- $w \in C$: an available wavelength
- $l \in E$: a network link
- $p \in P_{sd} \subset P$: a candidate path

Constants:

- Λ_{sd}: the number of requested connections from node s to d

Variables:

- $x_{p,w}$: a binary variable, equal to 1 if path p occupies wavelength w, and 0 otherwise
- W_l: the number of used wavelengths on link l
- S_p: the number of in-band lightpath interactions on path p, that is, the number of the different lightpaths that affect lightpath p through intra-channel crosstalk.

3.1   ILP Formulation

The problem is formulated as an ILP in order to handle high-power in-band jamming signal attacks. The formulation includes constraints for the traditional RWA problem plus additional constraints for in-band jamming attacks. In particular, a constraint for each lightpath (p,w) that counts the number of lightpaths that interact through intra-channel crosstalk with lightpath (p,w) in every network node traversed by lightpath (p,w), is inserted in the formulation.

The formulation of the attack-aware RWA problem is then as follows:

Objective

$$\text{Minimize}: \sum_l W_l + m \cdot \sum_p S_p \tag{1}$$

subject to the following constraints:

- Distinct wavelength assignment constraints,

$$\sum_{\{p | l \in p\}} x_{p,w} \leq 1, \text{ for all } l \in E, \text{ for all } w \in C \tag{2}$$

- Incoming traffic constraints,

$$\sum_{p \in P_{sd}} \sum_{w} x_{p,w} = \Lambda_{sd} \text{, for all } s\text{-}d \text{ pairs} \tag{3}$$

- Number of wavelengths per link

$$W_l = \sum_{p \| l \in p} \sum_{w} x_{pw} \text{, for all } l \in C \tag{4}$$

- Jamming attack related to intra-channel crosstalk

$$\sum_{\{p' \mid p' \in P_{pp'}^{cn}\}} x_{p',w} + B \cdot x_{pw} - S_p \leq B \text{, for all } p \in P \text{ and all } w \in C \tag{5}$$

where B, is a constant taking large values and is used to activate/deactivate the constraints of Equation (5). This means that if the variable $x_{p,w}$ in Equation (5) takes the value 1, then the above constraints are active and the in-band jamming attacks are taken into account, while if the variable $x_{p,w}$ takes the value 0, then these constraints are always true and do affect the objective function. $P_{pp'}^{cn}$ is the set of paths p' that have at least one common node with path p.

The first term of the objective accounts for the cost of the wavelength utilization on the links and the second term accounts for the in-band crosstalk interaction for each active lightpath as defined by the variables of the problem. The constant m is used to express the impact of each term to the objective function. Constraints (2) and (3) correspond to typical constraints of the traditional RWA problem. Specifically, Constraint (2) ensures that each wavelength is used at most once on each fiber and Constraint (3) ensures that all the incoming traffic is satisfied. Constraint (4) counts the number of the used wavelengths per link. The wavelength continuity constraint is implicitly taken into account by the definition of the $x_{p,w}$ variables. Constraint (5) counts the number of lightpaths that interact through in-band crosstalk with lightpath (p,w). For large network sizes, the complexity of the ILP problem is reduced by relaxing the integrality constraints of the variables $x_{p,w}$ and the corresponding Linear Programming (LP) problem is solved. Note that by minimizing the lightpath interactions through in-band crosstalk, the high-power attack propagation of a malicious signal is also minimized. Moreover, assuming that an affected signal can become an attacker (lightpath with high-power signal), the propagation of the secondary attacker is also minimized because all the lightpath interactions are minimized.

3.2   Variations of the ILP Formulation

In order to consider both factors of the objective function as described above, the following cost functions are studied, which try to penalize both the wavelength usage and the violation of in-band crosstalk propagation but differ in the number of additional variables they use:

- **Minimize:** $\sum_l W_l + \sum_{p \in P} S_p$, where S_p defines the number of in-band crosstalk interactions of path p.

- **Minimize:** $\sum_l W_l + \sum_{p \in P} \sum_{w \in C} S_{pw}$, where S_{pw} defines the number of in-band crosstalk

  interactions of path p on a specific wavelength w.   (6)

- **Minimize:** $\sum_l W_l + S$, where S defines the maximum number of in-band cross

  talk interactions over all paths.   (7)

The formulation presented in Section 3.1 uses one additional variable S_p per path p (irrespective of the chosen wavelength w); the modification needed to include one additional variable S_{pw} per lightpath (p,w) is done by replacing each additional variable S_p of each path in Constraint (5) with w additional variables S_{pw}. In addition, the modification needed to include only one additional variable S for all paths is done by replacing again the additional variables S_p of each path with one additional variable S for all connections. The algorithms that use one additional variable S for all paths, one additional variable S_p per path p, and one additional variable S_{pw} per lightpath are denoted by A-RWA, A-RWA-p and A-RWA-pw, respectively.

3.3   Variables and Constraints

Table 1 analyzes the variations of the formulation presented in the previous sections with respect to the number of variables and constraints that they require. These variations correspond to routing and wavelength assignment problems with the objective to minimize the high-power in-band jamming propagation. The formulations only differ in the number of the additional variables they utilize. These formulations use as input k-shortest paths for each requested connection in order to reduce the search space and as a consequence the complexity of the ILP formulations. By controlling the number of candidate paths k, the number of variables and constraints is also controlled. Other formulations, that do not depend on k-shortest paths [6] (used for routing sub-problem), [7] (used only for wavelength assignment sub-problem), are more sensitive to the used topology (number of nodes, connectivity degree, etc) and use more variables and constraints, even for the sub-problems, compared to the proposed formulation for the RWA problem. In Table 1, $k\rho N^2$ defines the number of the candidate paths for all requested connections. The network load ρ is denoted as the ratio of the total number of requested connections over the number of single requested connections between all possible source-destination pairs. Despite the fact that the number of requested connections (number of requested lightpaths) between a source-destination pair can be greater than 1 ($\rho > 1$), the number of the variables and the constraints, as described in Table 1, is not affected, because the algorithm calculates k candidate paths, irrespective of the number of requested lightpaths for each source-destination pair. For this reason, the maximum value of the load ρ in Table 1 is equal to one ($\rho = 1$).

Table 1. Number of variables and constraints of the formulations

Formulation	Number of Variables		Number of constraints	
	RWA Variables	Additional Variables	$=$	$\leq$
A-RWA	$k\rho N^2 W + W \cdot L$	1	$(\rho N^2)_1 + (L)_2$	$(L \cdot W)_3 + (k\rho N^2 \cdot W)_4$
A–RWA-p	$k\rho N^2 W + W \cdot L$	$k\rho N^2$	$(\rho N^2)_1 + (L)_2$	$(L \cdot W)_3 + (k\rho N^2 \cdot W)_4$
A–RWA-pw	$k\rho N^2 W + W \cdot L$	$k\rho N^2 W$	$(\rho N^2)_1 + (L)_2$	$(L \cdot W)_3 + (k\rho N^2 \cdot W)_4$

N: number of nodes
W: number of wavelengths
L: number of links
k: number of shortest paths for each connection
ρ: load (percentage of total connections)

Constraints:
1: incoming traffic constraints
2: wavelengths per link constraints
3: distinct wavelength assignment constraints
4: in-band jamming attack constraints

3.4 LP Relaxation Techniques

The high-complexity of the ILP problem makes the formulation intractable for large network sizes. In order to reduce the complexity of the ILP problem, the integrality constraints of the variables $x_{p,w}$ are relaxed, and the corresponding Linear Programming (LP) problem is solved by using the Simplex algorithm in combination with appropriate techniques to handle the non-integer solutions. If the Simplex algorithm yields a solution with integer and non-integer values, the variables with integer values are fixed, that is, the variables that are integer are treated as final and the reduced problem for the remaining variables is solved. Fixing variables does not change the objective cost of the LP solution, and as a consequence, with the fixing process, the previous solution is moved to a solution with equal or more integer variables that has the same cost. If after successive fixings an all-integer solution is reached, it is definitely an optimal solution. On the other hand, fixing variables is not guaranteed to return an integer optimal solution if one exists, since the integer solution might consist of different integer values than the ones gradually fixed. When a point is reached beyond which the process of fixing does not increase the integrality of the solution, a rounding process is performed. A single variable is rounded, the one closest to 1, and the reduced LP problem is solved. Rounding is inevitable when there is no integer solution with the same objective cost as the LP relaxation of the RWA instance. However, if after rounding the objective cost changes, there is no guarantee that the problem will end up with an optimal solution.

4   Simulation Results

To evaluate the performance of the proposed algorithms, a number of simulation experiments were performed. In the simulations two network topologies were considered as shown in Fig. 2; a small network topology that has 6 nodes and 9 links and the generic Deutsche Telekom network (DTnet). For solving the LP and ILP related formulations, the Gurobi library was used [9].

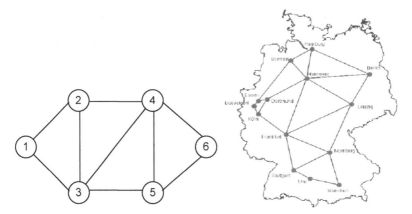

Fig. 2. 6-node network and DT network topologies

For solving each instance of the ILP formulations, a time limit of 3 hours (Gurobi running time) was set in both networks (a PC with Core i5-2400@3.1GHz and 4GB memory was used). First, the results for the 6-node network are presented. The network load ρ was assumed equal to 4.5. In Fig. 3(a), a comparison between the proposed ILP formulations and the traditional RWA that takes into account only the distinct wavelength assignment and continuity constraints is depicted. The objective of the traditional RWA algorithm is to minimize the total number of used wavelengths. On the other hand, the proposed ILP formulations minimize the effect of lightpath interactions due to in-band crosstalk. Fig.3(a) presents the number of lightpaths that interact through in-band crosstalk in relation with the number of available wavelengths. As can be seen, the performance of the traditional RWA algorithm is independent of the number of available wavelengths, while for the A-RWA-p and A-RWA-pw approaches, that exhibit similar performance, the number of interactions decreases significantly with increasing number of available wavelengths.

In Fig.3(b), the results in the form of histograms are presented, that show the effect of in-band jamming crosstalk on the solutions obtained by the RWA algorithms. Given the solution to an RWA instance, the distributions of the number of in-band interactions are plotted for every lightpath. The number of available wavelengths in this case was equal to 14. A left shift in the interactions among lightpaths is observed when attack-aware RWA algorithms and especially A-RWA-p and A-RWA-pw are used and as a consequence the possibility of a high-power in-band jamming attack is reduced. The performance of the A-RWA algorithm is worse than the other two proposed approaches, because the objective of this formulation is to minimize a single value for all the lightpaths. It is obvious from Fig. 3(b) that this value is equal to 2 for this RWA instance. A value equal to 2 of the cost objective means that the in-band interactions of all lightpaths will be from 0 to 2. This cost objective is determined by the lightpath with highest number of in-band interactions. Therefore, the distribution of the lightpaths between the values 0 and 2 does not affect the cost of the objective.

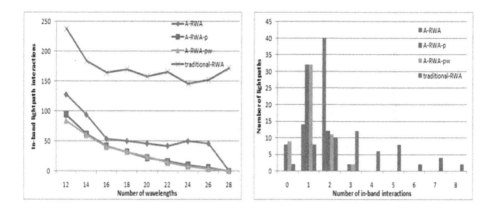

Fig. 3. (a) Number of lightpaths that interact through in-band crosstalk vs. number of available wavelengths – ILP formulations (6-node network). (b) Histogram for lightpath distribution related to in-band lightpath interactions (6-node network).

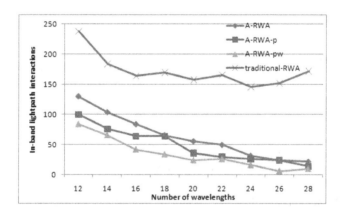

Fig. 4. Number of lightpaths that interact through in-band crosstalk vs. number of available wavelengths – Relaxed LP formulations (6-node network)

Fig.4 represents the same results as in Fig. 3(a), with the difference that the integer constraints were now relaxed to linear constraints as presented in Section 3.4. Comparing these two figures, a small increase to the number of in-band lightpath interactions is observed due to the fact that the LP relaxation technique can increase the cost of the objective function. However, this approach gives a solution much faster than the formulations with integer constraints. As demonstrated in the figure, the A-RWA-pw formulation gives better results than A-RWA-p, since A-RWA-pw minimizes the in-band interactions for all the lightpaths.

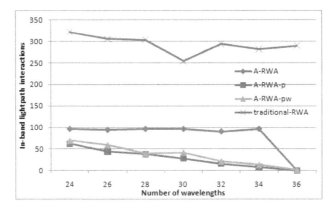

Fig. 5. Number of lightpaths that interact through in-band crosstalk vs. number of available wavelengths – ILP formulations (DT network)

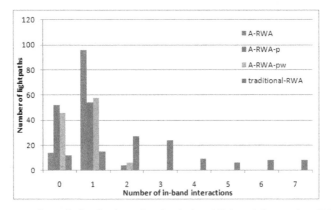

Fig. 6. Histogram for path distribution related to in-band lightpath interaction (DT network)

For the DT network, the load was assumed equal to 0.6. Figures 5 and 6 depict the results for the DT network in the same manner as the results presented for the 6-node network. For the results obtained in Fig. 6, the number of available wavelengths was equal to 24. The only difference between these two networks is that in the DT network the A-RWA-p approach has better performance than the A-RWA-pw approach in contrast to the results obtained for the 6-node network. This occurs due to the fact that in larger networks the number of variables for the A-RWA-pw algorithm is large and thus the complexity is increased in comparison with the A-RWA-p formulation.

5   Conclusions

This work proposed ILP formulations with different objective functions for solving the RWA problem during the design phase of a transparent WDM optical network with the objective of minimizing the high-power in-band crosstalk propagation which is caused when a high-power jamming signal is maliciously introduced in the network at a specific network node. Performance results indicate that the proposed solution outperforms the traditional RWA technique that does not account for the propagation of the jamming signal due to in-band crosstalk, significantly minimizing this propagation in the network and thus drastically containing the effect of the attack on the network infrastructure.

Acknowledgments. This work was supported by the Cyprus Research Promotion Foundation's Framework Programme for Research, Technological Development and Innovation (DESMI 2008), co-funded by the Republic of Cyprus and the European Regional Development Fund, and specifically under Grant Project New Infrastructure/ Strategic/0308/26.

References

1. Zang, H., Jue, J., Mukherjee, B.: A review of routing and wavelength assignment approaches for wavelength-routed optical WDM networks. Optical Net. Mag. 1(1), 47–60 (2000)
2. Ozdaglar, A., Bertsekas, D.: Routing and wavelength assignment in optical networks. IEEE/ACM Transactions on Networking 11(2), 259–272 (2003)
3. Mas, C., Tomkos, I., Tonguz, O.: Failure location algorithm for transparent optical networks. IEEE Journal on Selected Areas in Communication 23(8), 1508–1519 (2005)
4. Fok, M., Wang, Z., Deng, Y., Prucnal, P.: Optical Layer Security in Fiber-Optic Networks. IEEE Transactions on Information Forensics and Security 6(3), 725–736 (2011)
5. Jirattigalachote, A., Skorin-Kapov, N., Furdek, M., Chen, J., Monti, P., Wosinska, L.: Sparse power equalization placement for limiting jamming attack propagation in transparent optical networks. Optical Switching and Networking (OSN) 8(4), 249–258 (2011)
6. Skorin-Kapov, N., Chen, J., Wosinska, L.: A new approach to optical networks security: attack-aware routing and wavelength assignment. IEEE Trans. on Networking 18(3), 750–760 (2010)
7. Furdek, M., Skorin-Kapov, N., Grbac, M.: Attack-aware wavelength assignment for localization of in-band crosstalk attack propagation. IEEE/OSA Journal of Optical Communications and Networking 2(11), 1000–1009 (2010)
8. Skorin-Kapov, N., Furdek, M., Pardo, R., Pavón Mariño, P.: Wavelength assignment for reducing in-band crosstalk attack propagation in optical networks: ILP formulations and heuristic algorithms. European Journal of Operational Research 222(3), 418–429 (2012)
9. http://www.gurobi.com

The Role of Critical Infrastructures' Interdependencies on the Impacts Caused by Natural Disasters

Ana Laugé, Josune Hernantes, and Jose Mari Sarriegi

Tecnun - University of Navarra, San Sebastian, Spain
{alauge,jhernantes,jmsarriegi}@tecnun.es

Abstract. Recent natural disasters have highlighted society's dependency on the correct functioning of critical infrastructures (CIs). The existing interdependencies among CIs complicate matters further, since a failure in a CI can spread through cascading effects to other infrastructures or sectors. Thus society's welfare becomes severely affected, complicating emergency response and increasing the total impact of natural disasters. The aim of this paper is to illustrate the important role that affected CIs have on the overall impact of a natural disaster. We have developed a simulation model that represents a huge storm affecting the energy system, transport and food CIs on a small island. Through this simulation model we can show the effects associated with CIs and the effects of applying crisis management policies.

Keywords: Critical infrastructure, natural disaster, interdependencies, crisis management, impact analysis.

1 Introduction

The history of humanity includes repeated episodes of suffering through overcoming natural disasters. But, what makes people remember the occurrence of a natural disaster years later? Why have disasters such as hurricanes Sandy and Katrina, the Haitian and Japanese earthquakes and the eruption of the Eyjafjallajökull volcano had such a great impact on society?

The answer to these questions relies on the effect of natural disasters on critical infrastructures (CIs) such as transportation, energy, health and communication among others. Analysing natural disasters that have received most attention from the general public in recent years, there is a clear common aspect: they have significantly affected CIs, thus aggravating and prolonging disasters' impacts [1]. As a consequence recent natural disasters have significantly increased people's concern about CIs' vulnerabilities given that the welfare of society is dependent on CIs proper functioning [2-4].

Additionally, the complexity of CI systems and their interdependencies increase the difficulty of crisis management [5], [6]. It is necessary that crisis managers understand existing CIs interdependencies and their behaviour over time in order to effectively manage crisis phases and to identify current crisis management gaps [7-10]. Thus, including a dynamic perspective on this problem analysis is important [11].

Consequently, tools to understand the criticality of CIs and their interdependencies are needed in order to help crisis managers estimate, at least qualitatively, the global

E. Luiijf and P. Hartel (Eds.): CRITIS 2013, LNCS 8328, pp. 50–61, 2013.
© Springer International Publishing Switzerland 2013

impact of a negative event on interdependent CIs. Simulation modelling is an appropriate technique to study holistic CIs interdependencies due to system complexity and the need to include the system's dynamics through the analysis of variables' evolution [12], [13]. Furthermore, CIs modelling must adopt a holistic perspective including social, environmental and economic aspects in order to help crisis managers to have a complete view of the system they are managing and to guide them in implementing optimal policies.

The insights gained through modelling CIs interdependencies can help in developing new policies and legal and regulatory issues. Thus, special focus must be given to CIs and their interdependencies for effectively managing natural disasters [8], [9], [14-17].

The aim of this paper is to emphasise the important role of CIs and their interdependencies when a natural disaster occurs because when CIs are damaged the total impact of a disaster increases. Our approach includes the analysis of impact evolution over time through the development of a simulation model. This simulation model's behaviour is based on the effect of a natural disaster on CIs, the consequences of CIs interdependencies, and the effect of policies related to resource deployment to repair or reconnect CIs. The simulation model allows the analysis of how the presence of interdependencies between different CIs aggravates and prolongs disaster consequences.

2   CIs and Their Interdependencies

The CIs included in this research correspond to the list from the green paper on the European Programme for Critical Infrastructure Protection [18], which considers the following eleven infrastructures as critical: Energy, Information and Communication technologies (ICT), Water, Food, Health, Financial, Public and Legal Order and Safety, Civil Administration, Transport, Chemical and Nuclear Industry, Space and Research.

As the Council Directive 2008/114/EC of the European Union states, "critical infrastructure means an asset, system or part thereof located in Member States which is essential for the maintenance of vital societal functions, health, safety, security, economic or social well-being of people, and the disruption or destruction of which would have a significant impact on a Member State as a result of the failure to maintain those functions" [19]. This definition highlights the important role that CIs play in society's welfare. Therefore, current society is highly dependent on CIs [5], [12], [16], [20]. This dependency causes serious problems when a failure affects one or more CIs [12], [14], [16].

Furthermore, CIs are complex, connected and interdependent systems [1], [21]. These interdependencies can make failures spread from one to another making a short disruption in a CI cause important and long term effects in society [22] and disrupting society's welfare [12], [23], [24]. Researchers in CI protection use the term "cascading effects" to refer to the fact that one event affecting one CI can subsequently impact others [5], [8], [16], [21], [24-29]. For example, Hurricane Katrina directly affected electricity and transport, among other infrastructures, and these impacts spread to the water, telecommunications and gas distribution systems [30]. In the Haitian earthquake most of the CIs were severely affected but also months after, the devastation caused by the earthquake increased due to a cholera outbreak affecting health and water CIs [31]. Due to Eyjafjallajökull volcano's ash cloud in countries like Ireland and the United Kingdom, airports were closed for more than a week, which created a crisis in supply of medicines, fruits and vegetables [32]. In addition, after the Japanese earthquake, the tsunami critically damaged Fukushima nuclear plant creating a health alert due to radiation release [33]. Recent Hurricane Sandy provoked power supplies which affected CIs such as health services and communications systems [34].

The study of CIs interdependencies is a major challenge, however it is still immature and a growing research field [11], [12], [24], [35], [36]. Even though detailed information about individual CIs and their elements can be obtained, the understanding of interdependencies between different CIs is limited and often, experts are not completely aware of them [12], [20], [37].

However, CIs interdependencies research still needs to consider a long term perspective analysing how the effects of one CI on others can spread differently due to time delays. This can complicate crisis managers' understanding of causes and effects, affecting decisions or policies for crisis management [12]. Modelling and simulation can facilitate this understanding through the representation of different scenarios and the analysis of several policies' potential effectiveness.

3   CIs Interdependencies Modelling and Simulation Methodologies

Several authors have highlighted the importance of the analysis, modelling and simulation of CIs and their interdependencies for national and international security [9], [12], [17], [37-39]. Modelling and simulation of CIs interdependencies can help crisis management through prevention, preparation, response and recovery phases [5]. Even though progress has been made on research about CIs there is still more work to do due to the complexity of CI systems and their interdependencies [25], [40]. Furthermore, the criticality of CIs for society makes analysis and modelling of system behaviour a very relevant task [16].

However, CIs interdependencies modelling is not an easy task and several difficulties have been identified. One of the most important difficulties is the data gathering process [8], [11], [16], [17], [21], [41] as the relevant information is not easily available. Finding the appropriate level of abstraction for CIs modelling is also a hard task as at a very detailed level too much information and details would be required [20], [42] and a too aggregated level might not give significant results [41]. Furthermore, agents with different expertise have different points of view and information about the same CIs and therefore, multidisciplinary agents' participation is needed [12], [13], [41], [43]. Moreover, CIs owners have a good idea about the CIs they directly depend upon but they do not really know about the effects of higher order dependencies [27]. Additionally, due to CI systems complexity some of their interdependencies can be easily identified but others can produce unforeseen effects [9], [21], [41]. Finally, there is not an agreed upon or standard methodology for CIs modelling [9], [40], [41].

There are several modelling methodologies that have been used for CIs modelling [8], [11], [21], but agent based, input-output and dynamic simulation models have been identified as the most used methodologies.

Agent based models have been widely used for CIs modelling [9], [21], [44]. Agent based models can represent complex systems behaviour through the analysis of agents' interactions. It is appropriate mostly when the focus of the study is based on complex interactions among agents and the environment [12], [13], [45].

Input-output models [46] have been also applied to CIs modelling [47-49]. Input-output models rely on the flow of resources, providing an economic perspective [12], [13]. However, they are mostly focused on the economy, are heavily dependent on reliable data, and imply equilibrium conditions. Furthermore, equilibrium conditions are not useful when analysing the dynamics of systems produced for example, due to disasters' disruptions.

Dynamic simulation such as System Dynamics methodology [50], [51], which includes long term perspectives and impact evolution over time, has also been proposed by several authors as a proper tool for CIs modelling [8], [9], [12], [16], [21], [52-55]. It is based on feedback interactions which are analogous to CIs interdependencies. Furthermore, System Dynamics can model socio technical systems including not only technical details but also human and organizational aspects [12], [13], [45].

However, usually projects for analysing CIs interdependencies focus on the analysis of individual or few CIs and do not provide a complete picture of CIs as a system [5], [8], [12], [35], [40], [56], including interdependencies among CIs, which could lead to an improvement in crisis management [5], [24]. Therefore, there is still work to do in this research field [40].

4   CIs Interdependencies Simulation Model

This research includes a dynamic analysis of impacts generated by a crisis affecting CIs. This dynamic analysis illustrates the fact that CIs play a crucial role in subsequent impact generation. CIs interdependencies and cascading effects provoke that a damaged CI can affect others. Thus, the higher the level of interdependencies among CIs the more prolonged and aggravated the impacts. Therefore, we have developed a System Dynamics simulation model to show how the existing interdependencies of CIs can generate or extend the initial impact after a natural disaster. This model also enables crisis managers to understand how response policies may affect disaster impact evolution over time. This model represents an interesting scenario to show different behaviours and policies but it does not represent a real past scenario.

The developed simulation model represents the CIs interdependencies and their effects when one or more natural disasters occur. To solve the difficulties explained in section 3 we have included in the simulation model data gathered by Setola et al. [27], where surveys about CIs interdependencies were conducted to multidisciplinary CIs' agents. Other needed data have been estimated, based on the few real data available, in order to model a realistic scenario. Additionally, non linear look up tables have been included to calibrate the relation among variables. Furthermore, the aggregation level is quite high but it still allows including enough detail about CIs performance, their interdependencies and the effects of carrying out recovery policies.

It has to be pointed that even in the scientific literature most of authors use the concept "CIs interdependencies" for every dependency among CIs, without distinguishing between interdependencies and dependencies. For example, if two CIs (A and B) are interdependent, there will be a bidirectional effect as A will rely on B and vice versa. However, if A and B are dependent the effect will be unidirectional, for example A will be dependent on B but B will not be affected by A.

The model represents a small island in the Atlantic Ocean where a huge storm with devastating winds at the first hours and severe floods hours later, has affected some of its CIs. A representation of the CIs on the island is shown in Fig. 1 (lines connecting CIs show the degree of dependency among them). From Setola et al. [27], we have chosen electricity and air transportation which are the most influential and influenced CIs respectively (see dependency levels in Fig. 1). However, electricity and air transportation CIs are not interdependent as there is not a bidirectional dependency among them. If air transportation does not work electricity will not be affected but, if the opposite happens, airports' security systems and lighting could not work without power and the airports would have to shut down. Additionally, in order to show the effect of interdependent and dependent CIs in the simulation model, we have also included food as another affected CI. Food CI depends on electricity for production systems and on air transport as some food is produced inside the island but other must be supplied by this means of transport. In addition, even if the effect is not immediate, being shortage of food during some days it will have effect on other CIs such as electricity and air transport. The scarcity of food may cause a generalized public anxiety to get food and as consequence, electricity and air transport workers could not be able to continue with their normal activity.

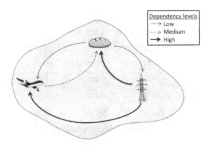

Fig. 1. Electricity is represented with a high voltage tower; a piece of bread corresponds to food infrastructure and a plain to the air transport CI

The structure of the System Dynamics simulation model is shown in Fig. 2. The model is composed of six stocks and several variables connected by arrow links. Each pair of stocks represents one of the three selected CIs. For example, the *Working electricity* stock represents the percentage of electricity that is working while the *Damaged electricity* shows the percentage that has failed. Additionally, there are variables and links connecting the stocks in the simulation model. The arrow links symbolize the existing causal influences among the parameters that are connected. Behind each variable, equations and data inputs are included. By changing the values of these parameters the model generates different behaviours that can be used for a deeper understanding of the system.

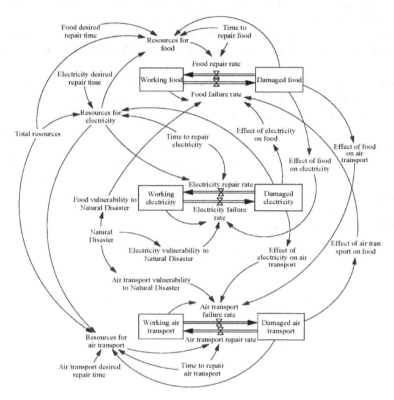

Fig. 2. Simulation model's structure

The input to the simulation model is the *Natural Disaster* variable which affects every CI depending on their vulnerability. For example, if electricity is affected by a natural disaster, the *Electricity vulnerability to Natural Disaster* variable will influence the *Electricity failure rate*. This *Electricity failure rate* makes some of the *Working electricity* fails and increasing therefore *Damaged electricity* stock. Furthermore, if food CI is also damaged, the dependency of electricity on food (*Effect of food on electricity*) will also affect electricity negatively increasing *Electricity failure rate* and therefore, decreasing the *Working electricity* stock and increasing the percentage of *Damaged electricity*. This effect on electricity will continue until the food system is restored. On the one hand, electricity is damaged by the natural disaster and furthermore, by the effect that food has on electricity. On the other hand, deployment of resources to repair is what triggers the flow from *Damaged electricity* to *Working electricity*. Thanks to the deployed *Resources for electricity* the electricity system will be repaired, increasing the *Working electricity* stock until the complete electricity system is recovered. A similar structure is represented for air transport and food considering their interdependencies with the other CIs.

The first scenario that has been simulated consists of two events. First, in hour 10, electricity and air transport CIs are severely affected by stormy winds. Then, in hour 20, only electricity CI is damaged due to floods. In this initial scenario resources are equally deployed to restore the three CIs. Fig. 3 shows the performance of the three CIs. The scale of the graph represents the percentage of CIs performance, meaning 100% that infrastructure works properly and 0% that CI does not wok at all. Each CI's behaviour is given a number, being 1 for electricity, 2 for food and 3 for air transport. In hour 10, both electricity and air transport fail due to winds. Food is also affected by its dependency on both CIs. As can be seen in the figure at hour 20 electricity has been affected by floods and even if air transport and food have not been damaged directly by floods their performance also goes down due to their dependency on electricity. Moreover, air transport and food do not fail as rapidly as electricity as they could have power generators that provide them with electricity at least for the most critical processes. Then, food's performance needs longer time to recover due to the high dependency on the other CIs. For example, time is needed to recover usual level of food supply after air transport has been recovered. Furthermore, raw materials that should have been processed could have been lost without electricity to refrigerate them. Therefore, firstly both CIs have to be restored and then could food improve its performance but it will not be immediate as time is needed to recover normal activity.

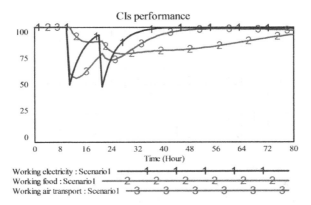

Fig. 3. Performance of electricity, air transport and food CIs affected by a natural disaster

The second simulation is based on the hypothesis that the three CIs are severely affected by winds and floods and crisis managers have to make decisions about resources deployment policies. There are two scenarios represented in Fig.4. On the one hand, "No priority" scenario shows the performance of the three CIs when no priority to restore any CI has been applied. On the other hand, "Priority to electricity" shows CIs performance when electricity repair has been prioritized in order to achieve a complete restoration of electricity faster. Giving priority to electricity shows better results as electricity is the most influential CI and its effects on other CIs are high. Therefore, the higher the time electricity is down, the higher its impact on air transport and food will be. To better represent this, we have measured the accumulated impact that each CI suffers through the "impact unit" (i.u.). "i.u." is used to compare the total impact of the three CIs (one "i.u." is equal to the impact of 1% of a CI which is down for 1 hour). As it can be seen in both graphs the total impact is much lower in the "Priority to electricity" scenario. If we could translate "i.u." to economic impact for each CI, the cost when prioritizing electricity would be six times lower for electricity and reduced to half for food and air transport CIs. Moreover, in "Priority to electricity" the complete recovery of CIs would take less than two weeks while "No priority" scenario would lead to a complete restoration of the three CIs in one month.

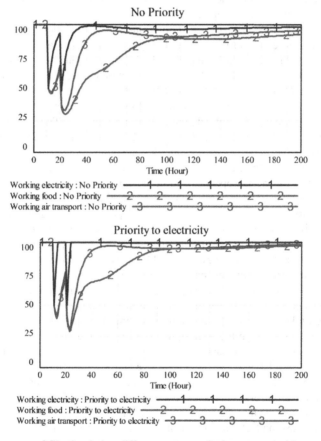

Fig. 4. Performance of CIs simulating different resource deployment priorities to recover them

The model allows managers to simulate different scenarios with short or long term perspectives and analyzing the effects of carrying out several crisis management policies. In light of the obtained results, this simulation model might be a valuable training tool to improve CIs management and their performance in face of future disasters.

5   Conclusion

Natural disasters can severely affect CIs and due to their interdependencies, disaster consequences can spread and prolong over time. A failure in a CI can spread through interdependencies affecting the whole region and society's welfare. Therefore, it is necessary to improve natural disasters management by paying more attention to CIs and their interdependencies system. This paper highlights the important role that CIs and their interdependencies play in the impacts a natural disaster generates.

A proper analysis of CIs interdependencies is an important issue to improve crisis management and impact assessment. Thus, research has to be done to identify and understand these interdependencies. The developed simulation model is a way to graphically represent CIs interdependencies and their effects' evolution over time in case of a natural disaster occurrence. The simulations show how natural disasters' effects can spread to different CIs, reducing their performance level, even if they are not directly affected by the disaster itself but by interdependencies on other CIs.

This simulation model has been developed with pedagogical purpose and it still has to be more accurately calibrated with real data for each scenario in order to be used by managers as training tool. It allows calibration to simulate several scenarios and their associated effects when CIs fail adversely affecting others. The simulation model presented in this paper is focused only in three CIs while our aim is to broaden it in order to represent the most important interdependencies among all the CIs. Further work has to be done on the development of this simulation model in order to include all CIs considered by the European Programme for Critical Infrastructure Protection [18] and other policies which can affect the prevention or response phases of crisis management. Furthermore, the implementation of policies, such as the resources deployment quantification or prioritization, can help crisis managers to understand this kind of complex systems evolution over time in order to improve their training for future events. Through this simulation model a better understanding is gained of how the effects, that interdependencies lead to, evolve over time.

The aim of this research is to develop a natural disaster impact dynamic framework in order to assist crisis managers with natural disasters management. Properly identifying, analysing and evaluating the impacts following a crisis helps managers to efficiently manage them through the development of preventive and response programs to mitigate the harshness of a disaster. The framework for evaluating natural disaster impact developed will have a holistic perspective and it will include all sectors affected by natural disasters such as the economy, environment, society, and, of course, CIs. Furthermore, the framework will have a dynamic perspective through the development of simulation models, such as the one presented in this paper. In these simulation models we include cause and effect relationships and crisis consequences evolution over time. In addition, these models can be used by crisis managers as a training tool to represent different scenarios where they make decisions. By analysing crisis evolution over time and how the consequences spread, managers can learn how decision making and the carrying out of different policies affect the final crisis impact.

Acknowledgements. Authors would like to thank Professors Murray Turoff and Starr Roxanne Hiltz for their valuable suggestions on this paper.

References

1. Chang, S.E., McDaniels, T.L., Mikawoz, J., Peterson, K.: Infrastructure failure interdependencies in extreme events: Power outage consequences in the 1998 ice storm. Nat. Hazards 41(2), 337–358 (2007)
2. Zimmerman, R.: Mass transit infrastructure and urban health. J. Urban Health 82(1) (2005)
3. Collier, S., Lakoff, A.: The vulnerability of vital systems: How 'critical infrastructure' became a security problem. In: Dunn, M., Kristensen, K.S. (eds.) The Politics of Securing the Homeland: Critical Infrastructure, Risk and Securitisation, pp. 40–62. Routledge (2008)
4. Croope, S.V., McNeil, S.: Improving resilience of critical infrastructure systems postdisaster. J. Transportation Research Board 2234(1), 3–13 (2011)
5. Dudenhoeffer, D.D., Permann, M.R., Manic, M.: CIMS: A framework for infrastructure interdependency modeling and analysis. In: Proceedings of the 2006 Winter Simulation Conference, pp. 478–485 (2006)
6. Zimmerman, R.: Understanding the implications of critical infrastructure interdependencies for water. In: Wiley Handbook of Science and Technology for Homeland Security (2009)
7. Peerenboom, J.P., Fisher, R.E., Rinaldi, S.M., Kelly, T.K.: Studying the chain reaction. EEI (2002)
8. Rinaldi, S.M.: Modeling and simulating critical infrastructures and their interdependencies. In: Proceedings of the 37th Annual Hawaii International Conference on System Sciences, vol. 8 (2004)
9. Pederson, P., Dudenhoeffer, D., Hartley, S., Permann, M.: Critical infrastructure interdependency modeling: A survey of US and international research. Idaho Idaho National Laboratory. INL/EXT-06-11464 (2006)
10. Oliva, G., Panzieri, S., Setola, R.: Fuzzy dynamic input–output inoperability model. IJCIP 4(3-4), 165–175 (2011)
11. Eusgeld, I., Nan, C., Dietz, S.: "System-of-systems" approach for interdependent critical infrastructures. Reliability Engineering & System Safety 96(6), 679–686 (2011)
12. Sarriegi, J.M., Sveen, F.O., Torres, J., Gonzalez, J.J.: Towards a research framework for critical infrastructure interdependencies. IJEM 5(3), 235–249 (2008)
13. Sarriegi, J.M., Sveen, F.O., Torres, J.M., Gonzalez, J.J.: Adaptation of modelling paradigms to the CIs interdependencies problem. Critical Information Infrastructure Security 5508/2009, 295 (2009)
14. Boin, A., McConnell, A.: Preparing for critical infrastructure breakdowns: The limits of crisis management and the need for resilience. J. Contingencies Crisis Manage. 15(1), 50–59 (2007)
15. Streips, K., Simpson, D.M.: Critical infrastructure failure in a natural disaster: Initial notes comparing kobe and katrina. Louisville (2007)
16. Min, H.S.J., Beyeler, W., Brown, T., Son, Y.J., Jones, A.T.: Toward modeling and simulation of critical national infrastructure interdependencies. IIE Transactions 39(1), 57–71 (2007)
17. Oliva, G., Panzieri, S., Setola, R.: Online distributed interdependency estimation for critical infrastructures. In: 2011 50th IEEE Conference on Decision and Control and European Control Conference (CDC-ECC), pp. 7224–7229 (2011)
18. Commission of the European Communities: Green paper on a european programme for critical infrastructure protection. Brussels (2005)

19. The Council of the European Union: COUNCIL DIRECTIVE 2008/114/EC of 8 december 2008 on the identification and designation of european critical infrastructures and the assessment of the need to improve their protection. European Union (2008)
20. Oliva, G., Panzieri, S., Setola, R.: Agent-based input-output interdependency model. IJCIP 3(2), 76–82 (2010)
21. Stapelberg, R.F.: Infrastructure systems interdependencies and risk informed decision making (RIDM): Impact scenario analysis of infrastructure risks induced by natural, technological and intentional hazards. Journal of Systemics, Cybernetics and Informatics 6(5), 21–27 (2008)
22. Conrad, S.H., LeClaire, R.J., O'Reilly, G.P., Uzunalioglu, H.: Critical national infrastructure reliability modeling and analysis. Bell Labs Technical Journal 11(3), 57–71 (2006)
23. President's Comission on Critical Infrastructure Protection: Critical foundations: Protecting america's infrastructures. Washington (1997)
24. Rinaldi, S.M., Peerenboom, J.P., Kelly, T.K.: Identifying, understanding, and analyzing critical infrastructure interdependencies. IEEE Control Systems 21(6), 11–25 (2001)
25. Peerenboom, J.P., Fisher, R.E.: Analyzing cross-sector interdependencies. In: 40th Annual Hawaii International Conference on System Sciences (HICSS), p. 112 (2007)
26. Duenas-Osorio, L., Vemuru, S.M.: Cascading failures in complex infrastructure systems. Struct. Saf. 31(2), 157–167 (2009)
27. Setola, R., De Porcellinis, S., Sforna, M.: Critical infrastructure dependency assessment using the input–output inoperability model. IJCIP 2(4), 170–178 (2009)
28. Theoharidou, M., Kotzanikolaou, P., Gritzalis, D.: A multi-layer criticality assessment methodology based on interdependencies. Comput. Secur. 29(6), 643–658 (2010)
29. Deshmukh, A., Oh, E.H., Hastak, M.: Impact of flood damaged critical infrastructure on communities and industries. Built Environment Project and Asset Management 1(2), 156–175 (2011)
30. Rahman, S.: Impact of natural disasters on critical infrastructures. In: The 1st Bangladesh Earthquake Symposium, BES-1 (2005)
31. NYU Law. NYU law students play key role in filing claims against the U.N. on behalf of cholera victims in haiti, http://www.law.nyu.edu/news/HAITI_CHOLERA
32. Hall, J.: volcanic ash cloud leaves shops facing shortages of fruit, vegetables and medicine, the telegraph (2010), http://www.telegraph.co.uk/finance/newsbysector/retailandconsumer/7599042/Volcanic-ash-cloudleaves-shops-facing-shortages-of-fruit-vegetables-and-medicine.html
33. Caro-Bejarano, M.J.: Algunas lecciones aprendidas del desastre de fukushima. Spain IEEE. ES. 9, 1 (2012)
34. Beck, C.: Critical infrastructure resilience: What we can learn from hurricane sandy, http://cnponline.org/ht/d/ViewBloggerThread/i/40897/pid/35636
35. Dunn, M., Wigert, I.: International CIIP handbook. ETH (2006)
36. Bologna, S., Di Costanzo, G., Luiijf, E., Setola, R.: An overview of R&D activities in europe on critical information infrastructure protection (CIIP). In: López, J. (ed.) CRITIS 2006. LNCS, vol. 4347, pp. 91–102. Springer, Heidelberg (2006)
37. Setola, R., Bologna, S., Casalicchio, E., Masucci, V.: An integrated approach for simulating interdependencies. Critical Infrastructure Protection II, 229–239 (2009)
38. Robinson, C.P., Woodard, J.B., Varnado, S.G.: Critical infrastructure: Interlinked and vulnerable. Issues Sci. Technol. 15(1), 61–67 (1998)
39. Department of Homeland Security: National infrastructure protection plan: Partnering to enhance protection and resiliency. Washington (2009)

40. Eusgeld, I., Henzi, D., Kröger, W.: Comparative evaluation of modeling and simulation techniques for interdependent critical infrastructures. Scientific Report, Laboratory for Safety Analysis, ETH Zurich (2008)
41. Beyer, U., Flentge, F.: Towards a holistic metamodel for systems of critical infrastructures. European CIIP Newsletter 2(3), 6–8 (2006)
42. Bloomfield, R., Chozos, N., Nobles, P.: Infrastructure interdependency analysis: Introductory research review. Adelard LLP. D/422/12101/4 (2009)
43. Peerenboom, J.: Infrastructure interdependencies: Overview of concepts and terminology. Infrastructure Assurance Center, Argonne National Laboratory, Argonne, IL (2001), http://www.pnwer.org/pris/peerenboom_pdf.pdf
44. Casalicchio, E., Galli, E., Tucci, S.: Federated agent-based modeling and simulation approach to study interdependencies in IT critical infrastructures. In: 11th IEEE International Symposium on Distributed Simulation and Real-Time Applications, DS-RT 2007, pp. 182–189 (2007)
45. Sveen, F.O., Torres, J.M., Sarriegi, J.M.: Modeling critical infrastructure interdependencies: Choosing a modeling technique. In: 15th TIEMS Annual Conference: Collection of Abstracts (2008)
46. Leontief, W.W.: Input-output economics. Sci. Am. 185, 15–21 (1951)
47. Haimes, Y.Y., Horowitz, B.M., Lambert, J.H., Santos, J.R., Lian, C., Crowther, K.G.: Inoperability input-output model for interdependent infrastructure sectors. I: Theory and methodology. J. Infrastruct Syst. 11(2), 67–79 (2005)
48. Setola, R.: How to measure the degree of interdependencies among critical infrastructures. IJSSE 2(1), 38–59 (2010)
49. Oliva, G., Panzieri, S., Setola, R.: Distributed synchronization under uncertainty: A fuzzy approach. Fuzzy Sets Syst (2012)
50. Forrester, J.: Industrial dynamics. MIT Press, Cambridge (1961)
51. Sterman, J.D.: Business dynamics: Systems thinking and modeling for a complex world. Irwin/McGraw-Hill, Boston (2000)
52. Zimmerman, R.: Decision-making and the vulnerability of interdependent critical infrastructure. In: IEEE International Conference on Systems, Man and Cybernetics, vol. 5, pp. 4059–4063 (2004)
53. Bush, B., Dauelsberg, L., LeClaire, R., Powell, D., Deland, S., Samsa, M.: Critical infrastructure protection decision support system (CIP/DSS) project overview. In: Proceedings of the 23rd International Conference of the System Dynamics Society (2005)
54. Zimmerman, R., Restrepo, C.E.: The next step: Quantifying infrastructure interdependencies to improve security. IJCIP 2(2), 215–230 (2006)
55. LeClaire, R.J., Hirsch, G.B., Bandlow, A.: Learning environment simulator: A tool for local decision makers and first responders. In: Proceedings of the 27th International Conference of the System Dynamics Society (2009)
56. Schmitz, W.: Analysis and assessment for critical infrastructure protection (ACIP). Ottobrunn, Germany ACIP consortium. Final report IST-2001-37257 Deliverable D7.5 (2003)

Analysis of Severe Space Weather on Critical Infrastructures

Francesco Gaetano[1], Gabriele Oliva[3,2], Stefano Panzieri[1], Claudio Romani[3,*],
and Roberto Setola[3,2]

[1] Dipartimento di Informatica e Automazione, University "Roma TRE",
Via della Vasca Navale, 79, 00146, Roma, Italy
{gaetano,panzieri}@dia.uniroma3.it
[2] Consorzio Nazionale Interuniversitario per i Trasporti e la Logistca,
Piazza dell'Esquilino 29, 00185 Roma, Italy
{Gabriele.oliva,roberto.setola}@nitel.it
[3] University Campus Biomedico of Rome, Italy
{g.oliva,c.romani,r.setola}@unicampus.it

Abstract. Space threats pose nontrivial issues to the safety of the population and to the correct functioning of critical infrastructures. In this paper we analyze the most significant threats posed by solar wind in terms of impact due to both direct consequences on satellite and critical infrastructure so as the subsequent domino effects. To this end we provide a model based on the CISIA platform with a case study related to the area of Rome, Italy.

Keywords: Critical Infrastructures, Solar Wind, Satellites, Space threats.

1 Introduction

Space threats are a big issue for the safety of nations and their citizens, as dramatically shown by the recent event occurred over Chelyabinsk (Russia) where a meteor with a mass of about 1000 tons exploded at approximately 15-25 kilometers above the ground [1]. 1491 people were injured and the shock wave damaged 3724 apartments, 671 educational institutions, 34 hospitals [2].
Even if the risk related to the impact with space object included the debris and a obsolete satellite can be estimated, it actually does not represent the most significant threat.

In fact Solar Wind – composed of particles flowing from the Sun to the Earth – could affect the ionoshpere, the Earth's magnetic field (e.g., causing auroras), telecommunication [7] and power electric grid (especially at the high latitude). The magnetic effects and the energetic particle flux are also able to cause a degradation of radio communications (both ground-to-ground and ground-to-space). For example airline routes and schedules were significantly affected because of

---

* Corresponding author.

E. Luiijf and P. Hartel (Eds.): CRITIS 2013, LNCS 8328, pp. 62–73, 2013.

communication problems and because of concerns about increased radiation exposure at high altitudes [30].

In 1859 a giant solar storm, in relation with a sequence of several extraordinarily intense solar flares, hit the earth's magnetosphere producing an impressive geomagnetic storm which lasted for several days. The astronomer Carrington was the first who connected the observed flares on the solar surface with the effects of the geomagnetic storm on the Earth [31].

In the middle of the XIX century, apart from the spectacular and diffused auroras (visible even in Cuba), the only infrastructures capable of detecting the geomagnetic storm were telegraph systems which experienced several anomalous and strange phenomena. In 1989, an electromagnetic storm, took place over the skies of Quebec, causing the aurora borealis visible to Texas. This strong solar storm with ground-level magnetic deflections of 500-1000 nT caused half-cycle transformer saturation to generate harmonics that improperly tripped five power lines, knocking out nearly 10 GW of generating capacity and collapsing the entire grid within a minute [11]. Less geo-effective than its predecessors was the event of 2003, called "Halloween Space Weather Storm" which lasted from late October to early November causing a considerable number of effects on electric grid.

It seems that such giant solar storm has a cyclical nature of events each about 60 years, hence it might happen in the first half of two century. However the most direct effect of Solar Storm is on satellite system which might experienced prolonged switch-off. Thus has consequences on ground infrastructure, especially telecommunications; some good examples are the *Synchronous Digital Hierarchy* (SDH) fiber connections and the UMTS infrastructure [5]. In order to transmit information, SDH systems need to be synchronized and require highly reliable clock sources. Analogously, most of the UMTS/CDMA mobile cellular networks use GPS as a precise clock reference. There are several approaches to study critical infrastructure interdependencies [15,16,14]; to date the study of the effects of space weather and satellites' failures has not been taken into account, except for the direct effects on power grids [7]. In this paper we analyze the most significant effects of solar wind on satellites and critical infrastructures as well as the consequences of a lack of satellite services, considering both direct and indirect effects.

In this paper we analyze the potential effect of solar wind considering a solar storm of comparable energy of those of Carrington using a framework based on the CISIA simulation platform [15,12], applied to a case study related to the area of Rome, Italy. The structure of the paper is as follow: section 2 focuses on modeling the effects of a solar storm on Ground Critical Infrastructures, section 3 explains the structure and functionality of the Cisia Simulator and section 4 provides a case study, displaying the structure of the area analyzed and the results of the simulations. Finally, section 5 provides some conclusions and topics for further discussion.

2   Modeling the Effects of a Solar Wind on Ground Critical Infrastructures

In this section we inspect the most relevant direct and indirect effects of solar wind. Figure 1 shows a synoptic view of such effects; specifically we have to consider both the effects caused directly by the solar radiations, represented by blue dotted lines, so as the indirect consequences , i.e. those induced by domino effects due the absence or degradation services, represented in the figure by black solid lines.

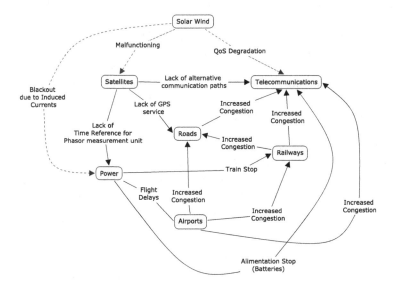

Fig. 1. Conceptual map that represents the direct (blu dotted arrows) and indirect (black solid arrows) effects of a solar storm on satellites and ground Critical Infrastructures

2.1   Direct Effects

The solar atmosphere emits radio waves at all wavelengths and at all times. Its total flux density varies with magnetic activity as manifest in sunspots. Abnormal emissions of microwaves and particles may sometimes occur, due to solar flares, coronal mass ejections, etc. Clouds of particles originated on the Sun during such extreme events may reach the Earth in 3-4 days and leak through the Earth's magnetic field.

Although effects on several other infrastructures such as pipelines and air transportation have been reported [8], in this paper we will focus on the direct effects on satellites, telecommunication equipment and power distribution grid. The reason for such a choice is twofold: the effects on such sectors are much more well documented [7], and are more likely to have severe effects in the short term, while other phenomena, such as pipeline erosion due to induced currents [9] are harder to assess and may have negligible effect when considering a narrow time frame.

Satellites are particularly vulnerable to solar blasts and several outages have been documented [23]. The most likely outcome of a solar storm on satellites is the complete unavailability of their provided services [23], while few cases of atmosphere heating resulting in satellite slow down and increased risk of being dragged down to the Earth have been documented [20,21]. Note that a common strategy to face such threats is to turn off the satellites in order to preserve the equipment or to move the satellites to upper orbits in order to prevent the risk of uncontrolled reentry [19]. In the following we will assume that the effect of a solar storm on the satellites consists in their temporary unavailability, while normal operations may be restored right after the event is concluded.

The presence of an unstable magnetic field in the vicinity of a conductor generates a so called *geomagnetic induce current* (GIC). The severity of such a phenomenon is especially relevant during geomagnetic storms. As a result, solar wind is likely to interfere with telecommunication equipment, and several cases have been reported [24].

GICs are harmful to electrical transmission equipment, especially generators and transformers. As a result, core saturation may occur, affecting performance and causing coils and cores to heat up. In extreme cases, this heat may disable or destroy equipment, inducing a chain reaction that may overload transformers [37]. One of the most relevant examples of induced failure on power grid occurred on March 1989, when a severe geomagnetic storm caused the collapse of Québec's power transmission system [25].

In the following we will assume that, in the event of a solar storm, the working condition of the elements in the power grid is progressively degraded while a progressive restoration occurs after the end of the solar event. We also assumed that the power grid's working condition was not affected in the very beginning of the event. For the telecommunication equipment we assume that a progressive degradation of the quality of service occurs during the event.

2.2   Indirect Effects

The unavailability of satellites' functions has manyfold downstream consequences on ground critical infrastructures, the most relevant being the lack of Global Navigation Satellite System (GNSS) signal (e.g. GPS). Such signal is used for both position estimation [26] and absolute time reference identification [27]. GNSS also provides very accurate (tens of nanoseconds) timing services, and several modern technological system use such data as a time reference for synchronization.

GNSS systems have the option of operating in a single frequency mode and are dependent on a compensating model of the signal delay due to the electron density in the ionosphere (on average, the model compensates for 50% of the ionospheric delay). At the start (and end) of an extreme event when the ionosphere is highly disturbed, the position and navigation solution from a single frequency GNSS receiver will be significantly degraded due to a large mismatch between the actual ionosphere and the average model assumed by the receiver, causing disturbances and failures on all the services that base their operation on the data provided by GPS.

A failure in the GPS positioning system indeed, among other it can detriment the economy and the safety of the nation's infrastructures [38] and may contribute to exacerbate the traffic in a given area, and such a result is more likely for highly congested zones such as densely populated cities [32]. Note that the U.S. is studying an alternative to GPS to be used as a backup, but to date no completely satisfactory solution has been developed [29]. GPS data is very often the sole way to understand the ongoing traffic situation, hence the lack of such an information [28] may result in the impossibility for the law enforcement and traffic managers to take adequate and quick decisions on the matter. The immediate effect of a lack of GPS signal to the transportation network is an inefficient distribution of the traffic flow, whose effects are particularly evident during rush hour. In the proposed model we represent such a phenomena with a slight increase in traffic both in highways and city streets.

Phasor Measurement Units (PMUs) is an efficient and cost-effective way to synchronize generators in a power grid and is becoming more and more adopted, in particular for smart grid applications [34,35]. However such a methodology heavily relies on the GPS time reference. This device normally allows to measure the electrical waves on an electricity grid, using a common time source for synchronization. Time synchronization allows synchronized real-time measurements of multiple remote measurement points on the grid, so the loss of synchronization leads to considerable problems to the whole system in terms of measurement (in the short term) and in terms of degradation of the power grid's performance (in the long term). In [36] an analysis of the vulnerability of PMUs with respect to GPS spoofing has been carried out. In the paper the authors found that inducing a slight time shift of about $2\mu s$ may lead to a complete failure in a given equipment after just $250s$, eventually leading to cascading effects across the power distribution network. In concordance with such a result in the proposed model, we consider a rapid decrease in the working condition of the power equipment just after the GPS outage, whose slope tends to reduce over time (in terms of hours). For what concerns telecommunications, satellites are often used as backup links and their unavailability has slight immediate effects, that may however become relevant when multiple failures are considered. For the sake of the proposed model we represented it with a generic slight reduction of the working capability of the telecommunication equipment.

Let us conclude the section describing some domino effects that are expected to occur over the system of systems. An outage on the power grid has severe effect on train transportations, and a sensible decrement of working condition has been considered, depending on the working condition of the power grid element that feed the train stations and lines. The degradation of the working condition of trains has further effect on the other infrastructures in terms of increased congestion on roads and increased telecommunication usage. Power outages have also effects on Airports, causing flight delays and on telecommunications (although such systems typically rely on batteries, hence in the short term few effects are experienced). The delays on air transportation also have effects on roads, trains and telecommunication. The different phenomena are showed in Figure 1.

3   Cisia Simulator

CISIA simulator (Critical Infrastructure Simulation by Interdependent Agents) [15,16] is a framework for modeling and simulating the interdependency phenomena that arise in tightly interconnected critical infrastructures. Within such a simulator (written in ANSI C++), each infrastructure is represented as a set of interconnected entities; each entity requires some resources to function correctly and provides its resources to the others according to a specific network topology that captures the interconnections among entities.

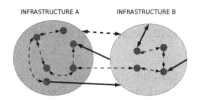

Fig. 2. Entities within CISIA may have heterogeneous levels of abstraction

Within CISIA, each entity is modeled with a high level of abstraction and, in order to reach an acceptable level of modularity and scalability. Each entity is described in terms of *operative level*, i.e., an abstract quantity that represents the percentage of working capability of an element. In this setting, the entities rely on the working capability of the others and provide information on their working capability to the others. Entities interact via the exchange of *resources* and *failures*. Resources are goods and services produced (or used) by the entity expressed in terms of their types, unit of measurements, nominal values and actual levels. Each entity may receive resources of a given type and produce some other kind of resource (i.e., a facility which receives power and produces actual goods). Moreover, some resources can be simply forwarded by the entity, i.e., in the case of a telecommunication fiber-optic wire which transmits data. The actual level of any resource is a function of the operative level the producer entity. Entities may also exchange failures of different types and severity. Failures are abnormal events, e.g. fire, explosion etc., which may affect an entity reducing its operational level. Generally any failure has its own dynamics which describe how it is generated, evolve over time and spread to other entities. To this end it implements a multitude of adjacency matrix in order to reproduce several concept of proximity. Notice that each link can be equipped with a defined delay in terms of timesteps required for the transmission of the resource/failure, and with an attenuation that represents a dissipation or attenuation of the quantity during the transmission.

CISIA allows the implementation of several mechanisms both resource transmission and failure propagation. Another peculiarity of CISIA is its capability to manage entities described with heterogenous level of abstraction. Indeed according to Mixed Holistic-Reductionistic (MHR) perspective (Figure 2), within CISIA the entities may have heterogeneous levels of abstraction, thus is possible to represent a specify equipment (e.g. generator) or a higher level system (e.g., electric grid). This allows to model complex dependencies that involve selected subsystems and higher level entities, as well as the overall interaction of different infrastructures and the low-level interaction among elements, either belonging to the same or different infrastructures.

4   Case of Study

We consider as a case study the areas of large Rome. Specifically, we take into account the effect of the malfunctioning of the satellites on a portion of the following infrastructures:

- *Power distribution grid*: 14 interconnected electrical cabins were considered;
- *Telecommunication Network*: 18 Base Transceiver Stations (BTS) and 7 Base Station Controllers (BSC);
- *Transportation Network*: 14 nodes representing important interconnections of urban routes and 8 highway nodes;
- *Railroads*: 3 Road stations;
- *Airports*: 2 airports.

Figure 3 shows the detail of the case study. Note that, for security reasons, the telecommunication and power distribution nodes, although being realistic in terms of dimensions and connections, are fictionally places over the map.

In addition to the elements, we also consider 4 high level entities:

- *Rome Area*: the entity summarizes the overall working condition of the infrastructures in the case study;
- *Power distribution*: the entity summarizes the overall working condition of the power distribution grid in the case study;
- *Telecommunications*: the entity summarizes the overall working condition of the telecommunications in the case study;
- *Transportations*: the entity summarizes the overall working condition of the transportations (including airports and railways) in the case study;

We consider a scenario over a time frame of 48 hours; specifically we consider that a solar storm occurs in t=0 and lasts 4 hours; we also assume that the services provided by satellites (power rephasing, GPS navigation and communication) are unavailable until t = 8 hours.

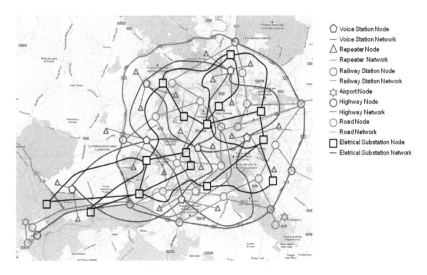

Fig. 3. Proposed case study

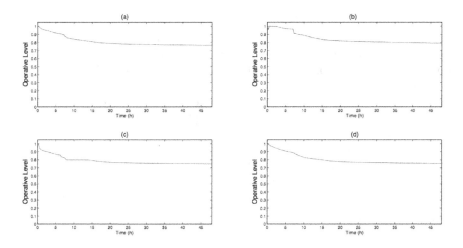

Fig. 4. Simulation results for a scenario where a solar storm occur in the a) area of Rome, in b) holistic transport, in c) holistic power and in d) holisitic node TLC

As it showed below in the Figure 4, the operative level of the holistic layers, included the whole area of Rome, is reduced to 80% of the nominal operational level due to the solar wind, and in particular the Holistic Power System affect directly the holistic layers of TLC and Transport. In Figure 5 there are curious trends, most of all Fiumicino Train Station decreases quickly the operative level reaching a value of 60%, while Fiumicino Airport keeps the operative level

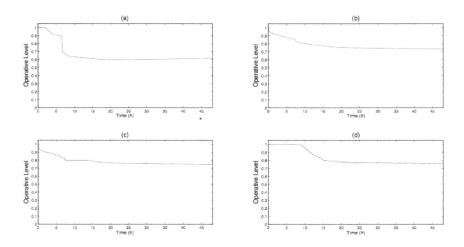

Fig. 5. Simulation results for a scenario where a solar storm occur in a) Fiumicino train station, in b) Fiumicino phone station, in c) electric substation and in d) Fiumicino airport

maximum until the $10th$ hour and decrease the operative level reaching a value of 80% after 18 hours. Regarding the holistic layer of TLC, we can see that, after a temporal range between 20 and 25 hours, characterized by a slow decrease of operative level, there is a recovery around the value of 75%. This result can be validated by the outage in January 1994 of one of two Canadian telecommunications satellites. This event brought to a disruption of communications services nationwide. The first satellite was recovered in a few hours while the recovery of the second satellite took 6 months and was costed 70 million [37].

The result of the simulation show that while the solar wind is occurring the effects on electricity last up to $8th$ hour and then there is a recovery.

5   Conclusions

In this paper we analyze the most significant effects of solar wind in terms of induced malfunctioning on satellites and critical infrastructures. We consider the consequences of the unavailability of satellite services, as well as the subsequent domino effects. Besides providing insights on the phenomenon, we give an although preliminary model based on the CISIA simulation platform and a case study related to the area of Rome, Italy. Future works will be aimed at enhancing the model involving the stakeholders, operators and technicians in the process. Another important aspect is to complement our study with an economic model in order to provide an estimation of potential economic loss. A crucial aspect will be the analysis of the effectiveness of possible counter-measurements. This latter aspect is of particular interest due to the periodicity of about 60 years in giant solar storm (hence the next one is foreseen in the first half of this century).

Indeed, even today a solar storm can be foreseen with hours or days in advance its effects reach the Earth. It is a short time, but if we know how to properly react it could be enough to mitigate the consequences.

Acknowledge. With the financial support of the Prevention, Preparedness and Consequence Management of Terrorism and other Security related Risks Programme European Commission – Directorate General Home Affairs – Project Space Awareness for Critical Infrastructures (SPARC).

References

1. Electronic Telegram, No. 3423, Central Bureau for Astronomical Telegrams, Inter- national Astronomical Union, http://www.cbat.eps.harvard.edu/iau/cbet/003400/CBET003423.txt
2. Zhang, Moran. Russia Meteor 2013: Damage To Top $33 Million; Rescue, Cleanup Team Heads To Meteorite-Hit Urals, International Business Times (February 16, 2013) (retrieved February 19, 2013)
3. Permanent Subcommittee on Investigations, Committee on Governmental Affairs, U.S. Senate, Critical Infrastructure Protection: Commercial Satellite Security Should Be More Fully Addressed, Report to the Ranking Minority Member, GAO-02-781 (2002)
4. Klinkrad, H.: Space Debris. Models and Risk Analysis, Springer-Praxis (2006)
5. U.S. Dept. of Transportation, Office of Commercial Space Transportation, Hazard Analysis of Commercial Space Transportation. Technical Report of Commercial Space Transportation (1995)
6. Setola, R., Oliva, G., Gaetano, F.: Space and Ground Critical Infrastructures- State of Art. Sparc D1 (2013)
7. McMorrow, D.: Impacts of Severe Space Weather on the Electric Grid. JASON, Virginia 22102-7508 (703) (2011)
8. Gummow, A.: GIC effects on pipeline corrosion and corrosion control systems. Journal of Atmospheric and Solar-Terrestrial Physics (2012)
9. Osella, A., Favetto, A., Lopez, E.: Currents induced by geomagnetic storms on buried pipelines as a cause of corrosion. Journal of Applied Geophysics 38 (1998)
10. Curry, C.: Dependency of Communications Systems on PNT Technology, rep., ChronosTechnology, GL179PD, UK (2010)
11. Boteler, D.H.: Geomagnetic hazards to conducting networks. Natural Hazards (2003)
12. Hollman, J.A., Martí, J.R., Jatskevich, J., Srivastava, K.D.: Dynamic Islanding of Critical Infrastructures, a Suitable Strategy to Survive and Mitigate Critical Events, CNIP, Rome, March 28-29 (2006)
13. Haimes, Y., Horowitz, B., Lambert, J., Santos, J., Lian, C., Crowther, K.: Inoperability Input-Output Model for Interdependent Infrastructure Sectors. I: Theory and Methodology. Journal of Infrastructure Systems 11(2), 67–79 (2005)
14. Kujawski, E.: Multi-Period Model for Disruptive Events in Interdependent Systems. Int. System Engineering 9(4), 281–295 (2006)
15. De Porcellinis, S., Panzieri, S., Setola, R.: Model Critical Infrastructure via a Mixed Holistic-Reductionistic Approach. Int. J. Critical Infrastructures (IJCIS) 5, 86–99 (2009)

16. De Porcellinis, S., Panzieri, S., Setola, R., Ulivi, G.: Simulation of Heterogeneous and Interdependent Critical Infrastructures. Int. J. Critical Infrastructures (IJCIS) 4(1/2), 110–128 (2008)
17. Stangalini, M., et al.: MHD wave transmission in the Sun's atmosphere. Astronomy & Astrophysics 534, 7 (2011)
18. Cliver, E.W., Svalgaard, L.: The 1859 Solar-Terrestrial Disturbance and the Current Limits of Extreme Space Weather Activity. Solar Physics 224(1-2), 407–422 (2004)
19. Linton, D.: Stormy weather: solar activity could wreak havoc on satellites, http://www.signal.army.mil
20. Mukai, K.: The Decay of ASCA's Orbit (2001), http://www.solarstorms.org/
21. Marshall Space Flt. Ctr. In: MSFC Skylab Mission Report: Saturn Workshop, NASA TM X-64818, pp. 3–30 (October 1974)
22. Gurgen, P.T.: Principal Regularities in the Distribution of Major Earthquakes Relative to Solar and Lunar Tides and Other Cosmic Forces. Icarus 9, 574–592 (1968)
23. Shue, J.-H., Song, P., Russell, C.T., Steinberg, J.T., Chao, J.K., Zastenke, G., Vaisberg, O.L., Kokubun, S., Singer, H.J., Detman, T.R., Kawano, H.: Magnetopause location under extreme solar wind conditions. Journal of Geophysical Research: Space Physics 103(A8), 17691–17700 (1998)
24. Radasky, W.A., Kappenman, J.G.: Impacts of geomagnetic storms on EHV and UHV power grids. In: 2010 Asia-Pacific Symposium on Electromagnetic Compatibility, APEMC (2010)
25. Geomagnetic Storms Can Threaten Electric Power Grid Earth in Space. American Geophysical Union 9(7), 9–11 (1997)
26. Mintsis, G., Basbas, S., Papaioannou, P., Taxiltaris, C., Tziavos, I.N.: Applications of GPS technology in the land transportation system. European Journal of Operational Research 152(2), 399–409 (2004)
27. Pullen, S.: Providing Integrity for Satellite Navigation: Lessons Learned (Thus Far) from the Financial Collapse of 2008–2009, International Technical Meeting of the Satellite Division of The Institute of Navigation (2009)
28. D'Este, G.M., Zito, R., Taylor, M.A.P.: Using GPS to Measure Traffic System Performance. Computer-Aided Civil and Infrastructure Engineering 14(4), 255–265 (1999)
29. Grant, A., Williams, P., Ward, N., Basker, S.: GPS Jamming and the Impact on Maritime Navigation. Journal of Navigation (2009)
30. Valsecchi, G., Rossi, A.: Analysis of the space debris impact risk on the International Space Station. Celestial Mechanics and Dynamical Astronomy 83(1), 63–76 (2002)
31. Cliver, E.W., Svalgaard, L.: The 1859 Solar-Terrestrial Disturbance and the Current Limits of Extreme SpaceWeather Activity. Solar Physics 224(1-2), 407–422 (2004)
32. Vulnerability Assessment of the Transportation Infrastructure relying on the Global Positioning System, Final Report, prepared by John A Volpe National Transportation Systems Center for Office of the Assistant Secretary for Transportation Policy, US Department of Transportation (August 29, 2001), http://www.navcen.uscg.gov/archive/2001/Oct/FinalReportv4.6.pdf
33. Adoption of a National Backup Service to GPS. United States Department of Homeland Security Press Release (February 2008)
34. Phadke, A.G.: Synchronized phasor measurements in power systems. IEEE Computer Applications in Power 6(2), 10–15 (1993)

35. Carta, A., Locci, N., Muscas, C., Sulis, S.: A Flexible GPS-Based System for Synchronized Phasor Measurement in Electric Distribution Networks. IEEE Transactions on Instrumentation and Measurement 57(11), 2450–2456 (2008)
36. Shepard, D.P., Humphreys, T.E., Fansler, A.A.: Evaluation of the Vulnerability of Phasor Measurement Units to GPS Spoofing Attacks. In: Sixth Annual IFIP WG 11.10 International Conference on Critical Infrastructure Protection Washington, March 19-21 (2012)
37. Severe Space Weather Events–Understanding Societal and Economic Impacts Workshop Report, http://www.nap.edu/catalog/12507.html
38. Understanding the Vulnerability & Building Resilience, developed by American Meteorological Society Policy Workshop Report (March 2011)

A Plug and Play, Approximation-Based, Selective Load Shedding Mechanism for the Future Electrical Grid

Yiannis Tofis, Yiasoumis Yiasemi, and Elias Kyriakides

Department of Electrical and Computer Engineering & KIOS Research Center for Intelligent Systems and Networks, University of Cyprus, 1678 Nicosia, Cyprus
{ytofis01,yiasemi.yiasoumis,elias}@ucy.ac.cy
http://www.ucy.ac.cy/
http://www.kios.ucy.ac.cy/

Abstract. As soon as a load disturbance occurs in a power system, such as the unexpected outage of a generation unit or the introduction of a big load, the electric frequency declines from its nominal value. This is a highly unwanted situation that limits machine and other power system auxiliaries life time. Contemporary power systems employ conventional load shedding practices as a last resort, in order to achieve frequency stability. However, these practices, which are determined a priori, are very conservative and result in over-shedding. In this paper, an intelligent load shedding scheme that combines approximation-based feedback linearization and load disturbance adaptive bounding is presented. The proposed scheme provides the minimum amount of load that should be shed in order to maintain the power system stability. It prevents over-shedding practices as a result of conventional load shedding that the proposed scheme is compared with. Furthermore, the mechanism under consideration provides smooth and seamless load restoration, preventing oscillations between shedding and restoration. It is robust to functional approximation errors, measurement noise and sudden load disturbances.

Keywords: Load shedding, load restoration, feedback linearization, adaptive disturbance bounding, power system frequency stability.

1 Introduction

Load shedding is the procedure of disconnecting the power supply to a portion of the transmission and/or distribution network when the demand exceeds the supply. Load shedding intents to achieve the balance of the current demand with the available generation. The need for a fast and optimal load shedding is imperative in the future grid in order to accommodate unforeseen or unexpected load disturbances due to the outage of large generation units or the excessive power demand at peak times. Electric utilities currently employ brutal load shedding techniques based on predetermined load tripping via the employment of under-frequency relays. Brutal load shedding is the massive load shedding of a certain sufficient magnitude to ensure the operation of

E. Luiijf and P. Hartel (Eds.): CRITIS 2013, LNCS 8328, pp. 74–83, 2013.
© Springer International Publishing Switzerland 2013

essential loads, allowing at the same time the system to recover from the under-frequency operational condition [1].

The system could be an interconnected power network or an islanded portion thereof. In the case of an interconnected network, the need for a uniform automatic load shedding program is imperative. This requires a service level agreement between the interconnected utility companies, indicating the number of steps, how these are associated with the frequency levels and the amount of load that should be shed at each of these levels [6].

Apart from the frequency levels, the frequency decay rate has also been used in order to determine the amount of load that should be shed [2]. Further, in [3] Artificial Neural Networks (ANNs) are employed taking as input neurons the total power generation, total power demand and frequency decay rate. The output neuron is the minimum amount of load shedding that maintains the stability of the power system. Moreover, ANNs have been employed in order to design power system controllers [3].

The proposed scheme is plug and play, providing online adaptive learning of the system as well as online adaptive bounding of the system load disturbances. In this manner, the non-linear relation of the frequency decay rate is related –using linearly parameterized approximators– to the amount of load that should be shed in order to maintain the stability of the power system.

2   Conventional Load Shedding Practices

According to the conventional load shedding practices followed by system operators, load shedding is designed and performed on a trial and error basis. The load is shed in steps in order to avoid over-shedding because of the oscillatory nature of the frequency decay rate as a result of frequency characteristic variations observed at each bus of the system as soon as a disturbance occurs.

Load shedding schemes are usually pessimistic regarding the load that should be shed in order to ensure that at the end of the transient event the frequency settles at a level above 59 Hz (in this paper the nominal frequency is assumed to be 60 Hz). This is due to two reasons (a) the governor action of each generator will be able to stabilize the frequency at the nominal levels if the frequency is above 59 Hz and (b) the steam turbines can be permanently damaged in the case that they operate under 59 Hz for a certain time period [6]. The following table presents estimates of steam-turbine limitations as far as the under-frequency time of operation is concerned. The times shown are cumulative for the life of a certain unit.

Table 1. Cumulative time-frequency limitation for steam-turbines [6]

Frequency at Full Load - Hz	Cumulative Time to Damage
59.4	continuous
58.8	90 minutes
58.2	10 minutes
57.6	1 minute

Current load shedding practices keep performing shedding in successive steps, determined from the equipment limitations, until the frequency is restored back to its normal value. Power plant auxiliaries such as boiler feedwater pumps, coal pulverizing and feeding equipment [6], present under frequency operating limitations. These limitations determine the number and the size of the steps that the load should be shed. The performance degradation of these components starts below 59 Hz while the limiting condition is reached between 53-55 Hz. For this reason –and in order to provide some margin- the frequency decay is limited to 57 Hz [6]. In order not to exceed downwards this limit, the load shedding steps are defined in higher levels in order to accommodate the time delays as a result of delays in the operation of relays and circuit breakers.

Load shedding schemes are designed in order to accommodate a maximum level of disturbance or overloading condition. The number of load shedding steps is also determined based on this level, but usually it is limited to three to six steps. Reference [1] proposes two load shedding approaches: a Four and a Six Step Plan. In this work we compare the proposed load shedding scheme to the Six Step Plan. The Six Step plan is shown in Table 2 for the convenience of the reader. It should be noted that the number and the size of load shedding steps that are used by the utilities are in general arbitrarily chosen and there are several proposed approaches in the literature.

Table 2. Frequency settings for a Six Step Load Shedding Plan

Relay	Frequency	Load Trip	Delay
f1	59.5 Hz	0.048 per unit	0.1 s
f2	59.3 Hz	0.048 per unit	0.1 s
f3	59.1 Hz	0.042 per unit	0.1 s
f4	58.8 Hz	0.040 per unit	0.1 s
f5	58.5 Hz	0.036 per unit	0.1 s
f6	58.2 Hz	0.036 per unit	0.1 s
	Total	**0.25 per unit**	

3   Proposed Load Shedding Practice

This section presents a method that enables the online learning of the nonlinear function that relates the frequency rate of change with the amount of load that should be shed. The online learning is based on the real time measurement of the electrical frequency of the grid. The nonlinear function depends on the total generation capacity of the generation units, the governor action, as well as the topology of the power system regarding the degree of connectivity of transmission system buses.

The uniform or average electrical frequency of an isolated system [7] is given by the equation [4]

$$\frac{2H}{f_{syn}^2} f(t) \frac{df(t)}{dt} = p_{mp.u.}(t) - p_{ep.u.}(t) - \frac{Df(t)}{f_{syn}} \tag{1}$$

where H is the total normalized inertia constant in joules/VA or per unit-seconds, f_{syn} is the synchronous electrical frequency, $f(t)$ is the average electrical frequency, $p_{mp.u.}$ is the per unit mechanical power supplied by the prime movers minus mechanical losses, $p_{ep.u.}$ is the per unit electrical power output of the generators plus electrical losses and D is the damping factor. Equation (1) can be rewritten in the following form:

$$\begin{aligned}
\frac{df(t)}{dt} &= \frac{f_{syn}^2}{2H} \left(\frac{p_{mp.u.}(t)}{f(t)} - \frac{p'_{ep.u.}(t) + \Delta p'_{ep.u.}(t)}{f(t)} - \frac{D}{f_{syn}} \right) \\
&= \underbrace{\frac{f_{syn}^2}{2H} \left(\frac{p_{mp.u.}(t) - p'_{ep.u.}(t)}{f(t)} - \frac{D}{f_{syn}} \right)}_{g_1^*(f)} + \underbrace{\frac{f_{syn}^2}{2Hf(t)}}_{g_2^*(f)} \underbrace{\Delta p'_{ep.u.}(t)}_{u(t)}
\end{aligned} \tag{2}$$

where $p_{ep.u.}(t) = p'_{ep.u.}(t) + \Delta p'_{ep.u.}(t)$. Through load shedding we can change/control the quantity $\Delta p'_{ep.u.}(t)$. The proposed scheme decides the value of this quantity in order to maintain the stability of the system, i.e. it decides the amount of load that should be shed $\left(\Delta p'_{ep.u.}(t) > 0 \right)$ or restored $\left(\Delta p'_{ep.u.}(t) < 0 \right)$, in order to achieve the frequency stability of the grid.

Based on the aforementioned analysis, equation (2) can be approximated by the following relation:

$$\dot{f}(t) = g_1^*(f) + g_2^*(f)u(t) \tag{3}$$

where $f(t)$ is the per unit average electrical frequency of the power system, $g_1^*(f)$ and $g_2^*(f)$ are unknown nonlinear functions of $f(t)$ to be approximated and u is the control output indicating the per unit amount of load that should be shed or restored in order to achieve the control objective which is the system output $f(t)$ to be equal to the nominal value, i.e., equal to unity.

The two unknown functions can be approximated with linearly parameterized approximators:

$$g_{1(2)}^*(f) = \hat{g}_{1(2)}\left(f, \theta_{g_{1(2)}}^* \right) + \delta_{g_{1(2)}}(f) \tag{4}$$

where $\theta_{g_{1(2)}}^* = \arg \min_{\theta_{g_{1(2)}} \in R^N} \left\{ \sup_{f \in D} \left| g_{1(2)}^*(f) - \hat{g}_{1(2)}\left(f, \hat{\theta}_{g_{1(2)}} \right) \right| \right\}$, $\delta_{g_{1(2)}}(f)$ is the minimum functional approximation error, A is the $f(t)$ region of interest [0.95-1.02], i.e., in natural units [57-61.2 Hz] and N is the number of approximators that the functions are approximated with, such as:

$$\hat{g}_{1(2)}\left(f, \theta_{g_{1(2)}}^* \right) = \Phi_{g_{1(2)}}(f)^T \theta_{g_{1(2)}}^* = \sum_{i=1}^{N} \theta_{g_{1(2)i}}^* \varphi_{g_{1(2)}}(\| f - c_i \|) \tag{5}$$

The centers c_i of the approximators vector $\Phi_{g_{1(2)}}(f)$ are chosen uniformly distributed in the region of interest A.

If we demand the system output $f(t)$ to be equal to the nominal frequency, then

$$u = \frac{-a_m (f-1) - \Phi_{g_1}(f)^T \hat{\theta}_{g_1} - v_g}{\Phi_{g_2}(f)^T \hat{\theta}_{g_2}} \tag{6}$$

where a_m is a design constant, and v_g is used to deal with the functional approximation errors and load disturbances. All the quantities are included in a time function $\delta(t)$. Further, by demanding the suitable Lyapunov functions to be negative semi-definite we derive the following parametric adaptive laws:

$$\dot{\hat{\theta}}_{g_1} = \Gamma_{g_1} \Phi_{g_1}(f)(f-1) \tag{7}$$

$$\dot{\hat{\theta}}_{g_2} = \Gamma_{g_2} \Phi_{g_2}(f)(f-1)u \tag{8}$$

as well as the adaptive laws regarding the lower and upper bounds of $\delta(t)$, i.e. $\delta_L(f) \leq \delta(f,u,t) \leq \delta_U(f)$:

$$\dot{\hat{a}}_u = \begin{cases} \gamma_u (f-1)\delta_u(f) & \text{if } f > 1 \\ 0 & \text{if } f < 1 \end{cases} \tag{9}$$

$$\dot{\hat{a}}_L = \begin{cases} 0 & \text{if } f > 1 \\ \gamma_L (f-1)\delta_L(f) & \text{if } f < 1 \end{cases} \tag{10}$$

Finally v_g is chosen as:

$$v_g = \begin{cases} \hat{a}_u \delta_u(f) & \text{if } f > 1 \\ \hat{a}_L \delta_L(f) & \text{if } f < 1 \end{cases} \tag{11}$$

In the above expressions $\Gamma_{g1(2)}$ is the learning rate of the parametric laws in (7) and (8) respectively, $\hat{a}_u$ and $\hat{a}_L$ are unknown parameters multiplying the bounding (lower and upper) disturbance functions $\delta_L(f)$ and $\delta_u(f)$. Finally, γ_u and γ_L are the learning rates of $\hat{a}_u$ and $\hat{a}_L$ respectively.

4   Implementation of the Methodology

The 9-bus 3-machine system transient stability study is applied in this validation case. The system is documented in [4]. The system includes three generators and three large equivalent loads connected in a meshed transmission network through transmission lines as shown in Figure 1. The generators are dynamically modeled with the classical equivalent model.

The load disturbances are taking place at bus 8 by introducing step changes at the connected load. The controllable load is the one connected to bus 5 and represents the portion of load in the system which can be managed. The load connected to bus 6 is kept constant during the transient analysis simulations and represents the loads that cannot be shed due to their high importance.

The test system of Figure 1 is simulated using DigSilent PowerFactory [5]. Figure 2 presents the load values and frequency variations in three different scenarios: the case of conventional load shedding, the proposed load shedding case and the case without any load shedding. The frequency is measured at bus 8. Figure 3 presents the frequency variations in case of a sudden load increase and decrease respectively, in all three aforementioned scenarios.

In the case of the conventional load shedding, the load shedding scheme of Table 2 with a total delay (including the time delay of relays and circuit breaker time) of 0.1 s is implemented. It is clearly obvious that the 0.1 s of delay, obtains a reasonably accurate indication of the true rate of decay and thus a good indication of the amount of load that should be shed in order to keep the frequency stability of the system.

In the proposed scheme scenario, the aforementioned mechanism that has been presented in Section 3 is implemented. The proposed scheme because of its adaptive online nature mitigates potential communication delays and achieves identical performance as far as frequency response is concerned.

Regarding the third scenario where no load shedding takes place, it should be stressed that the conventional controllers of the generators, such as VARs and governors, are activated during the simulation time.

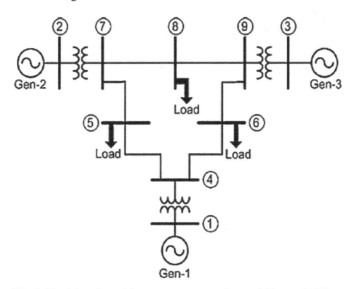

Fig. 1. The 9-bus 3-machine test system transient stability study [4]

The two consecutive load disturbances at bus 8 are simulated as a step load change of the load connected to the bus 8. In the conventional load shedding program implementation of Table 2, a load amount of about 95 MW is shed in order to prevent under-frequency operation. Because of this brutal action of excessive load shedding, the frequency recovers fast at the 59.5 Hz level when the first load shedding step of Table 2 is activated, causing an overshooting of about 0.25 Hz before reaching the steady state.

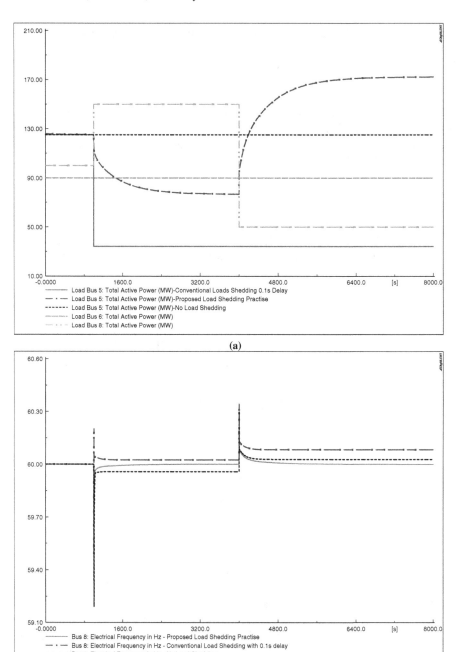

Fig. 2. (a) Load and (b) Frequency variations in the case of: (1) conventional load shedding, (2) proposed load shedding and (3) without load shedding

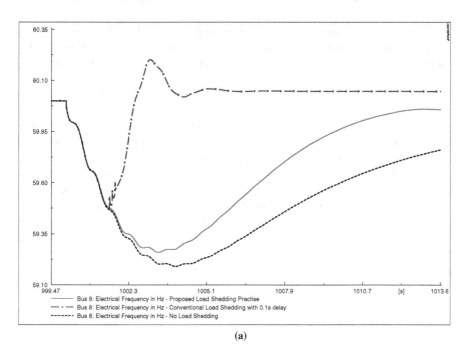

(a)

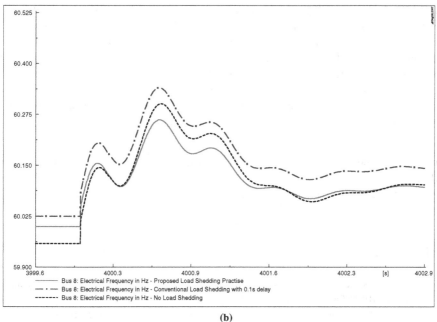

(b)

Fig. 3. Frequency variations in case of (a) Load Increases and (b) Load Decreases in the case of (1) conventional load shedding, (2) proposed load shedding scheme, and (3) without any load shedding

In the proposed scheme, a load amount of 55 MW is shed, significantly less than the conventional load shedding program. The frequency decays as low as 59.2 Hz. Further, frequency restoration is achieved in a seamless manner without causing any overshooting, which is the case in the previous scenario.

Finally, in the case that the frequency exceeds its nominal value, indicating a situation of lack of load or excessive generation, smooth load restoration and/or energy device charging are enabled, preventing over-frequency operation. Load restoration or energy storage device charging start immediately as soon as the frequency recovers, facilitating and expediting the entire system recovery to the normal operation. This is in contrast with the conventional load shedding practice, where load restoration constitutes a separate procedure that takes place after the transients have subsided.

In the last scenario, where no load shedding is applied, the frequency response characteristic has the worst performance as expected. As soon as the spinning reserve is exhausted, a portion of the kinetic energy of the rotating masses of the generators is used to feed the extra demand (the lack of generation capacity). As a result of this, the power balance is achieved at a lower level of the system frequency, causing a permanent frequency deviation from the nominal value.

5   Conclusions

An intelligent load shedding mechanism has been presented which approximates on-line the system's swing equation. It is robust to the system load disturbances and determines efficiently the optimum amount of load that should be shed in order maintain the nominal value of the frequency. It outperforms the conventional load shedding practices since it prevents over-shedding and provides smooth load restoration. It provides supplementary control to the governor action that achieves higher availability levels of the power grid, minimizing the discomfort and inconvenience of the customers in the case of a contingency scenario or an unforeseen load event.

Acknowledgements. This work was developed from the FP7 Network of Excellence CIPRNet, which is being partly funded by the European Commission under grant number FP7-312450-CIPRNet. The European Commission's support is gratefully acknowledged.

References

1. Anderson, P.M., Mirheydar, M.: An adaptive method for setting under-frequency load shedding relays. IEEE Trans. Power Syst. 7(2), 647–655 (1992)
2. Chuvychin, V.N., Gurov, N.S., Venkata, S.S., Brown, R.E.: Adaptive approach to load shedding and spinning reserve control during under-frequency conditions. IEEE Trans. Power Syst. 11(4), 1805–1810 (1996)
3. Hsu, C.T., Kang, M.S., Chen, C.S.: Design of adaptive load shedding by artificial neural networks. IEE Proc. Gene. Trans. Distrib. 152, 415–421 (2005)

4. Anderson, P.M., Fouad, A.A.: Power system control and stability. IEEE Press Power Eng. Ser. (2003)
5. DigSilent PowerFactory, http://www.digsilent.de
6. Berdy, J.: Load Shedding – An Application guide. Electric Utility Engineering Operation, Schenectady, N.Y
7. Anderson, P.M., Mirheydar, M.: A low-order system frequency response model. IEEE Trans. Power Syst. 5(3), 720–729 (1990)

A Framework for Risk Analysis in Smart Grid
Perspective Based Approach

Rani Yesudas and Roger Clarke

College of Engineering and Computer Science, The Australian National University,
Canberra, Australia
{rani.yesudas,roger.clarke}@anu.edu.au

Abstract. Smart Grids have great potential for the management of energy consumption. However, moving from a traditional grid to a smart grid introduces significant new risk to the energy sector that were not present in the power grids that operated in isolation. The data that is generated in the smart metering systems can possibly harm its stakeholders. Hence it is important to protect all the stakeholders by providing effective controls to the vulnerable elements in the smart metering system. This highlights the necessity to conduct a risk analysis to evaluate the harms, threats and vulnerabilities that are introduced into this critical infrastructure by modernization. Currently there are numerous risk analysis methodologies available; there are many differences among them, and hence selecting an appropriate one is challenging. Risk that technical experts perceive to be minor often elicits strong public concerns. Consequently during risk analysis, different perspectives need to be considered. This article reports on an extensive analysis of risk management frameworks, which resulted in a framework specifically targeted at smart grid and smart metering systems. Perspective of risk analysis is a key element in this framework.

Keywords: smart meter, smart grid, security, risk assessment, risk analysis, framework.

1   Introduction

Smart grids, including smart meters, offer great promise for the efficient management of energy. However, concerns remain about the security of smart meter designs, and the potential negative impacts on householder privacy. These could slow adoption of the technologies, and threaten return on the considerable investments involved.

Like any infrastructure, smart grid is also prone to attacks. Moving systems from a manual process to an automated process creates new vulnerabilities. As systems are added, complexities and functionalities increase making it more difficult to address security. Increasing connection to previously isolated systems and networks expands the threat surface. Connection points between different networks become access points for interception and for the infiltration of malware. The dependence on networking technologies introduces new threats to service reliability [1].

Confidentiality, integrity and availability are the commonly used terms in security. In the electrical power system, availability of electricity is considered as the most

E. Luiijf and P. Hartel (Eds.): CRITIS 2013, LNCS 8328, pp. 84–95, 2013.

critical element and a disruption in communications can cause a blackout to a vast region. So a secure power grid should have the best control measure to ensure that availability of electricity is protected. Secondly, a smart grid uses data collected by various sensors and agents and this data is used for number of functionalities which include automated billing, peak usage determination, power outage tracking etc. The integrity of this data is very important. Unauthorized modification of the data or insertion of data from unknown sources can cause loss and damage to the system. Next is confidentiality. Customer information, general corporation information, and electric market information are some of the areas that need to be confidential. In smart grid, detailed information of electricity usage is recorded in the smart meter and this information is transmitted at certain intervals to the remote system via different communication methods [2].

Having identified availability as the top priority in a power system, does not deem integrity and confidentiality as elements of less importance. The system should ensure that the customer privacy is not violated and that the consumer is well informed of what could happen to their utility usage and personal data. Ultimately it will be the consumer who will have to bear the cost of running such a system and if the system can't guarantee safety and security they can backlash the system with the help of consumer advocacy groups. Risk that technical experts perceive to be minor, and even non-existent, often elicit strong public concerns and have even resulted in systems being discarded after huge investments have been made [3].

In various countries, after the initial roll out of smart metering systems there have been protests and demonstrations against them. The main reasons for their protests have been media reports regarding health hazards and privacy breaches that smart meters cause to its consumers. The smart meter has been described as a spy in the home [4]. This was based on a report that found that detailed smart meter data at one-minute intervals could provide insights into a household's living patterns to the extent that it could reveal the appliances used and activities conducted by the household [5]. It was completely misleading, as mostly the smart meters were read on half-hourly basis and it was almost impossible to deduce such information. Even if the meter was read at one minute intervals, detailed knowledge of the appliances present in the home and the habits of the consumer would be required to deduce living patterns [4]. Nonetheless, the perceptions of health and privacy threats persist.

If erroneous information sources find ready access to the mass media without effective remedies, then large social impacts, even for minor events, becomes possible [3]. This demonstrates the need to take security and privacy more seriously. In order to avoid any public resistance towards the Smart Grid especially from poorly drawn evidence, risk from the system should not only be analysed and managed but also effectively communicated.

Though over years, experts have stressed the need to have risk analysis embedded into design, it seldom happens. Even if risk analysis is done during design or after deployment; it requires distinct steps or processes that can be followed effectively. A good framework should make its processes transparent and understandable to all its stakeholders. It should also be adaptable and extensible as the system grows or modifies. A great many frameworks are available. They have a lot of commonality, but also differences, some of which are significant in the context of smart meters.

This paper reports on an extensive study of frameworks for the assessment and management of risk, whose purpose was to produce a framework specifically targeted at smart grid and smart metering systems. Following a brief introductory section on smart grids, a summary and comparison of existing smart grid models are presented, followed by a presentation of a method that is proposed as an effective but efficient approach to risk assessments for smart grid projects generally, and is illustrated by means of application to smart meter projects.

2   Background

2.1   Current Smart Grid Scenario

All around the globe, utilities and government have identified that the traditional energy grids needs to be replaced by Smart Grids. It emerged as a need to effectively manage the electricity requirements from the needs of an increasingly large world population. Though the initial interests were limited to accurately measuring the power usage, the focus has shifted to environmental gains through the reduction of peak demand and hence lower production cost and lower carbon emissions [6, 7].

As smart meters were identified as a primary requirement in a smart grid, many countries have started the smart meter roll-out for residential customers, in some cases mandated.

During and after roll-out, many schemes have been subjected to considerable criticism in relation to security and privacy aspects of the design. In many cases, public concerns have been exacerbated by the discovery that the risk assessments had been performed solely from the perspective of the utility provider [8, 9, 10]. Also by narrowing down the context, most of the documents have failed to consider vulnerabilities of the new system to different kinds of threats.

2.2   Models for Smart Grids

As a part of the realignment of the utility industry to support a smart grid, various countries and organisations have developed architectural and conceptual models to plan, evaluate and monitor the success of transformation from the traditional to a modern grid. Two popular models are Smart Grid Conceptual Model (SGCM) established by the National Institute of Standards and Technology (NIST) and Smart Grid Architecture Model (SGAM) established by the Working Group Reference Architecture (SG-CG/RA).

SGCM provides a visualized diagram explaining how different components of smart grid can be integrated and organised into seven Domains: Bulk Generation, Transmission, Distribution, Customers, Markets, Service Providers and Operations [11].

SGAM has a Smart Grid Plane. Zones are present in additions to the Domains to form a matrix, distinguishing between electrical process and information management viewpoints. The Domains encompass the complete electrical energy conversion chain (Bulk Generation, Transmission, Distribution, Distributed Electrical Resources (DER) and Customers Premises) and the Zones represent the hierarchical levels of power system management (Process, Station, Operation, Enterprise and Market) [12].

SGAM provides a better basis for risk assessment, because it provides more comprehensive coverage of parties than SGCM, and its structuring of the area into Domain/Zone cells assists the analyst in identifying the relevant scenarios.

3   Preparation for the Risk Analysis Framework

3.1   Chaos in Risk Terms

Before entering a discussion on risk analysis it is important to have the terminologies correct. Over years different entities have developed many standards and methods for risk analysis, and the terms and definitions used for risk elements and processes vary.

Most commonly used risk process terms are 'Risk Analysis', 'Risk Assessment' and 'Risk Management'. Some of the descriptions given by few standards and organizations are as follows:

- In ISO/IEC 27005, 'Risk Assessment' consists of 'Risk Analysis' and 'Risk Evaluation'. 'Risk Analysis' is then further divided into 'Risk Identification' and 'Risk Estimation' [13].
- In SP 800-30 by NIST, 'Risk Management' is said to encompass three processes, namely 'Risk Assessment', 'Risk Mitigation', and 'Risk Evaluation' [14].
- According to a Working Group (WG) established by European Network and Information Security Agency (ENISA), 'Risk Management' consists of 'Definition of Scope', 'Risk Assessment', 'Risk Treatment', 'Monitoring' and 'Communication' [15].
- Society of Risk Analysis (SRA) defines 'Risk Analysis' to broadly include 'Risk Assessment', 'Risk Characterization', 'Risk Management', 'Risk Communication', and policies [16].

In one definition, 'Risk Assessment' encompasses 'Risk Analysis' and in another one it is the reverse. Similarly 'Risk Management' in one interpretation includes all activities from scope definition to monitoring whereas in another it refers only to the planning and implementation phases.

Reference [17] drew attention to the problems inherent in defining the key term 'risk'. This article adopts a similar approach to the other key terms in the area; rather than attempting a universal definition, each term needs to be defined within the risk assessment document and used consistently within that document.

It is also important not to confuse one risk element with others. The Expert Group of the European Commission's Smart Grid Task Force prepared a Data Protection Impact Assessment Template for Smart Grid and Smart Metering Systems ('DPIA Template') in 2012. The main flaw that was highlighted by the Working Party against the DPIA template was that it often confused risk and threats [18].

3.2   Defining Elements of Risk

In this section the key elements of risk are defined. They variously adopt and adapt definitions found in the most relevant sources found during the conduct of the research [13, 14, 19, 20, 21, 22]. The terms used for each risk element by different entities have been tabulated in Table 1.

Table 1. Terminologies used for Risk Elements

Risk Elements	Different Terminologies Used
Stakeholder	User, Party
Asset	Resource, Property
Threat	Hazard
Vulnerability	Weakness, Susceptibility
Harm	Impact, Consequence, Damage, Effects of Unwanted Incident
Control	Safeguard, Treatment , Countermeasure
Risk	Probability, Chance

1. **Stakeholder:** Any entity that has interests in the target of evaluation, and whose interests are taken into account during the process.
2. **Asset:** Anything to which a stakeholder assigns value and which therefore requires protection. An asset can be physical or intangible. Assets include people, property, information and reputation.
3. **Threat:** Any circumstance that can potentially cause an event (sometimes referred to as an 'unwanted incident') that can result in harm or damage to an asset. A threat can be intentional (in which case it is referred to as an attack) or unintentional (an accident).
4. **Vulnerability:** A feature of a system that represents a susceptibility to a threat. A vulnerability may be a weakness, flaw or deficiency, or it may be an intentional aspect of the system.
5. **Harm:** The impact or damage to an asset arising from a threatening event.
6. **Controls:** A Countermeasure or safeguard against a threat or a vulnerability. Four types of control are commonly distinguished:
   — Preventative controls to protect vulnerabilities.
   — Corrective controls to reduce the effect of harm.
   — Deterrent controls to reduce the likelihood of unwanted incident.
   — Detective controls to discover threats and trigger preventative or corrective controls.
7. **Risk:** A risk is the probability of the occurrence of a harmful event. It can be considered as a function of threats exploiting vulnerabilities to create unwanted incidents to harm assets.

4   Proposed Framework

4.1   Purpose

The quality of security and privacy risk assessments conducted on smart meter projects has generally not been sufficient to satisfy the public [9, 23]. A framework is needed that enables efficient conduct of risk assessment, and that produces understandable results that convince all stakeholders, including consumers who are suspicious about the compulsory installation of a smart device on their premises.

4.2   Framework Description

Standards like ISO/IEC 2700x, NIST SP 800-30, BSI 100-x and methods like CORAS and OCTAVE have been exhaustively analysed, with the specific needs of smart meter projects in mind, in order to develop this framework [13, 14, 19, 20, 21]. We choose to use the terminology 'Risk Analysis' for this entire decision-making and management process and hence the framework is termed 'Risk Analysis Framework'. The proposed framework has a set of optimal steps that can be used to identify, evaluate and control risk to mitigate potential negative effects in Smart Grid. Fig. 1 provides a visual presentation of the framework.

Definition of Scope
The risk analysis process starts with the definition of scope. To define the scope, the target of evaluations should be identified. Each target will have involvement with one or many stakeholders. To identify the target of evaluation in a smart grid, the Smart Grid Architecture Model (SGAM) is used. There are few ways in which the target can be chosen:

- Each Domain/Zone cell can become a target. For example in the Customer Premises/Process cell the target will be a smart meter. For a smart meter there are multiple stakeholders like customer, utility provider, etc. Choosing a stakeholder helps to narrow down the analysis to how the meter hardware and the data that exist within the meter affect that particular stakeholder.
- Zone to Zone for a particular domain helps to target data in transmission from one zone to another. So if we consider the zones Process and Field we can target the data transmitted from the smart meter to the concentrators/collectors and vice versa.
- Domain to Domain for a particular zone helps to identify the target of interaction between each domain.

We can identify a number of targets and the stakeholders involved. Then the next step is to choose the target for assessment. We have found that each target may have more than one stakeholder, hence a stakeholder must also be chosen from those identified for the target. Narrowing down the target and stakeholder enables to easily identify the assets involved. At the end of this step we can identify targets, their stakeholders and assets involved.

Risk Identification
In this step for each asset identified, all possible threats will be listed. Using the threats identified, all possible vulnerabilities and unwanted incidents can be identified. Using the unwanted incidents list, the harms on the assets can be extracted. Activities should be conducted to ensure stakeholder participation in this phase of risk analysis in particular.

Risk Characterization
This is vital step in risk analysis. The results from this step will vary based on the perspective of analysis. We have mentioned earlier how risk factors that have been assessed as minor by technical experts had elicited strong public concerns. For example, an unauthorized party gaining access to the meter data may occur as a minor risk to a utility provider if the access is read-only but from the perspective of the consumer it is still a major risk. So in this step, the perspective of analysis is vital. Based on the perspective, severity levels and likelihood levels need to be identified and tabulated. A risk matrix can be generated using this information.

Risk Evaluation
In this step the unwanted incidents and the harmful impacts that were identified are evaluated using the established levels for severity and likelihood. A likelihood level is assigned to the unwanted incident listed and a severity level assigned to the harms listed. Based on the values of likelihood and severity given, a risk value can be assigned to each case. This risk value can be used to prioritise the risks identified.

Risk Mitigation Plan
This section specifies the treatment that needs to be provided to the identified risks. It begins with the identification of existing controls. The suitability of the control for the target of evaluation is then evaluated. Common factors affecting suitability are cost and resource limitations. For example, there are strong and complex encryption techniques available to protect data, but it may not be feasible to apply them on a smart meter with a limited processor. Based on the evaluation, a list of applicable controls can be specified, and the residual risk determined. Apart from countermeasure, contingency response also needs to be identified so that those actions can be taken should the risk event actually occur.

Risk Management
With all the risks and countermeasures identified, the next step is to plan and implement the safeguards. The implementation needs be tested to ensure that the risk have been mitigated as expected during the analysis.

Risk Communication
A planned communication process is very important to improve the awareness of risk to all its stakeholders. In addition, education of the media is needed, in order to avoid negative impacts caused by erroneous information sources.

Monitoring and Review
All identified unwanted incidents, harm and their controls need to be documented and then to be reviewed regularly in order to adapt to new threats and vulnerabilities and to improve control measures and find better ways of implementing and maintaining them.

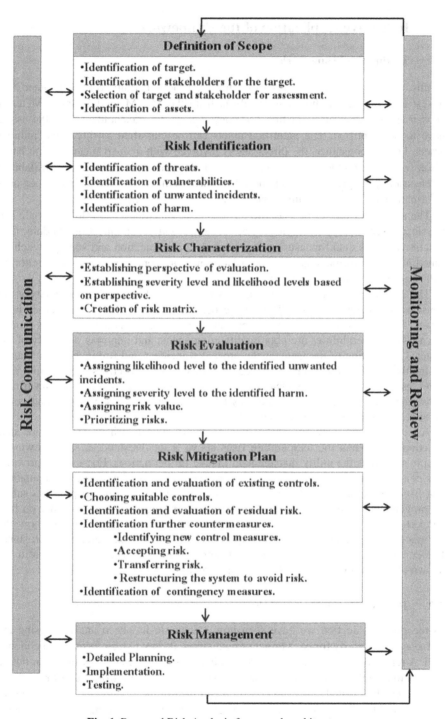

Fig. 1. Proposed Risk Analysis framework and its steps

5   Indicative Application of the Framework

5.1   Testing the Framework

In this section we analyse a scenario using the proposed framework. Customer Premises/ Process cell is chosen for analysis from the SGAM model. Smart Meter is chosen as the target of evaluation and consumer as the stakeholder. Then the assets have to be identified. The identified assets can be classified as direct and indirect assets. For the consumer, the direct assets involved with a smart meter are the hardware, firmware and the information stored. Some of the indirect assets are availability of electricity; integrity of billing and other functionalities; confidentiality of personal information and safety of human and non-human elements involved.

The assets can further be classified as physical, functional and informational. The physical assets comprise of the meter hardware and communication module. The functional assets entail measuring, conversion, communication and supply-switching functions. The informational assets consist of measurement, configuration, monitoring and consumer's personal information data.

The next step is to identify threats, vulnerabilities and harms. For this analysis we consider the meter hardware. There have been few reports that power surges have caused the smart meters to overheat and start a fire [24]. Power surge is a non-human threat. The vulnerabilities are poor quality components and improper assembly of the meter. Overheating of the meter is the unwanted incident and fire is the harm caused by the threat. This risk can be analyzed from different perspectives. For a utility provider, as there were only few incidents reported, the risk value will be low. But from a consumer perspective it is very high as there is always a chance of fire that could damage their property and even cause death.

As a control measure to overheating, some smart meters have temperature alert functionality. When the temperature rises above a set threshold, it shuts down the supply and alerts the utility management to take further actions. For a utility provider this control is sufficient as it prevents a fire and there is no harm to their reputation. But from the perspective of a consumer there is still residual risk. It provides safety by preventing the fire, but the power supply is disrupted. If it is a consumer on life-support machine, it could even cause death. This scenario clearly shows how the perspective of analysis changes the requirements in control measures for each stakeholder. Diagrammatic representations of some of the elements of the scenario are shown in the following figures (Fig. 2, Fig. 3 and Fig. 4).

5.2   How to Use the Framework

In the previous section we have seen how a scenario has been analysed using the framework. Similarly for each target of evaluation, its key risk elements can be identified. A repository can be created for assets, harms, risk and controls. Both quantitative and qualitative risk analysis can be carried out using this framework. A risk register or risk log can be created using the criteria mentioned in the framework. For qualitative risk register descriptive terms are used where as in a quantitative risk register numerical quantities will be used.

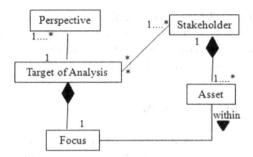

Fig. 2. Defining Scope for Analysis

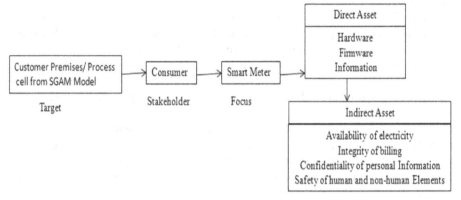

Fig. 3. Choosing Focus of Analysis

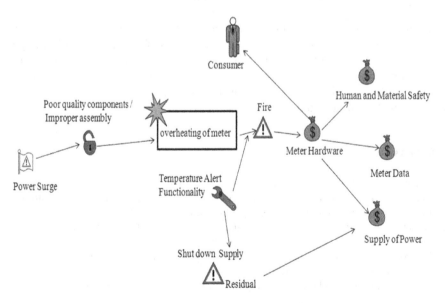

Fig. 4. Scenario Analysis

Alternately, tools like CORAS can be modified to satisfy the framework and then used for conducting security analyses. This model-based approach, improves communication and interaction between parties involved in the analysis. It will help in easily identifying the missing links and errors [19].

6   Conclusion and Discussion

Smart grids, and their critical sub-element smart meters, have great potential, but harbour risk to various stakeholders. The perception by householders that they are subject to significant security and privacy risk has proven to be a significant impediment to progress.

The field of risk assessment suffers from an excess of frameworks and a great deal of terminological ambiguity. The risk evaluation framework proposed in this paper reflects the substantial accumulated literature on risk assessment, and is sculpted to the needs of smart grid projects. It is now being applied to existing AMI systems and will then be applied to other categories of project within the smart grid arena. Experience gained from its use will result in clarifications and improvements to the framework.

Also there are some of the directions in which we can expand this work. We have mentioned in the definition of scope that the stakeholder needs to be identified. It has been conventional to identify consumers or customers as a large number of homogeneous entities. But can all the consumers be considered the same? Even if residential purpose alone is considered, a free-standing house requirement will vary from those of residential apartments and those of holiday apartments. Hence there will be value for all parties from deepening risk evaluation from a consumer perspective and comparing the results with the current, provider-focused system.

Though this proposed framework is intended for the smart grid, it may have implications for other critical infrastructures as well. The 'definition of scope' changes based on the choice of infrastructure and except for that one process all the other processes remains the same. The SGAM model is only used as a plug-in to define the targets in the Smart Grid. So even if the model changes or a new model is used the framework will not be affected.

References

1. Danahy, J., Bochman, A.: Smart Grid for the CSO (2009)
2. Baumeister, T.: Literature Review on Smart Grid Cyber Security, Department of Information and Computer Sciences. University of Hawaii, Hawaii (2010)
3. Kasperson, R.E., Renn, O., Slovic, P., et al.: The Social Amplification of Risk - a Conceptual-Framework. Risk Analysis 8, 177–187 (1988)
4. Roberts, S., Redgrove, Z.: The smart metering programme: a consumer review. The Centre for Sustainable Energy, Bristol (2011)
5. Quinn, E.L.: Privacy and the new energy infrastructure. SSRN eLibrary (2009)

6. Fang, Y.D.: Smart Grid – The New and Improved Power Grid. IEEE Communications Surveys Tutorials PP, pp. 1–37 (2011)
7. Farhangi, H.: The path of the smart grid. IEEE Power and Energy Magazine 8(1), 18–28 (2010)
8. Deloitte, Department of Treasury and Finance- Advanced metering infrastructure cost benefit analysis- Final Report, Victoria (2011)
9. Lockstep Consulting, Privacy Impact Assessment Report - Advanced Metering Infrastructure (AMI), Victoria, Australia (2011)
10. Rambi, J.: Lessons learned from the new Smart Meter Risk Analysis Methodology in the Netherlands, Chairman Policy Committee Privacy & Security Netbeheer Nederland (January 16, 2013)
11. NIST, National Institute of Standard and Technology, NIST Framework and Roadmap for Smart Grid Interoperability Standards Release 1.0, Office of the National Coordinator for Smart Grid Interoperability (2010)
12. CEN-CENELEC-ETSI, Smart Grid Coordination Group Smart Grid Information Security (2012)
13. ISO/IEC 27005, ISO/IEC 27005 Information technology - Security techniques - Information security risk management, ISO/IEC 2008 (2008)
14. Stoneburner, G., Goguen, A., Fering, A.: Risk Management Guide for Information Technology Systems. NIST Special Publication 800-30, VA 22042 (2002)
15. ENISA, Risk Management: Implementation principles and Inventories for Risk Management/Risk Assessment methods and tools, http://www.enisa.europa.eu/activities/risk-management (2005-2013)
16. SRA, Society for Risk Analysis (SRA) (2013), http://www.sra.org/
17. Kaplan, S.: The words of risk analysis. Risk Analysis 17(4), 407–441 (1997)
18. WP 29, Opinion 04/2013 on the Data Protection Impact Assessment Template for Smart Grid and Smart Metering Systems ('DPIA Template') prepared by Expert Group 2 of the Commission's Smart Grid Task Force, Article 29 Data Protection Working Party (2013)
19. Dimitrakos, T., Raptis, D., Ritchie, B., Stølen, K.: Model based Security Risk Analysis for Web Applications: The CORAS approach (2002)
20. Marek, P., Paulina, J.: The OCTAVE methodology as a risk analysis tool for business resources. In: International Multi-Conference on Computer Science and Information Technology (2006)
21. BSI, BSI-Standard 100-3: Risk analysis based on IT-Grundschutz (2008)
22. Security Risk Analysis Group, Introduction to Risk Analysis (2003), http://www.security-risk-analysis.com/introduction.htm
23. NRECA, Guide to Developing a Cyber Security and Risk Mitigation Plan, National Rural Electric Cooperative Association/Cooperative Research Network, Arlington, VA (2011)
24. EMF Safety Network, Smart Meter Fires and Explosions (2012), http://emfsafetynetwork.org/?page_id=1280

Physical Attestation of Cyber Processes in the Smart Grid

Thomas Roth and Bruce McMillin

Computer Science Department, Missouri University of Science and Technology,
Rolla, MO 65409, USA
{tprfh7,ff}@mst.edu

Abstract. Cyber-physical system security must consider events in both the cyber and physical layers. This paper proves that a cyber process in the smart grid can lie about its physical behavior and remain undetected by its peers. To avoid this scenario, physical attestation is introduced as a distributed mechanism to validate the behavior of a cyber process using physical measurements. A physical attestation protocol is developed for the smart grid, and the protocol is proven to expose malicious cyber behavior. Through the use of physical attestation, the behavior of cyber processes in cyber-physical systems can be verified.

Keywords: power grid, information flow security, remote attestation.

1 Introduction

A cyber-physical system (CPS) embeds cyber controls into physical infrastructures to enhance performance and reliability. Due to the tightly coupled nature of a CPS, security over such systems must adopt a unified approach that considers both the cyber and the physical layers. If an algorithm is analyzed using purely cyber information, then the analysis ignores physical actions performed during the algorithm's execution. Consider the case of Stuxnet, which resulted in the wide-spread infection of Siemens programmable logic controllers [2]. Stuxnet faked the process control signals in infected systems to appear indistinguishable from normal system operation. However, it performed malicious physical actions that were undetected by the system operator. When thought of in cyber-physical terms, the cyber process falsified the state of the physical system in its communications. Such an attack was possible because the behavior of the cyber process was not validated on the physical layer.

One prominent CPS is the future smart grid, which proposes the use of distributed cyber intelligence to manage energy resources at the residential level. Within smart grid literature, new attack scenarios are starting to emerge where the cyber control lies about its physical state to affect state estimation. Most of these attack scenarios are based on the false data injection attack, where an adversary compromises a subset of smart meters to report the incorrect physical state of the system [4]. It has been shown that the current smart meter infrastructure is vulnerable to this attack scenario [6]. There is a large field of research

E. Luiijf and P. Hartel (Eds.): CRITIS 2013, LNCS 8328, pp. 96–107, 2013.

that focuses on bad data detection in power system state estimation [12], but recent work has shown that attack vectors exist which cannot be handled using these approaches [4]. For instance, an attack might be unidentifiable in the sense it that is impossible to determine the correct system state [9]. One solution for false data injection attacks has been proposed that utilizes dynamic detection based on control theory [7]. This paper considers an alternative approach which attempts to validate a cyber process' behavior on the physical layer.

The cyber realm has the concept of attestation to test the correctness of a cyber process based on peer evaluations [8]. Software based attestation protocols evaluate processes for malicious behavior by examining memory and byte code, but have severe limitations when it comes to processes that exhibit intermittent behavior [5]. Within a CPS, however, cyber processes issue commands that modify the state of the physical layer. Because the physical layer is a shared medium, its state can be read by all the controllers, and the behavior of a cyber process can be derived from the current physical state of the system. And due to the tightly coupled nature of a CPS, a cyber action can have a unique physical footprint [3]. This allows a controller to determine the behavior of its peers through observation of the physical system.

The main contribution of this paper is a distributed attestation protocol to validate the behavior of a cyber process using feedback from the physical system. Section 2 introduces the smart grid architecture and attack model used to present physical attestation. Section 3 summarizes the results of prior work that prove that the adversary cannot be identified without physical attestation. Section 4 introduces the concept of physical attestation, and Section 5 applies it to the smart grid model. The paper is concluded with Section 6.

2   System Overview

This section presents an overview of a future smart grid based on the architecture developed by the FREEDM Systems Center [1]. It then introduces an attack scenario against the smart grid model.

2.1   Smart Grid Architecture

A smart grid consists of the set of houses in a neighborhood. Each house has local energy production and consumption, and the houses are connected by a shared distribution line. Houses are classified as in supply due to an excess of generation or in demand due to an excess of load. Figure 1 shows the structure of a smart grid neighborhood.

A house can push its excess generation to the shared distribution line, or pull power from the distribution line to satisfy its load. These pushes and pulls of power are governed by a distributed cyber intelligence embedded in power-electronics controllers at each house. Migration contracts are formed between pairs of controllers which migrate some amount of power from one house to another. A migration is a sequence of a push from a supply house followed by

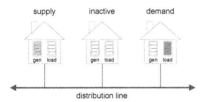

supply   inactive   demand

gen   load   gen   load   gen   load

distribution line

1. Supply house advertises its excess generation
2. All demand houses request power from supplier
3a. Supply house *selects* one demand house
3b. Supply house *increases* its local generation
4. Selected demand house increases its local load

Fig. 1. Smart Grid Architecture   **Fig. 2.** Power Migration Steps

a pull from a demand house. A physical representation of a migration is that a supply house discharges its energy storage, causing power to flow into the shared distribution line, and a demand house schedules some power consumption. This creates a natural flow of power from the supply house to the demand house.

Figure 2 enumerates the steps of a power migration. A migration is a combination of an increase in generation followed by an increase in load. If these two steps are not performed together, then there will be an imbalance between generation and load in the system. One attack scenario would be to maximize this imbalance.

2.2   Fake Supply Attack

Consider a malicious supply house that compromises its controller to change how it executes power migrations. During a migration, the malicious supplier does not *increase* its generation, skipping step 3b in Figure 2. If the selected demand house cannot distinguish this malicious behavior from a supplier who commits to the *increase* in generation, then the malicious supply house has successfully deviated from the protocol. This attack is called a fake supply attack and was analyzed in prior work [10]. A summary of the analysis is included in Section 3.

2.3   Formal System Model

A formal system model must be developed for the smart grid architecture to prove whether the system is secure with respect to the fake supply attack. Henceforth, the system will be defined as a microgrid consisting of a single neighborhood. The houses of the neighborhood will be referred to as nodes of the system. Each node i has two local state variables, P_i and $\hat{P}_i$. P_i is the net generation at node i and is calculated as $P_i = generation_i - load_i$. $\hat{P}_i$ is the advertised generation of node i broadcast to other nodes by the embedded controller. The difference between these state variables is that P_i is private information of the actual generation at node i, while $\hat{P}_i$ is a cyber message that may be falsified. A node can detect changes in the physical system through observation of its local variables such as voltage and phase angle. This is modeled as a single state variable P_B, which represents the individual physical measurements made by each power-electronics controller.

Suppose a system contains n nodes, then a state Q is defined as $Q = \{\hat{P}_1, \ldots, \hat{P}_n, P_1, \ldots, P_n, P_B\}$. A state transition $Q \rightarrow Q'$ occurs when a node performs a command drawn from Table 1. An assumption is made that each node participates in the cyber communication protocol. It is therefore assumed that a node cannot issue an *increase* command without a corresponding *select* command.

Table 1. State Transition Commands

command	description	state transition
select(i,j)	node i starts a migration with node j	$\hat{P}_i' \leftarrow \hat{P}_i + 1$
increase(i)	node i increases its local generation	if $P_i < \hat{P}_i$ then $P_i' \leftarrow P_i + 1$ and $P_B' \leftarrow P_B + 1$

Given this formulation of the system model, a power migration is the command sequence *select* $\rightarrow$ *increase*, while the fake supply attack is the sequence *select*. The fake supply attack succeeds if the demand node cannot distinguish between these two event sequences.

3   Nondeducible Attack

This section proves that it is nondeducible whether a supply house has chosen to commit to an increase in generation during a power migration. It first defines nondeducibility, and then applies the definition to the formal system model.

3.1   Nondeducibility

Nondeducibility is an information flow property introduced by Sutherland to analyze system security [11]. A low-level observation z is nondeducible if:

$$(\forall w \in W)(\exists w' \in W : f_1(w) = f_1(w') \wedge f_2(w') = z) \tag{1}$$

Equation 1 is satisfied if all possible high-level command sequences $f_1(w)$ are able to produce the low-level observation z using the information function $f_2()$. If a single command cannot produce the observation z, then it is deducible that at least one command was not issued, and the Sutherland definition is violated.

3.2   Attack Analysis

Given the fake supply attack introduced in Section 2, a malicious supply node wants to perform a power migration without an *increase* in its generation. The system is secure against this attack only if the demand node can deduce whether a *increase* command has been issued. Thus, for the system to be secure, nondeducibility must be violated between the pair of nodes involved in the migration.

Table 2. Nondeducible Attack

cmd	P_1	$\hat{P}_1$	P_2	$\hat{P}_2$	P_3	$\hat{P}_3$	P_B
init	0	0	0	0	0	0	0
select(2,3)	0	0	0	1	0	0	0
select(1,3)	0	1	0	1	0	0	0
increase(2)	0	1	1	1	0	0	1

Define a high-level view for the system that consists of the sequence of *increase* commands issued during execution. Define a low-level view that consists of a sequence of states with the form $Q = \{\hat{P}_1, \ldots, \hat{P}_n, P_B\}$. Consider the attack sequence shown in Table 2 in which malicious node 1 performs the fake supply attack *select*(1, 3) during the power migration *select*(2, 3) → *increase*(2). The low-level view of this execution consists of a sequence of states $Q = \{\hat{P}_1, \hat{P}_2, \hat{P}_3, P_B\}$:

$$\{0,0,0,0\} \rightarrow \{0,1,0,0\} \rightarrow \{1,1,0,0\} \rightarrow \{1,1,0,1\} \tag{2}$$

Theorem 1. *An attacker who launches a fake supply attack concurrent with another migration in the system is nondeducible and thus unidentifiable.*

Proof. If this execution was deducible, then it would be possible to deduce which node executed the *increase* command from the low-level view in Equation 2. However, both the *increase*(1) and *increase*(2) commands are enabled during the last state transition. This is because the guard $\hat{P}_i > P_i$ holds for both $i = 1$ and $i = 2$. Both commands also result in the same final state $\{1, 1, 0, 1\}$ according to Table 1. Therefore, it cannot be deduced which command caused the final state transition, and the execution is nondeducibility secure.   □

One solution to the nondeducible attack is to prevent concurrent migrations in the system. This approach was used by the paper that introduced the fake supply attack [10]. An alternative solution, which is the focus of this paper, is to increase the amount of information available to each node during execution. Rather than relying solely on the local measurement P_B, a distributed algorithm can combine the physical observations of multiple peers to determine whether an *increase* has occurred.

4   Physical Attestation

A single node does not have sufficient information to deduce the origin of a power change. It must collect additional information using a distributed algorithm that combines the observations of multiple nodes. This will allow the demand node to attest to the behavior of its supplier.

4.1   Conservation of Power

An attestation framework requires an invariant that evaluates to either true or false in order to determine if a node is honest. Within a smart grid, the law of the conservation of power can be used as such an invariant. Consider the circuit in Figure 3. For this circuit, the invariant I_b must hold that:

$$\{I_b : P_{ab} + P_b - P_{bc} = 0\} \tag{3}$$

Now suppose that the values for Equation 3 are obtained as inputs from potentially malicious nodes. The value P_b is the advertised generation $\hat{P}_B$ broadcast by the cyber controller. P_{ab} and P_{bc} must be calculated using physical measurements made by two nodes:

$$P_{ab} = \frac{V_a V_b}{X_{ab}} sin(\theta_b - \theta_a) \tag{4}$$

According to Equation 4, the value for P_{ab} can be calculated using the voltages (V) and phase angles (θ) at the points a and b. An assumption is made that each house has a means to measure the voltage and phase angle at the point where it connects to the shared distribution line. Under this assumption, node B can measure both V_b and θ_b at point b in Figure 3.[1] Each house stores a history of its voltage and phase angle measurements, and broadcasts them to the system in the same manner as $\hat{P}_i$. The invariant in Equation 3 can then be instantiated using the measurements broadcast by each node. If the invariant is violated, then one of the nodes that provided measurements must be dishonest.

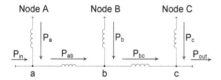

Fig. 3. Attestation Invariant

Bad Values	Invariant Violations
P_b	I_b
$V_b\theta_b$	$I_a I_b I_c$
$P_b V_b\theta_b$	$I_a I_c$

Fig. 4. Impact of Malicious Node B

4.2   Malicious Participants

The attestation framework should tolerate a single malicious node. That node can falsify its advertised net generation, as well as its measurements for voltage and phase. Consider the basic network of Figure 3 under the assumption that node B is malicious. Table 4 enumerates all the permutations of malicious values that can be produced by node B. Because V and θ have the same impact on line power, all permutations of these two values produce the same set of invariant violations. Note that in this table, I_a refers to the conservation of power invariant at point a, and I_c refers to the invariant at point c. These invariants have the same formulation as I_b from Equation 3 using their respective power flows.

---

[1] A phasor measurement unit (PMU) or similiar method can realize this assumption.

Theorem 2. *Table 4 lists the complete set of invariant violations produced by a malicious node B when the listed values are falsified.*

Proof. Suppose node B falsifies the value for only P_b. Because V_b and θ_b are not falisfied, and nodes A and C are honest, Equation 4 will yield the correct values for both P_{ab} and P_{bc}. Thus, I_a and I_c are calculated using the same power flows as the ideal case and retain their truth. However, I_b is violated due to the malicious value P_b'. This set of invariant violations corresponds to the first row in Table 4.

Suppose node B falsifies the value for both V_b and θ_b. In this case, the values for both P_{ab}' and P_{bc}' will be affected by the falsified values. Both invariants I_a and I_c are calculated using one of these malicious values, causing both invariants to be violated. The invariant I_b is also violated when using one correct value for P_b and two malicious values for P_{ab}' and P_{bc}'. This produces the second row of the table.

Suppose node B falsifies all three of its values. Both I_a and I_c are violated for the same reason as the prior case. However, now I_b is calculated using malicious values for P_b', P_{ab}', and P_{bc}'. If node B chooses these values with the invariant in mind, it is possible for the invariant I_b to be satisfied by the set of malicious values. This produces the third row of the table.   □

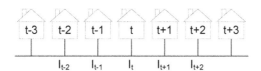

Fig. 5. 7-Node Attestation Framework

Table 4 shows that the actions of a malicious node cause invariant violations centered at its location in the power network. Provided that there are sufficient observation points to detect all of the invariant violations, a malicious node can be identified based on its invariant violation pattern. Consider the physical network represented by Figure 5. Through repeated application Theorem 2, the set of invariable violations for this network are listed in Table 3. Node t has a unique violation pattern that no other node can replicate. This allows the 7-node physical network to attest to the behavior of node t in the presence of one malicious node.

The 7-node framework cannot detect if nodes other than node t are dishonest. Given the invariant violation pattern I_{t-2}, it is not clear whether node $t-3$ or $t-2$ contributed the malicious measurements. It is therefore necessary to build the framework dependent on the target of attestation. For example, if the attestation protocol needed to validate the behavior of node $t+1$, then it would shift the attestation framework one node to the right and consider observations produced

Table 3. 7-Node Invariant Violations

Node	Bad Values	Violations		Node	Bad Values	Violations
1	$V_1\theta_1$	I_{t-2}			P_5	I_{t+1}
	P_2	I_{t-2}		5	$V_5\theta_5$	$I_tI_{t+1}I_{t+2}$
2	$V_2\theta_2$	$I_{t-2}I_{t-1}$			$P_5V_5\theta_5$	I_tI_{t+2}
	$P_2V_2\theta_2$	I_{t-1}			P_6	I_{t+2}
	P_3	I_{t-1}		6	$V_6\theta_6$	$I_{t+1}I_{t+2}$
3	$V_3\theta_3$	$I_{t-2}I_{t-1}I_t$			$P_6V_6\theta_6$	I_{t+1}
	$P_3V_3\theta_3$	$I_{t-2}I_t$		7	$V_7\theta_7$	I_{t+2}
	P_4	I_t				
4	$V_4\theta_4$	$I_{t-1}I_tI_{t+1}$				
	$P_4V_4\theta_4$	$I_{t-1}I_{t+1}$				

by node $t + 4$. As such, the attestation framework is capable of verifying the behavior of the center node and will change based on the target of the attestation protocol.

4.3 Physical Attestation Algorithm

A physical attestation algorithm can be developed using the 7-node attestation framework to validate the behavior of a target cyber process in the presence of one malicious node. The attestation algorithm will receive as input a target cyber process t, a *time* used to synchronize the physical measurements, and some small value ϵ to be used as a tolerance. An attestation framework is built around node t to gather the required physical measurements. The attestation algorithm follows as Algorithm 1.

Lines $1 - 2$ gather the required physical measurements from each node in the attestation framework. Using these values, lines $3 - 9$ calculate the truth of each invariant using the conservation of power. Line 6 uses the ϵ value as a tolerance for the invariant because the honest power flow values are unlikely to result in an exact sum due to measurement error. Line 10 determines if the violation pattern of the invariant indicates that the target t is malicious based on the results from Table 3. If t is malicious, then lines $11 - 13$ calculate P_t using honest values provided by other nodes in the attestation framework. If t is not malicious, then the advertised value $\hat{P}_t$ is returned directly.

Theorem 3. *The secure power calculation algorithm returns the actual generation P_t for some target node t even in the presence of a single malicious node.*

Proof. Assume t is malicious. Then according to the 7-node attestation framework, the invariant violation pattern will be either I_t, $I_{t-1}I_{t+1}$, or $I_{t-1}I_tI_{t+1}$. All of these violation patterns will cause line 10 of the algorithm to evaluate *true*. Lines $11 - 12$ calculate $P_{t-1,t}$ and $P_{t,t+1}$ using values from nodes $\{t-2, t-2, t+1, t+2\}$. Because none of the nodes in this set are malicious, the calculations will produce the actual power flows for the system. Line 13 then returns the actual value for P_t using the calculated values for $P_{t-1,t}$ and $P_{t,t+1}$. No

---

Algorithm 1. Secure Power Calculation

Data: Index t of the node to attest
Data: The *time* of the attestation
Data: A small tolerance ϵ
Result: Actual generation P_t at node t

1 get values $\{\hat{P}_{t-2}, \ldots, \hat{P}_{t+2}\}$ for given *time*
2 get values $\{V_{t-3}\theta_{t-3}, \ldots, V_{t+3}\theta_{t+3}\}$ for given *time*
3 **for** $i \leftarrow t - 2$ **to** $t + 2$ **do**
4      $\quad P_{i-1,i} \leftarrow \frac{V_{i-1}V_i}{X_{i-1,i}} sin(\theta_i - \theta_{i-1})$
5      $\quad P_{i,i+1} \leftarrow \frac{V_i V_{i+1}}{X_{i,i+1}} sin(\theta_{i+1} - \theta_i)$
6      $\quad$ **if** $|P_{i-1,i} + \hat{P}_i - P_{i,i+1}| < \epsilon$ **then**
7      $\quad\quad I_i \leftarrow true$
8      $\quad$ **else**
9      $\quad\quad I_i \leftarrow false$

10 **if** $\neg I_{t-1}$ **and** $\neg I_{t+1}$ **OR** $\neg I_t$ **and** $(\forall k \neq t)(I_k)$ **then**
11     $\quad P_{t-1,t} \leftarrow P_{t-2,t-1} + \hat{P}_{t-1}$
12     $\quad P_{t,t+1} \leftarrow P_{t+1,t+2} - \hat{P}_{t+1}$
13     $\quad$ **return** $P_{t,t+1} - P_{t-1,t}$
14 **else**
15     $\quad$ **return** $\hat{P}_t$

---

measurements from t are used in these calculations, and thus the final calculated value is correct regardless of which values t falsifies.

Assume t is honest. Then line 10 will evaluate to *false* because no other malicious node can exhibit the violation pattern unique to node t. The output of the algorithm will be $\hat{P}_t$. Because t is an honest node, it holds that $\hat{P}_t = P_t$. Therefore, the output of the algorithm will be the actual generation P_t. □

The secure power calculation algorithm assumes that each node maintains a history of past measurements to be able to calculate the actual generation of a node at a particular point in time. Each cyber process must therefore store a history of the most recent values observed on the physical layer. Also note that due to the existence of a tolerance ϵ, the algorithm allows nodes to be dishonest within some small tolerance. ϵ can be thought of as a security parameter that determines how much malicious generation a node can perform on the physical system. However, the value for ϵ must be chosen based on experimental values to prevent false positives of invariant violations.

5 Making It Deducible

This section uses the physical attestation algorithm to break the nondeducible fake supply attack.

5.1 System Modifications

Augment the system with a new state variable P_i^a for the value of P_i as calculated by the attestation algorithm. A new *attest* command is defined in Table 4 to set the value of this state variable. In order to use the physical attestation algorithm, a modification must be made to the migration protocol. Before a demand node increases its local load, it will run the attest command on the supply node that issued the select command. This will allow a demand node to verify that its supplier is honest, and to abort the migration if the attestation fails. One assumption is made to reduce the length of the security analysis. It is assumed that, during the initialization stage, the attestation protocol is run on each node in the system to verify their initial value. This prevents the need to attest to the value of a node both before and after its advertised change in generation. These modifications are sufficient to introduce physical attestation into the system model.

Table 4. Modified State Transition Commands

command	description	state transition
select(i,j)	node i starts a migration with node j	$\hat{P}_i' \leftarrow \hat{P}_i + 1$
increase(i)	node i increases its local generation	if $P_i < \hat{P}_i$ then $P_i' \leftarrow P_i + 1$ and $P_B' \leftarrow P_B + 1$
attest(i)	perform physical attestation on node i	$P_i^{a'} \leftarrow P_i$

Table 5. Deducible Attack using Attestation

cmd	P_1	$\hat{P}_1$	P_1^a	P_2	$\hat{P}_2$	P_2^a	P_3	$\hat{P}_3$	P_3^a	P_B
init	0	0	0	0	0	0	0	0	0	0
select(2,3)	0	0	0	0	1	0	0	0	0	0
select(1,3)	0	1	0	0	1	0	0	0	0	0
increase(2)	0	1	0	1	1	0	0	0	0	1
attest(2)	0	1	0	1	1	1	0	0	0	1
attest(1)	0	1	0	1	1	1	0	0	0	1

5.2 Attack Analysis

Given the changes to the system model, Table 5 shows the fake supply attack when launched in the presence of physical attestation. The low-level view consists of states $Q = \{\hat{P}_1, P_1^a, \hat{P}_2, P_2^a, \hat{P}_3, P_3^a, P_B\}$:

$$\{0,0,0,0,0,0,0\} \rightarrow \{0,0,1,0,0,0,0\} \rightarrow \{1,0,1,0,0,0,0\} \rightarrow$$
$$\{1,0,1,0,0,0,1\} \rightarrow \{1,0,1,1,0,0,1\} \rightarrow \{1,0,1,1,0,0,1\} \tag{5}$$

Theorem 4. *An attacker who launches a fake supply attack in a system with physical attestation is not nondeducible and thus identifiable.*

Proof. Recall that the high-level command sequence consists of a set of *increase* commands issued by supply nodes. The attack scenario is nondeducible only if the low-level view is compatible with all possible sequences of *increase* commands. Consider the alternative high-level command sequence $increase(1)$ instead of $increase(2)$ in Table 5. In this sequence, $P_1 = 1$ and $P_2 = 0$ after the increase command is performed. When the $attest(2)$ command is issued, $P_2^a \leftarrow P_2 = 0$. This produces the low-level state $\{1, 0, 1, 0, 0, 0, 1\}$. Then when the $attest(1)$ command is issued, $P_1^a \leftarrow P_1 = 1$ to produce the state $\{1, 1, 1, 0, 0, 0, 1\}$. This is not the same low-level view as Equation 5 since it results in a different final state. It is therefore deducible that the $increase(1)$ command did not produce the trace in Equation 5. This is sufficient to claim that the execution is not nondeducibility seceure.

6 Conclusion

This paper presented the notion of physical attestation in the smart grid. The behavior of a cyber process can be validated using physical measurements made by its peers. A physical attestation framework was developed for the smart grid that was resilient against a single malicious node. Using this framework, an attestation algorithm was presented to calculate the actual physical contribution of a target node. The algorithm was proven to handle an attack scenario that was nondeducible prior to the introduction of physical attestation.

The physical attestation algorithm has several limitations. It is not resilient against multiple attackers that cooperate to affect the violation pattern of the invariants. It also requires physical measurements from 7 consecutive nodes on the physical layer. This requirement limits its use in certain physical topologies and makes it difficult to perform attestation when the cyber processes cannot communicate due to network partitions. Possible future research directions to overcome these limitations are to expand the attestation framework to be resilient against multiple attackers and consider attestation by non-adjacent nodes.

The main contribution of this paper is the concept of physical attestation of cyber-physical systems. Distributed attestation of cyber processes in current literature uses the physical memory of a process to determine if the process is malicious. However, this approach allows a malicious process to duplicate its memory and simulate honest behavior even under attestation. In a cyber-physical system, the physical layer represents a shared memory between all the processes that cannot be hidden by a malicious node. A cyber-physical attestation protocol is therefore much stronger than its cyber counter-part since a process cannot lie about its influence on the physical layer. Although the focus of this paper was on the smart grid, physical attestation should be possible in any system where cyber processes share a physical resource. The main future direction of this work is a generalization of the attestation framework that allows it to apply to a generalized cyber-physical system.

References

1. Akella, R., Meng, F., Ditch, D., McMillin, B., Crow, M.: Distributed power balancing for the FREEDM system. In: First IEEE International Conference on Smart Grid Communications, SmartGridComm, pp. 7–12 (October 2010)
2. Falliere, N., Murchu, L., Chien, E.: W32.stuxnet dossier (February 2011), http://www.symantec.com/content/en/us/enterprise/media/security_response/whitepapers/w32_stuxnet_dossier.pdf (accessed April 19, 2013)
3. Gamage, T., McMillin, B.: Nondeducibility-based analysis of cyber-physical systems. In: Palmer, C., Shenoi, S. (eds.) Critical Infrastructure Protection III. IFIP AICT, vol. 311, pp. 169–183. Springer, Heidelberg (2009)
4. Liu, Y., Ning, P., Reiter, M.K.: False data injection attacks against state estimation in electric power grids. In: Proceedings of the 16th ACM Conference on Computer and Communications Security, CCS 2009, New York, NY, USA, pp. 21–32 (2009), http://doi.acm.org/10.1145/1653662.1653666
5. Mallela, S., Masson, G.: Diagnosable systems for intermittent faults. IEEE Transactions on Computers C-27(6), 560–566 (1978)
6. McLaughlin, S., Podkuiko, D., McDaniel, P.: Energy theft in the advanced metering infrastructure. In: Rome, E., Bloomfield, R. (eds.) CRITIS 2009. LNCS, vol. 6027, pp. 176–187. Springer, Heidelberg (2010)
7. Pasqualetti, F., Dorfler, F., Bullo, F.: Cyber-physical attacks in power networks: Models, fundamental limitations and monitor design. In: 2011 50th IEEE Conference on Decision and Control and European Control Conference (CDC-ECC), pp. 2195–2201 (December 2011)
8. Preparata, F.P., Metze, G., Chien, R.T.: On the connection assignment problem of diagnosable systems. IEEE Transactions on Electronic Computers EC-16(6), 848–854 (1967)
9. Qin, Z., Li, Q., Chuah, M.C.: Unidentifiable attacks in electric power systems. In: Proceedings of the 2012 IEEE/ACM Third International Conference on Cyber-Physical Systems, ICCPS 2012, Washington, DC, USA, pp. 193–202 (2012), http://dx.doi.org/10.1109/ICCPS.2012.27
10. Roth, T., McMillin, B.: Breaking nondeducible attacks on the smart grid. In: Seventh CRITIS Conference on Critical Information Infrastructures Security. Springer, Lillehammer (2012)
11. Sutherland, D.: A model of information. In: Proceedings of the 9th National Computer Security Conference, pp. 175–183 (September 1986)
12. Van Cutsem, T., Ribbens-Pavella, M., Mili, L.: Bad data identification methods in power system state estimation-a comparative study. IEEE Transactions on Power Apparatus and Systems PAS-104(11), 3037–3049 (1985)

QSec: Supporting Security Decisions on an IT Infrastructure

Fabrizio Baiardi[1], Federico Tonelli[1], Fabio Corò[1], and Luca Guidi[2]

[1] Dipartimento di Informatica, Università di Pisa
[2] ENEL Engineering and Research SpA, Pisa, Italy
{baiardi,tonelli,fcoro}@di.unipi.it, luca.guidi@enel.com

Abstract. A global vulnerability of an IT infrastructure is a set of vulnerabilities in its nodes that enables a sequence of attacks where an agent acquires the privileges that each attack requires as a result of the previous attacks in the sequence. This paper presents QSec, a tool to support decision on the infrastructure security that queries a database with information on global vulnerabilities and the corresponding attack sequences. QSec can return information on, among others, global vulnerabilities, the corresponding attack sequences and the infrastructure nodes that are the target of a sequence. This information is fundamental to evaluate in more details the security of the infrastructure and to support decisions on vulnerabilities to be removed.

Keywords: Vulnerability Assessment, Risk evaluation, Attack Chain, Privilege Escalation, Remote Attack, SCADA System.

1 Introduction

A fundamental step to assess the security of an IT infrastructure is the one that discovers the attacks against its nodes. This analysis is supported by several tools that scan, e.g. analyze, each infrastructure node and return its local vulnerabilities and the *elementary* attacks they enable. Starting from these elementary attacks, an assessment has to determines the **complex attacks** that a threat agent may implement. A complex attack is a **sequence**, e.g. a **chain**, of elementary attacks where a threat agent acquires the privileges to implement each attack through the previous attacks in the chain. A complex attack is enabled by a **global vulnerability**, a set of local vulnerabilities that are correlated because the attacks they enable can be composed into a sequence. By implementing a complex attack, an agent owning some privileges on a node can acquire further privileges even on a distinct node. The analysis that returns the global vulnerabilities of an IT infrastructure is highly complex and produces a large amount of intermediate results.

To minimize the overall complexity of the assessment, we have designed and implemented QSec, a tool to support decisions to evaluate and improve the security of an IT infrastructure. QSec properly structure the analysis that returns

E. Luiijf and P. Hartel (Eds.): CRITIS 2013, LNCS 8328, pp. 108–119, 2013.

the global vulnerabilities of the infrastructure and stores its intermediate results in a database. Useful information for a security assessment is produced by querying the database.

This paper describes QSec and it is organized as follows. Sect. 2 briefly reviews related works. Sect. 3 discusses the correlation of local vulnerabilities and presents the solutions we propose and Sect. 4 describes QSec. Sect. 5 presents a case study to test the proposed approach. Finally, Sect. 6 draws some conclusions and outlines future developments.

2   Related Works

[2] describes a preliminary version of the analysis and of the tool discussed in this paper. Other works have already introduced and discussed the correlation of vulnerabilities and the complex attacks they enable without defining or developing tools to automate the correlation. As an example, the taxonomy in [8] is focused on a series of use case events. [1] shows a theoretical approach to analyze complex attacks involving distinct nodes of an infrastructure and it is focused on the compromised level of a node. The resulting approach is rather efficient, but it does not enumerate all complex attacks. [3] defines a language to model attack scenarios that includes several steps. It uses dictionaries and predicates. [14] defines a run time algorithm to detect stepping stones. [11] specifies a formal data model for IDS alert correlation called M2D2. The discovery of global vulnerability is strongly related to attack graphs and attack trees that formally represent how a complex attack can be decomposed into simpler ones [12], [4], [3], [9], [7] and [16]. These structures support a security assessment in terms of attacks and vulnerabilities. Lastly, [6] and [15] applying attack surface method to a computer network.

3   The Problem

We briefly outline the analysis we propose to discover the global vulnerabilities of an IT infrastructure to show how its intermediate results can support a security assessment of the infrastructure to improve the security it offers.

The first step to compute the global vulnerabilities of an infrastructure is a vulnerability scanning of each infrastructure node that returns the local vulnerabilities that affect it. After scanning all the nodes, the local vulnerabilities of same or of distinct nodes are correlated to determine whether the elementary attacks they enable can be sequentialized to enable an agent to acquire the privileges to implement the j-th attack in the sequence as a results of the previous attacks in the same sequence. After all sequences have been determined each is mapped into the set of vulnerabilities that enable its attacks and all the resulting sets are returned. To correlate the vulnerabilities, e.g. to build the attack sequences, we need to know, for each vulnerability, the attacks it enables and the privileges each of these attacks requires and those it grants. In the following, we say that a vulnerability v requires a privilege p if one of the attacks that v

enables can be implemented only by an agent that owns p. In a similar way, we say that v grants a privilege p if a threat agent may acquire p by successfully implementing one of the attacks that v enables. As discussed in the following, we deduce the privileges that each vulnerability requires and those that it grants through a classification of the vulnerabilities.

At first, the correlation considers those global vulnerabilities that only include the local vulnerabilities of the same node. Each of these global vulnerabilities enables an attack sequence that results in a privilege escalation within the node. Then, the correlation considers those sequences of elementary attacks that target several nodes. Each of these sequence includes at least a remote attack where agent uses some privileges on a node to attack another node. Here and in the following, we assume that only an agent that has the control of n_s can implement an attack from n_s against a distinct node n_d. However, even an agent that control n_s may need to attack several further nodes, the intermediate ones, before being able to attack n_d. These attacks are required to violate the constraints introduced by the logical topology of the interconnection network of the infrastructure. This topology specifies the subnets, their connections, the network routing, and the connection privileges for each node interface and it may forbid a direct connection between n_s and n_d. To violate this constraint, a threat agent has to attack and control one or more intermediate nodes to built a chain of nodes from n_s to n_d such the logical topology of the interconnection network allows a direct connection between each pair of nodes in the chain. This shows the strong relation between the correlation and the logical topology of the interconnection network.

The previous discussion shows that a global vulnerability gv allows an agent that owns some privileges on a source node n_s to acquire some privileges on a destination node n_d that, in general, is distinct from n_s. The sequence of elementary attacks enabled by gv may be partitioned into an *initial* sequence, a *final* one and some intermediate sequences. The initial sequence is the one that implements the privilege escalation where the agent exploits the local vulnerability of n_s to control it, while the final one enables the agent to acquire the privileges of interest on n_d. Each intermediate sequence attacks and controls a node in the chain from n_s to n_d. Hence, the sequence of attacks enabled by a global vulnerability may include:

1. a final sequence only,
2. an initial sequence immediately followed by a final one,
3. an initial sequence, followed by one or more intermediate sequences and then by a final one.

In the first case, $n_s = n_d$ while in the second one the topology enables a direct connection from n_s to n_d. In the third and last case, the agent attacks and controls some intermediate nodes to violate a topology constrain that forbids a direct connection from n_s to n_d.

All the sequences of elementary attacks and the corresponding global vulnerabilities can be computed provided that we know, for each ordered pair of nodes, the elementary sequences of attacks that enable an agent that control the first node to control the second one as well. Obviously, no elementary sequence exists anytime the infrastructure topology prevents direct interactions between the two nodes. By properly sequentializing these elementary sequences, we can built longer sequences and detect further global vulnerabilities that enable an agent to control a node even starting from the control of a source node that cannot directly interact with the one of interest.

We can now sketch an algorithm to correlate local vulnerabilities. At first, the algorithm classifies the vulnerabilities of the various nodes to pair each vulnerability with the privileges it requires and with those it grants. Then, the algorithm builds a square matrix A where $A[i,j]$ includes all and only the sequences of elementary attacks that an agent that controls n_i can exploit to directly attack n_j. $A[i,j]$ is empty if no sequence exists. To build all the sequences that an agent that controls n_i can implement to attack n_j, even those that involve further nodes, we compute the closure of A, i.e. we compute the power 2^m of A where m is the logarithm ceiling of n. Finally, the algorithm computes all the *initial* and the *final sequences* for each node. An initial sequence involving a node n_i and a final one involving a node n_j can be composed with any sequence in $A[i,j]$ to determine how an agent owning some privileges on n_i can acquire some privileges on n_j.

To estimate the complexity of correlation, we consider the worst case of an infrastructure with a flat, e.g. unstructured, interconnection network where the topology enables a direct interaction between any pair of nodes and where each node n has v vulnerabilities. The complexity of vulnerability classification is $n \cdot v$. To identify any *initial* or *final* sequence we need $n \cdot v^2$ operations because the correlation of the local vulnerabilities of a node requires at most v^2 operations. The correlation of vulnerabilities of two distinct nodes requires $n \cdot v$ operations. The complexity of computing the matrix closure is $n^3 \cdot \log n$ where the basic operation determines whether the sequences in two positions of A can be sequentialized. Since a position of an intermediate matrix to compute the closure includes, at most, v^n elements, the resulting complexity is $v^n \cdot n^3 \cdot \log n$

Given the complexity of the correlation even for a small infrastructure, it is worth saving all its intermediate results in a database to avoid repeating some computations. For this reason, QSec stores this intermediate results in a database and then queries it to compute information to support security decisions on the infrastructure.

3.1   The Proposed Solution

In the following, we give some more details on the correlation of local vulnerabilities. Then, we describe the implementation of the relational database and how QSec queries it not only to deduce information on global vulnerabilities but also to implement some focused analyses to support security decisions. As an example, an analysis returns the local vulnerabilities that should be patched to remove a global one.

To show an application of QSec, we consider the simple infrastructure in Fig.1, where a node n_5 is logically connected to n_1, n_2, n_3, n_4 and n_6. n_5 is affected by 4

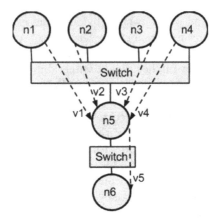

Fig. 1. Example of a network

local vulnerabilities v_1,v_2,v_3,v_4 that may be exploited by an agent that controls, respectively, n_1, n_2, n_3, and n_4. n_6 is affected by a local vulnerability v_5 that may be exploited by an agent that controls n_5. Since any local vulnerability enables a threat agent to fully control the attacked node. The overall infrastructure is affected by nine global vulnerabilities:

GV1: $\{v_1\}$, **GV2:** $\{v_2\}$, **GV3:** $\{v_3\}$, **GV4:** $\{v_4\}$, **GV5:** $\{v_5\}$, **GV6:** $\{v_1, v_5\}$, **GV7:** $\{v_2, v_5\}$, **GV8:** $\{v_3, v_5\}$, **GV9:** $\{v_4, v_5\}$.

Let us suppose that we want to remove any global vulnerability involving n_6 because it is critical. Furthermore, we aim to minimize the security investement, e.g. the number of local vulnerabilities to be patched. While this information cannot be deduced from the global vulnerabilities of the infrastructure, the information returned by QSec shows that by patching v_5 we remove all the global vulnerabilities involving n_6. Further analyses can be run to minimize the costs of patching and of hardening. As an example, some of these analyses may point out critical nodes from a security perspective by ranking all the nodes according to their betweenness, e.g. the number of distinct attack sequences involving the considered node, or evaluate the quality of a provider by considering which local vulnerabilities are more frequent in the global ones.

4   QSec

This section outlines the implementation of QSec. QSec builds a relational database with information to classify and correlate the local vulnerabilities and then offers pre-built queries and mechanism to compute information to support a security assessment.

4.1   Detecting Global Vulnerabilities

As previously discussed, to correlate local vulnerabilities, each of them has to be paired with the privileges it grants. In particular, we need to determine whether these privileges enable the full control of a node to use it as a stepstone [14] to attacks other nodes. QSec adopts an abstract view of this problem as it correlates vulnerabilities only after their classification in terms of the privileges each requires and grants. In this way, we can determine whether the attacks enabled by two local vulnerabilities can be sequentialized by checking the classes of these vulnerabilities.

The adopted classification partitions vulnerabilities into three classes:

1. those that grant privileges that enable the full control of a node,
2. those that grant privileges that enable the full control of a node if paired with those granted by further vulnerabilities,
3. those that grant privileges that cannot enable the full control of a node.

Vulnerabilities in the second class are further partitioned *subclasses* according to the privileges each of them grants. Each subclass is associated with other subclasses with the intended meaning that, given a set of associated subclasses, an agent can control a node by exploiting one vulnerability for each subclass.

The classification determines the class of a vulnerability by searching some *patterns* in its CVE [10] description that it uses as a standard reference model. Each pattern consists of predefined terms and phrases and the class of the vulnerability depends upon the patterns that its description matches. Even if CVE descriptions are not fully formal, they define the effect of an attack by combining a small number of predefined keywords. Hence, in general, the same keywords describe vulnerabilities that enable attacks that require and grant the same privileges. Besides using these keywords, QSec also uses the information provided by CVE details [13], a de facto standard in terms of vulnerability information repository. This noticeably improves the overall accuracy of the classification with respect to one that only uses pattern matching. Fig.2 compares the accuracy of the classification in terms of the percentage of vulnerabilities not classified for each year when using the CVE description only, [2], against the QSec classification that integrates CVE description and CVE details.

Currently, QSec retrieves information on the local vulnerabilities of a node either in a Nessus report or in a MySQL database. In the latter case, the information in the database that may have been produced by applying distinct scanners to distinct infrastructure nodes. The user can add, eliminate or edit some vulnerabilities for any node.

After loading the scanner reports, QSec classifies the vulnerabilities that have not been classified yet. The CVE database can be accessed either via web or locally. The user can check and update the final classification.

After classifying all the vulnerabilities, QSec correlates the local vulnerabilities of the same node. In this ways, it detects any global vulnerability that enables a sequence of attacks resulting in a privilege escalation against the considered node. Each of these sequences may appear as the initial sequence or the final one in the sequences of a complex attack. Then, QSec builds the attack surface of each infrastructure node. This surface includes all the attacks that can be implemented against the node by an agent that controls some other node. Given the node surfaces, QSec can compute the basic sequences for each pair

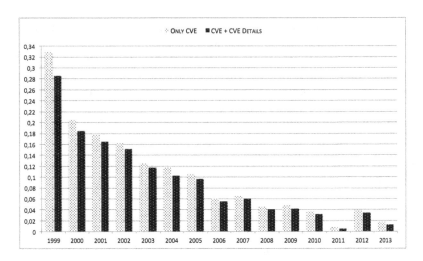

Fig. 2. Classification accuracy improvement between Qsec and GVScan

of nodes. Each of these sequences allows an agent controlling the first node in the pair to attack the second one. By composing these sequences, QSec builds longer sequences that target several nodes. For each distinct sequence built in this process, QSec signals a global vulnerability. The sequence building process corresponds to the initialization of the matrix A with the basic sequences and then to its closure previously outlined. The user can bound the length of an attack sequence or the number of stepping stones, e.g. of intermediate nodes, to neglect those sequences that will be implemented with a very low probability.

4.2   QSec Database

The user describes the network topology and the vulnerabilities of each node through a MySQL database. In this way, the user provides the information on the topology only once. Furthermore, anytime some new local vulnerabilities are discovered in some nodes, only these vulnerabilities have to be correlated to compute any further global vulnerability. Starting from this database, QSec computes the correlation and updates the database with partial and final results. Taking into account input and output information, the database includes the following 14 tables:

a) The **network, subnet, node, subnetConnection, nodeConnection**, and **routing** tables store information about the QSec project name and the network physical and logical topology including routing and filtering policies.
b) The **rights, accounts**, and **daemons** tables store information about the initial privileges on the network nodes. Rights are described as a tuple <source interface, destination interface, port, protocol>.
c) The **vulnerability** table stores information about each local vulnerability affecting the infrastructure nodes. It records the CVE number, the CVE

description, the class, the port, the protocol and the CVSS score. A vulnerability affecting several nodes is stored only once because the table **nodeVuln** links for each node its vulnerabilities.

d) The **hop** table stores information on the elementary attacks in the sequence of a complex one. The fields of a record are: a unique id, the source and the destination interface of the elementary attack and the position of the elementary attack in the sequence of the complex one. The **hopvuln** table relates each elementary attack to the vulnerability it exploits.

e) The **correlation** table stores information on the complex attacks returned by the correlation. This relation and the *hop* one may be seen as an implementation of the transitive closure previously described.

The first three groups of tables describe the infrastructure to be assessed, the remaining tables store the partial results computed by GVScan during the correlation. The tables in the last three groups are the most important ones for our purposes because we query them to compute information of interest.

4.3   Database Query Analysis

QSec provides a php script that loads and runs a query from a text file. QSec is interactive so the user can specify some further query arguments, if requested. At first, the query is parsed and a user input is requested anytime a special marker is found. Then, the query as modified through the user input is run. Lastly, the results are visualized (Fig.3).

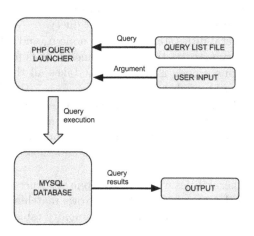

Fig. 3. Execution scheme of QSec

QSec has a set of pre-built queries to implement the most important analysis introduced in Sect. 3.1. In the following, we denote the user input in bold, e.g. **n**, $\mathbf{n}_s$, **v**. Currently, the following information can be deduced:

a) The local vulnerabilities that belong to at least a global vulnerability. This query joins the rows in *vulnerability* and *nodeVuln* tables and it discards those where the vulnerability id belongs to a row in the *hopvuln* table.

b) The local vulnerabilities that do not belong to a global vulnerability. This query joins the rows in *vulnerability* and *nodeVuln* tables and it discards those where the vulnerability id does not belong to any row in the *hopvuln* table.

c) The number of attack paths involving a node **n**. This query counts the number of rows in the *hop* table where the destination is **n**.

d) The local vulnerabilities that may be exploited to attack a node **n**. This query extracts all attack sequences from the *hop* table where the destination node is the one given as input. Then, it joins the results with the rows in the *hopvuln* and *vulnerability* tables.

e) The elementary attacks from a node n_s to a distinct node n_d that exploits a local vulnerability **v**. At first, this query extracts all the attack sequences from the *hop* table where the destination node is n_d and then it joins the results with the rows in the *vulnerability* table where the cve number is the one of v.

f) All the elementary attacks that an agent controlling a node n_s may implement against a node n_d. After extracting all the attack sequences from the *hop* table, this query joins the results with the rows in the tables *hopvuln* and *vulnerability*.

g) The number of global vulnerability involving a local vulnerability **v**. At first, the query extracts the vulnerabilities in the *nodeVuln* table where the cve number is the one of **v**. Then, it extracts from the *hopvuln* table the rows with the vulnerabilities returned by the first query.

h) All the global vulnerabilities starting from a node n_s and targeting a distinct node n_d. This query extracts the global vulnerabilities from the *correlation* table where the source node is n_s. Then, it takes all those where the last hop of the sequence is equals to n_d.

i) All the global vulnerabilities where at least one sequence of attacks starts from a node n_s and where n_i is an intermediate node. This query extracts from the *correlation* table the rows match n_s and from the *hop* table the rows matching n_i. Then, it joins these rows and those in the *hopvuln* and *vulnerability* tables ones.

j) All the global vulnerabilities where at least one sequence starts from **n**. This query extracts in the *correlation* table the rows matching **n**. Then, it joins these rows with the *hop, hopvuln,* and *vulnerability* tables ones.

Further queries may be run to rank the various global vulnerabilities according to the CVSS score of each local vulnerability it includes. As an example, the user can deduce the largest score of the local vulnerabilities enabling a given attack sequence or a sequence to attack a node from another one.

The user can defined further queries and insert them into the QSec query text-file. Each row of this file defines a query and QSec executes the query at the command-line specified row.

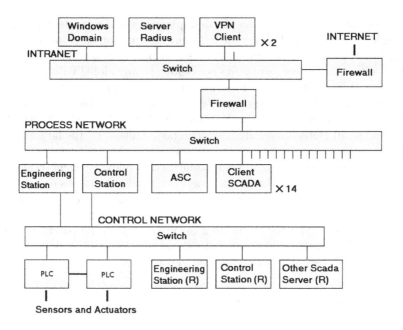

Fig. 4. Network architecture of the experimental IT infrastructure

5   The Case Study

We have applied QSec to an experimental IT infrastructure [5] that implements a supervision and control system in a thermoelectric plant for electric power production. As shown in Fig 4, the infrastructure backbone includes a switch and some firewalls that interconnect the switch and three subnets: the *intranet* network, the *process* network and the *control* one. The perimeter of each subnet is defined by a firewall that also acts as a router. While the switch and the firewall filter communications among subnets, each subnet is flat as any two of its nodes can interact. The business processes of the organization use the *intranet* network that interfaces the nodes in an external production plant with access privileges to some *control* network nodes. This subnet has 6 nodes, its main components are a Windows Domain and two VPN Clients that remotely access the *process* network. The *process* network includes 17 nodes that run SCADA servers and clients that act as the supervision and control system of the electric power production process. Some nodes are redundant for safety reasons. Lastly, the 7 nodes in the *control* network simulate the electric power production plant through proper hydraulic circuits and PLC systems.

The infrastructure is affected by about 2700 local vulnerabilities, about 900 local vulnerabilities per subnet. QSec signals that these local vulnerabilities result in 648 global vulnerabilities. Fifty of these global vulnerabilities enable attack sequences that begins in the *intranet* network and ends in the PLC System. We have manually checked these vulnerabilities to confirm the accuracy of QSec.

By adopting QSec, an assessment can implement some more detailed analyses of the infrastructure and discover the following information on vulnerabilities and nodes. There are 1238 local vulnerabilities that belong to a global vulnerability, whereas 1566 local vulnerabilities do not belong to any global vulnerability. The local vulnerability appearing in most global ones is *"CVE-1999-0504"* described as *"A Windows NT domain user or administrator account has a default, NULL, blank, or missing password"*, classified as "ADMIN LOGIN GUESSABLE". It is involved in 20 global vulnerabilities. The node crossed by the largest number of attack paths, i.e. with the largest betweenness, is the ASC server.

Lastly, we consider the global vulnerabilities that allow an agent owning some privileges on the nodes of the intranet network or of the process one to control the PLC system. QSec signals that these global vulnerabiities can be removed by patching two local vulnerabilities only. We remove all the global vulnerabilities where that attack sequence starts from an *intranet* node by patching one vulnerability and we remove all the global vulnerabilities enabling attacks starting from the *process* network by patching the second one.

6   Conclusion and Future Works

This work has described the specification and the development of QSec, a tool to automate vulnerability assessment analysis on an IT infrastructure by building and querying a database with information on the global vulnerabilities of the infrastructure. The information QSec returns is essential to assess the infrastructure security, because its analyses compute all the local vulnerabilities involved in a global one or that have to be patched to remove a global one. QSec can return further information that concerns the infrastructure nodes such as the node betweenness, e.g. the number of global vulnerabilities that enables to attack a given node.

QSec may be easily customized to develop further versions for different application scenarios because the queries are stored in a *plaintext files* and the user can update them according to the scenario of interest. In particular, we are currently developing a version that uses the output of the analyses to compute a set of cost effective countermeasures to deploy.

References

1. Ammann, P., Pamula, J., Street, J., Ritchey, R.W.: A host-based approach to network attack chaining analysis. In: ACSAC, pp. 72–84. IEEE Computer Society (2005)
2. Baiardi, F., Corò, F., Tonelli, F., Guidi, L.: Gvscan: Scanning networks for global vulnerabilities. In: First International Workshop on Emerging Cyberthreats and Countermeasures, Regensburg, Germany (September 2013)
3. Cheung, S., Lindqvist, U., Fong, M.W.: Modeling multistep cyber attacks for scenario recognition. In: DISCEX (1), pp. 284–292. IEEE Computer Society (2003)
4. Cuppens, F., Autrel, F., Miege, A., Benferhat, S.: Correlation in an intrusion detection process. In: SECI 2002: Sécurité des Communications sur Internet, Tunis, Tunisie, Septembre 19-21, pp. 153–172 (2002)

5. Fovino, I.N., Masera, M., Guidi, L., Carpi, G.: An experimental platform for assessing SCADA vulnerabilities and countermeasures in power plants. In: 3rd International Conference on Human System Interaction, pp. 679–686. IEEE (May 2010)
6. Han, Z., Cheng, L., Zhang, Y., Feng, D.: Measuring and comparing the protection quality in different operating systems. In: Lopez, J., Huang, X., Sandhu, R. (eds.) NSS 2013. LNCS, vol. 7873, pp. 642–648. Springer, Heidelberg (2013)
7. Harrison, L., Spahn, R., Iannacone, M., Downing, E., Goodall, J.R.: Nv: Nessus vulnerability visualization for the web. In: Proceedings of the Ninth International Symposium on Visualization for Cyber Security, VizSec 2012, pp. 25–32. ACM, New York (2012)
8. Howard, J.D.: An analysis of security incidents on the Internet 1989-1995. PhD thesis, Carnegie Mellon University, Pittsburgh, PA, USA, UMI Order No. GAX98-02539 (1998)
9. Jajodia, S., Noel, S.: Topological vulnerability analysis: A powerful new approach for network attack prevention, detection, and response, pp. 285–305. World Scientific Press (2009)
10. MITRE. Cve, a dictionary of publicly known information security vulnerabilities and exposures. Technical report, MITRE (1999)
11. Morin, B., Mé, L., Debar, H., Ducassé, M.: M2d2: A formal data model for ids alert correlation. In: Wespi, A., Vigna, G., Deri, L. (eds.) RAID 2002. LNCS, vol. 2516, pp. 115–127. Springer, Heidelberg (2002)
12. Noel, S., Robertson, E., Jajodia, S.: Correlating intrusion events and building attack scenarios through attack graph distances. In: ACSAC, pp. 350–359. IEEE Computer Society (2004)
13. Ozkan, S.: Cve details, the ultimate security vulnerability datasource. Technical report, Serkan Ozkan (1999)
14. Paxson, V., Zhang, Y.: Detecting stepping stones. In: USENIX (2000)
15. Stuckman, J., Purtilo, J.: Comparing and applying attack surface metrics. In: Proceedings of the 4th International Workshop on Security Measurements and Metrics, MetriSec 2012, pp. 3–6. ACM, New York (2012)
16. Wang, S., Zhang, Z., Kadobayashi, Y.: Exploring attack graph for cost-benefit security hardening: A probabilistic approach. Computers and Security 32, 158–169 (2013)

Structural Controllability of Networks for Non-interactive Adversarial Vertex Removal

Cristina Alcaraz[1,4] and Estefanía Etchevés Miciolino[2] and Stephen Wolthusen[3,4,*]

[1] Computer Science Department, University of Málaga, Spain
[2] Complex Systems & Security Laboratory, Universitá Campus Bio-Medico di Roma, Italy
[3] Norwegian Information Security Laboratory, Gjøvik University College, Norway
[4] Information Security Group, Department of Mathematics, Royal Holloway,
University of London. Egham TW20 0EX, United Kingdom
alcaraz@lcc.uma.es,
e.etcheves@unicampus.it,
stephen.wolthusen@rhul.ac.uk

Abstract. The problem of controllability of networks arises in a number of different domains, including in critical infrastructure systems where control must be maintained continuously. Recent work by Liu *et al.* has renewed interest in the seminal work by Lin on structural controllability, providing a graph-theoretical interpretation. This allows the identification of *driver nodes* capable of forcing the system into a desired state, which implies an obvious target for attackers wishing to disrupt the network control. Several methods for identifying driver nodes exist, but require undesirable computational complexity. In this paper, we therefore investigate the ability to regain or maintain controllability in the presence of adversaries able to remove vertices and implicit edges of the controllability graph. For this we rely on the POWER DOMINATING SET (PDS) formulation for identifying the control structure and study different attack strategies for multiple network models. As the construction of a PDS for a given graph is not unique, we further investigate different strategies for PDS construction, and provide a simulative evaluation.

Keywords: Structural Controllability, Attack Models, Complex Networks.

1 Introduction

Controllability theory offers a general, rigorous, and well-understood framework for the design and analysis of not only control systems, but also of networks in which a control relation between vertices is required [1]. The seminal work by Lin [2] provided a graph-theoretical formulation that has only recently become the renewed focus of research [3], which aids in understanding criteria for establishing control over networks. Both the work by Liu *et al.* [3] and subsequent work focuses on the identification of so-called *driver nodes* using non-rigorous maximum matching (to find subset of driver nodes that do not share input vertices) [4,5]. In this paper, we study an alternative approach based on the POWER DOMINATING SET (PDS) problem, which gives an equivalent

---

* Corresponding author.

E. Luiijf and P. Hartel (Eds.): CRITIS 2013, LNCS 8328, pp. 120–132, 2013.

formulation for identifying minimum driver node subsets (denoted N_D in the following discussion) sufficient to reach a desired configuration from an arbitrary configuration in a finite number of steps; for a time-dependent linear dynamical system (equation 1):

$$\dot{x}(t) = \mathbf{A}x(t) + \mathbf{B}u(t), \qquad x(t_0) = x_0 \qquad (1)$$

where $x(t)$ is a vector $(x_1(t), \ldots, x_n(t))^T$ representing the current state of a system with n nodes at time t; $\mathbf{A}$ is an adjacency matrix $n \times n$ giving the network topology identifying interaction among nodes, $\mathbf{B}$ an *input* matrix $n \times m$, where $m \leq n$, identifying the set of nodes controlled by a time-dependent *input vector* $u(t) = (u_1(t), \ldots, u_m(t))$ which forces the system to a desired state. The system in eq. 1 is *controllable* if and only if $\text{rank}[\mathbf{B}, \mathbf{AB}, \mathbf{A}^2\mathbf{B}, \ldots, \mathbf{A}^{n-1}\mathbf{B}] = n$ (Kalman's rank criterion). Whilst straightforward, for large networks the exponential growth of input values as a function of nodes is problematic, giving importance to the work on *structural controllability* by Lin [2].

The robustness of such networks has been studied by Pu *et al.* [5] *inter alia*, while work by both Liu *et al.* [3] and Wang *et al.* [4] has shed light on the effects of attacks (edge and vertex removal) on the network and the subgraph representing the controlling structures, clearly identifying the effect that network topology has on the impact achievable by such removal attacks. One problem immediately arising from vertex removal from a minimal power dominating set is the *reconstruction* and recovery of control.

Direct computation is undesirable as the PDS problem in general graphs has been shown to be $W[2]$-hard by Downey and Fellows [6], also showing that PDS is only $\Theta(\log n)$-approximable for general graphs. However, we argue that sub-optimal approximations are of considerable interest if this allows the efficient re-construction of a power dominance relationship that has only been partially severed.

In this paper we therefore study the effects of different non-interactive attack patterns (i.e. attackers are assumed to choose only a single set of vertices) resulting in vertex and edge removal from control graphs and interactions with the choice of equivalent PDS. For critical infrastructure networks, such as electric power networks or information networks, several topologies are of interest in which the concept of controllability underlines the importance of the technique itself for protection. We therefore study elementary (*Erdős-Renyi*) random graphs, but also small-world (*Watts-Strogatz*) and scale-free (*Barabási-Albert*) graphs, also with preferential attachment and provide simulation results for different parameter sets.

The remainder of this paper is structured as follows: Section 2 briefly reviews related work and the relationship between structural controllability and power dominance while section 3 describes the network models and resulting topologies as well as the derivation of control networks and strategies for attack based on limited vertex removal. We then proceed to study the impact of such attacks on different network and equivalent control topologies simulatively in section 4 before discussing the results and giving our conclusions together with an outlook on our on-going work.

2   Structural Controllability and Power Domination

In eq. 1, the matrix $\mathbf{A}$ gives the network topology, and the matrix $\mathbf{B}$ can be interpreted as the set of nodes with the capacity to drive control. Lin [2] gives the interpretation of

$G(\mathbf{A},\mathbf{B}) = (V,E)$ as a digraph where $V = V_\mathbf{A} \cup V_\mathbf{B}$ the set of vertices and $E = E_\mathbf{A} \cup E_\mathbf{B}$ the set of edges. In this representation, $V_\mathbf{B}$ comprises nodes able to inject control signals into the entire network, i.e. those constituting $u(t)$ in eq. 1.

Two main approaches for determining $V_\mathbf{B}$ have been studied; most attention has been paid to the *maximal matching* approach. Liu *et al.* [3] have recently observed that in directed networks, cacti (interconnection point between systems) and matchings in certain bipartite graphs are in a one-to-one correspondence and have gained considerable attention from their study of these structures, using the non-rigorous *cavity method* (applied to solve mean field approaches in statistical physic) for different classes of random directed graphs, notably directed versions of random regular graphs, the Erdős-Renyi random graph, and power-law random graphs. Of particular interest is the identification of minmum subsets of unmatched (*driver*) nodes N_D not sharing input vertices. Matchings in graphs is a well-studied problem, and polynomial algorithms exist [7,8], but this is not matched by understanding of graphs with fixed degree sequence and is the subject of on-going research that is both of mathematical interest and for motivated by the characteristics of networks as recent work by Pósfai *et al.* shows [9].

The robustness of controllability of several random graph classes including degree sequences found in existing (i.e. complex) networks has been investigated by Wang *et al.* [4], describing a perturbation strategy based on adding edges to graphs, while Pu *et al.* describe the effect of random and targeted vertex removal on matchings in Erdős-Renyi random graphs and scale-free graphs, although we note that the underlying results have been proven rigorously previously by Bollobás and Riordan [10]. We also note the results by Sudakov and Vu on graph resilience for both local and global properties [11].

In this paper, however, we concentrate on an alternative approach to the study of structural controllability, POWER DOMINATING SET (PDS). This problem was introduced by Haynes *et al.* [12] as a variant of the well-studied problem of domination motivated in part by the structure of electric power networks and the efficient monitoring of such networks. The basic decision problem (DOMINATING SET, DS) is NP-complete with a polynomial-time aproximation factor of $\Theta(\log n)$ as shown by Feige [13]. The PDS problem can be summarised by two rules, simplified by Kneis *et al.* [14] from the original formulation by Haynes *et al.*:

OR1 A vertex in the N_D observes itself and all its neighbours.
OR2 If an observed vertex v of degree $d \geq 2$ is adjacent to $d - 1$ observed vertices, the remaining un-observed vertex becomes observed as well.

which is reduced to DOMINATING SET by the omission of **OR2**; whilst we are also interested in the digraph formulation, for an undirected graph $G = (V,E)$ and an integer $k \geq 0$, PDS seeks a set $N_D \subseteq V$ with $|N_D| < k$, which can observe all vertices in V satisfying **OR1** and **OR2**. As can be seen, this also gives an intuitive formulation for control networks. However, for the general case, Haynes *et al.* have shown the NP-hardness of PDS, which is also the case for bipartite and chordal graphs; as noted above, PDS is also only $\Theta(\log n)$-approximable with recent results by Aazami bounding this to a factor of $2^{\log^{1-e} n}$ [15] unless NP $\subseteq$ DTIME($n^{\text{polylog}(n)}$), and the parameterised intractability results for DS imply $W[2]$-hardness [16]. Moreover, PDS is a non-local problem in that correctness of PDS cannot be checked by only considering a graph neighbourhood, and while it is polynomial-time solvable for max-degree 2 graphs, the best current result for cubic graphs due to Binkele-Raible and Fernau is exponential (in polynomial space) [17]. Guo *et al.* give complexity results for a number of graph classes including circle, planar, split, and partial k-tree graphs [16], while Pai *et al.* give recent results on grid graphs [18] and Atkins *et al.* on block graphs [19]. We now give pseudocode for a simple algorithm to determine the DS based on **OR1** in algorithm 2.1:

Algorithm 2.1: OR1 $(G(V,E))$

---

output $(DS = \{v_i,\ldots,v_k\}$ where $0 \le i \le |V|)$

Choose vertex $v \in V$
$DS \leftarrow \{v\}$ *and* $N(DS) \leftarrow \{v_i,\ldots,v_k\} \, \forall \, i \le j \le k / (v,v_j) \in E$
while $V - (DS \cup N(DS)) \ne \oslash$
$\quad$**do** $\begin{cases} Choose \ vertex \ w \in V - (DS \cup N(DS)); \ \Longleftarrow \\ DS \leftarrow DS \cup \{w\} \\ N(DS) \leftarrow N(DS) \cup \{v_i, \ldots, v_k\} \ where \ \forall \, i \le j \le k \setminus (w,v_j) \in E; \end{cases}$
return (DS)

The PDS algorithm 2.2 is analogously derived from **OR2**:

Algorithm 2.2: OR2 (DS)

---

output $(N_D = \{v_i,\ldots,v_k\}$ where $|N_D| \ge |DS|)$

$N_D \leftarrow DS$;
$i \leftarrow 1$;
while $i \le |N_D|$
$\quad$**do** $\begin{cases} Choose \ vertex \ w \in N_D \ with \ degree \ d \ge 2; \\ \textbf{if} \ (d-1 \ vertices \in N(w) \ and \subseteq N_D) \ \textbf{and} \\ (\exists \ vertex \ w_1 \in U \ where \ w_1 \in N(w)) \\ \quad \textbf{then} \begin{cases} N_D \leftarrow N_D \cup \{w_1\}; \\ U \leftarrow U \setminus \{w_1\}; \\ i \leftarrow 1; \\ \quad \textbf{else} \ \{i \leftarrow i+1; \end{cases} \end{cases}$
return (PDS)

---

3   Network and Attack Models

We now describe the graph classes and variants studied subsequently along with the variants of algorithm 2.1 and several attack strategies:

3.1 Network Models

As a baseline we consider the Erdős-Renyi (ER) random graph class [20], often constructed as $ER(n, p)$ with n vertices where each edge included in the graph is determined independently with probability p, as this has also been studied intensively for other approaches described in section 2.

We also consider the simple Watts-Strogatz (WS) random graph model [21], which is given as a construction beginning with a ring lattice of n vertices connected to k neighbours as determined by path lenghts, and with independent probability p choosing an edge of the graph where one vertex to which the edge is incident is chosen uniformly at random, but disallowing duplicate edges (ensuring the graph is simple). These so-called "small world" networks are connected, and have a vertex distance of $\frac{\log n}{\log z}$ (where z is the vertex mean degree), but unlike the Erdős-Renyi random graph exhibit significant clustering, making it an appropriate model e.g. for social networks where the degree distribution following a Dirac delta function centered on the median degree K is suitable. For a considerable number of networks, however, this is not the case, and we chose to include the popular Barabási-Albert (BA) model exhibiting a power-law degree distribution [22]. A construction giving a BA random graph starts with an initial graph of at least 2 vertices with degree ≥ 1 and proceeds to add vertices where each new vertex is connected to existing ones with a probability proportional to the number of edges that existing vertices have of $p_i = \frac{k_i}{\sum_{1 \leq j \leq m} k_j}$ where k_j is the degree of vertex i and m the number of vertices at the time that vertex i is added. The resulting degree distribution follows a power law, giving a small number of nodes with high degree. Empirical studies by Cohen *et al.* give an exponent between 2 and 3 when analysing a number of actual networks, which also have a small diameter $d \sim \ln \ln n$ [23] and a low vertex clustering coefficient. Finally, we also study a further power-law graph model (PLOD), but with lower clustering coefficient [24]. As noted in section 2, we require connected acyclical graphs without self-loops following Lin's structural controllability theorem.

3.2 Vertex Choices

The rules **OR1**, **OR2** do not identify a single power dominating set (or set of driver nodes N_D) for a given graph; we therefore have chosen three generation strategies:

1. Beginning with a vertex of *maximum out-degree*,
2. beginning with a vertex of *minimum out-degree*, and
3. randomly choosing an initial vertex

We note that these also do not identify unique sets for given graph instances. For simplicity, we describe strategies based on algorithm 2.1 satisfying **OR1**. For a given *strategy* we assume that an instance $\mathbf{N}_D^{strategy}$ is represented by a partial order given by the out-degree ($\leq$ or $\geq$) in case of $\mathbf{N}_D^{max}$ or $\mathbf{N}_D^{min}$, respectively; in case of $\mathbf{N}_D^{rand}$, no such relation exists; however, we do assume vertices to be enumerated regardless of the above in the following for each individual instance as we will need to reason over specific instances in the following section.

$\mathbf{N}_D^{\max}$ Obtains N_D based on vertices with maximum out-degree, defining a vertex choice sequence generating the set of DS for **OR1**. All vertices with maximum degree d are considered before those with degree $d' < d$ following **OR1** (see algorithm 3.1).

$\mathbf{N}_D^{\min}$ Generates N_D analogous to $\mathbf{N}_D^{\max}$, but using vertices ($\in W$) with the minimum out-degree d until these are exhausted before identifying nodes with degree $d' > d$ (see algorithm 3.1).

$\mathbf{N}_D^{\mathrm{rand}}$ Obtains N_D satisfying **OR1** defined in algorithm 2.1 in which the set of DS is generated by randomly choosing a vertex $v \in V$ in each iteration.

3.3   Attack Models

The strategies defined in section 3.2 for obtaining N_D are analysed according to five attack models (denoted here as $\mathbf{AM}_i$) described below. For the analysis, we assume that the attacker has full knowledge of the network and N_D, and will seek to remove vertices from N_D but cannot remove arbitrary numbers of vertices. In this paper we study five different models (see also algorithm 4.1):

$\mathbf{AM}_1$ This strategy attacks the first driver node v in a given ordered set $\mathbf{N}_D^{\mathrm{strategy}}$. The attack consists of removing edges until isolating v from the network, which may also result in isolating several vertices with dependence (i.e. also control relation) on v or partitioning of the underlying graph.

$\mathbf{AM}_2$ Seeks to delete vertices $v \in PDS$ positioned in the middle of the ordered set obtained for a given $\mathbf{N}_D^{\mathrm{strategy}}$.

$\mathbf{AM}_3$ Removes last element v in ordered set given by $\mathbf{N}_D^{\mathrm{strategy}}$.

$\mathbf{AM}_4$ Removes vertices $v \in V$ with highest *betweenness centrality* of the graph.

$\mathbf{AM}_5$ Randomly deletes a vertex $v \in V$ not within $\mathbf{N}_D^{\mathrm{strategy}}$ in order to analyse the behaviour of the entire graph after the isolation/removal of the target v.

Algorithm 3.1: MAXIMUM/MINIMUM STRATEGIES FOR OR1 $(G(V,E))$

---

output $(DS = \{v_i, \ldots, v_k\}$ where $0 \le i \le |V|$ with max./min. out-degree$)$;

$d \leftarrow$ *Obtain max./min. out-degree in* V;
$DS \leftarrow \{\}; N(DS) \leftarrow \{\};$
while $(V - (DS \cup N(DS)) \ne \oslash)$

do $\begin{cases} W \leftarrow \textit{Obtain the set of vertices} \in V \textit{ of degree } d; \\ \textbf{for each } w \in W \textit{(chosen randomly)} \\ \quad \textbf{do} \\ \quad \begin{cases} \textbf{if } w \notin (DS \cup N(DS)) \\ \quad \textbf{then } \begin{cases} DS \leftarrow DS \cup \{w\}; \\ N(DS) \leftarrow N(DS) \cup \{z_i, \ldots, z_k\} \, \forall \, i \le j \le k \setminus (w, z_j) \in E; \end{cases} \end{cases} \\ d \leftarrow U\textit{pdate } d \textit{ with next-smaller/-larger out-degree in } V; \end{cases}$

return (DS)

---

4 Structural Controllability under Vertex Removal

To evaluate the three types of structural controllability strategies ($\mathbf{N}_D^{\mathrm{max}}$, $\mathbf{N}_D^{\mathrm{min}}$ and $\mathbf{N}_D^{\mathrm{rand}}$) described in section 3.2, several attack patterns were studied for the graph topologies described in section 3.1. As large-scale networks are of particular interest, networks with $50\ldots2000$ vertices were studied. The focus has been on *sparse* graphs that are representative of critical infrastructures such as power networks, this is reflected in the parameter choice for the different topologies (e.g. $p_k = 0.3$ in ER/WS; $d^- = 2$ in BA for $\alpha \approx 3$). Under these conditions, robustness is evaluated from two perspectives:

Algorithm 4.1: ATTACK MODELS ($\mathscr{G}(V,E), AM, \mathbf{N}_D^{\mathrm{strategy}}$)

---

output (*Isolation of a vertex for a given $\mathscr{G}(V,E)$*);
local *target* $\leftarrow 0$;

if $AM == \mathbf{AM}_1$
  then $\{target \leftarrow \mathbf{N}_D^{\mathrm{strategy}}[1]$;
  else $\Big\{$ **if** $AM == \mathbf{AM}_2$
      then $\{target \leftarrow \mathbf{N}_D^{\mathrm{strategy}}[(\mathrm{SIZE}(\mathbf{N}_D^{\mathrm{strategy}}))/2]$;
      else $\Big\{$ **if** $AM == \mathbf{AM}_3$
          then
          $\{target \leftarrow \mathbf{N}_D^{\mathrm{strategy}}[(\mathrm{SIZE}(\mathbf{N}_D^{\mathrm{strategy}}))]$;
          else $\Big\{$ **if** $AM == \mathbf{AM}_4$
              then
              $\{target \leftarrow$ BETWEENNESS CENTRALITY$(\mathscr{G}(V,E))$;
              else $\{target \leftarrow$ OUTSIDE $\mathbf{N}_D^{\mathrm{strategy}}(\mathscr{G}(V,E), \mathbf{N}_D^{\mathrm{strategy}})$;
ISOLATE VERTEX$(\mathscr{G}(V,E), target)$;
return $(\mathscr{G}(V,E))$

---

1. *degree of connectivity*, and
2. *degree of observability*.

For the former case, diameter (Dm), density, and average clustering coefficient (CC) are considered. These values should maintain small values in proportion to the growth and the average degree of links (AD), and more specifically after an attack. For observability, we consider the remaining observable network as a percentage (**OR1**).

The diameter for ER graphs remains broadly stable for larger numbers of nodes as is well-known; however, the density and CC (see figures 1 and 2) for small networks (with $50\ldots500$ vertices) is significantly reduced after the attack. This reduction is even more notable when the perturbation is targeted, i.e. to locations with maximum out-degree ($\mathbf{AM}_1$ on $\mathbf{N}_D^{\mathrm{max}}$, $\mathbf{AM}_3$ on $\mathbf{N}_D^{\mathrm{min}}$) or with the highest betweenness centrality inside the network ($\mathbf{AM}_4$ on $\mathbf{N}_D^{\mathrm{max}}$, $\mathbf{N}_D^{\mathrm{max}}$, and $\mathbf{N}_D^{\mathrm{rand}}$). With a similar behaviour for small networks, WS topology behaviour may appear somewhat confusing as it does not fully capture

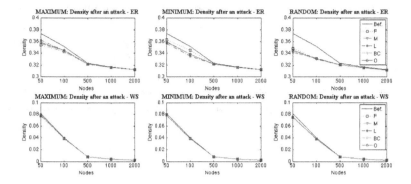

Fig. 1. Global density after attack in ER and WS networks

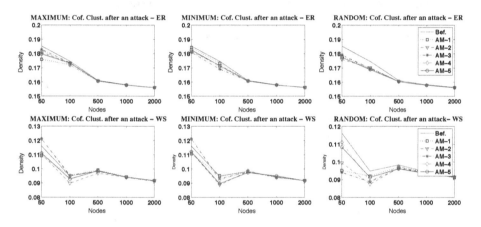

Fig. 2. Clustering coefficient after attack in ER and WS networks

small-world behaviour in which network diameter is significant. The reason for this lies in the fact that we work with small connectivity probabilities ($p_k = 0.3$) where the average degree of links reaches small values (≈ 2) regardless the network dimension (see table 1). On the other hand, although table 1 and figure 2 also highlight that small WS networks lose diameter values and CC with respect to the initial network, this does not affect to the global network density. Therefore, this type of topology is resilient to PDS vertex isolation, and more particularly to those vertices with the maximum out-degree or with the highest betweenness centrality.

For power-law distributions, parameters for BA distributions remain almost invariant for both small networks and large networks (cf. figures 3 and 4), confirming overall resilience but some sensitivity in observability (table 3) to attacks of type $\mathbf{N}_D^{\max}$ on small networks (50 nodes). Table 3 shows the fraction of observed nodes for each topology and shows observability remaining high ($\simeq 90\%$ and 100% of observability) after attack. Similar to the base BA distribution, low-exponent power-law networks appear

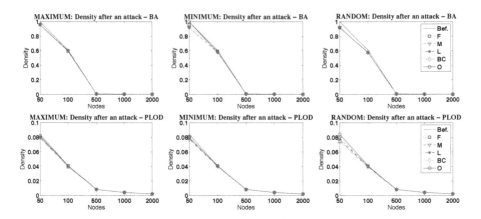

Fig. 3. Global density after attack in BA and low-exponent power-law networks

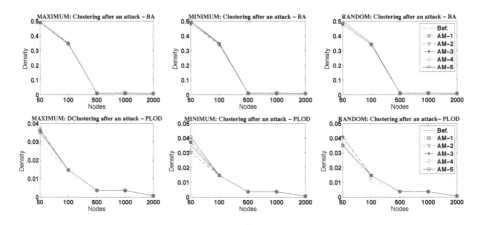

Fig. 4. Local density after attack low-exponent power-law networks

robust except to AM_4 attacks where the network diameter varies for any distribution $(50 \ldots 2000)$ when the node with the highest centrality is targeted. In contrast, AM_5 attacks do not present major risks with respect to intentional threats, but can have an impact on observability with 90% of observation in the worst case. This means that observability is a factor not only dependent on the network topology and construction strategies of driver nodes (N_D^{max}, N_D^{max} and N_D^{rand}), but also on the nature of the attack or perturbation [5] where degree-based attacks are more significant.

Varying the exponent of the power-law distribution ($\alpha = 0.1, 0.3$ and 0.5), we observe no significant change in global density after perturbation (cf. figures 3 and 5), even when the diameter vary after an **AM-4** threat with respect to the rest of threats (see table 2); a relevant datum highlighting the above analysis. Even so, tables 3 and 2 show that the observation percentage remains high with varying exponents independent of connectivity.

Table 1. Network diameter before and after a perturbation or attack

		ER					WS					BA with $alpha \simeq 3$					PLOD with $\alpha \simeq 0.3$				
		50	100	500	1000	2000	50	100	500	1000	2000	50	100	500	1000	2000	50	100	500	1000	2000
											Before Attack										
	DA	6.66	17.39	80.03	157.86	312.17	1.66	2.00	1.97	1.99	1.99	24.50	30.16	1.97	1.99	1.99	2.06	2.04	2.08	2.10	2.11
	Dm	3	4	5	5	5	12	14	38	78	78	1	4	9	11	13	6	12	28	35	46
											AM_1										
N_D^{max}	Dm	3	4	5	5	5	12	16	38	78	78	1	4	9	11	13	6	12	28	35	46
N_D^{min}	Dm	3	4	5	5	5	12	14	38	78	78	1	4	9	11	13	6	12	28	35	46
N_D^{rand}	Dm	3	4	5	5	5	12	14	39	68	78	1	4	9	11	13	7	12	28	35	46
											AM_2										
N_D^{max}	Dm	4	4	5	5	5	12	14	38	78	78	1	4	9	11	13	6	12	28	35	46
N_D^{min}	Dm	3	4	5	5	5	12	14	37	78	78	1	4	9	11	13	6	12	28	35	46
N_D^{rand}	Dm	3	4	5	5	5	12	14	39	78	78	6	6	9	11	13	6	12	28	35	46
											AM_3										
N_D^{max}	Dm	3	4	5	5	5	9	14	38	78	78	1	4	9	11	13	7	12	28	35	46
N_D^{min}	Dm	4	4	5	5	5	9	14	38	78	78	1	4	9	11	13	6	12	28	35	46
N_D^{rand}	Dm	3	4	5	5	5	12	16	39	78	78	1	4	9	11	13	6	11	28	35	46
											AM_4										
N_D^{max}	Dm	4	4	5	5	5	9	15	45	78	78	1	4	9	11	13	8	11	25	33	51
N_D^{min}	Dm	4	4	5	5	5	9	15	45	78	78	1	4	9	11	13	9	11	25	33	51
N_D^{rand}	Dm	4	4	5	5	5	9	15	45	78	78	1	4	9	11	13	9	11	25	33	51
											AM_5										
N_D^{max}	Dm	4	4	5	5	5	12	14	38	78	78	1	4	9	11	13	6	12	28	35	46
N_D^{min}	Dm	4	4	5	5	5	12	14	38	78	78	1	4	9	11	13	6	12	28	35	46
N_D^{rand}	Dm	3	4	5	5	5	12	16	39	78	78	1	4	9	11	13	6	12	28	35	46

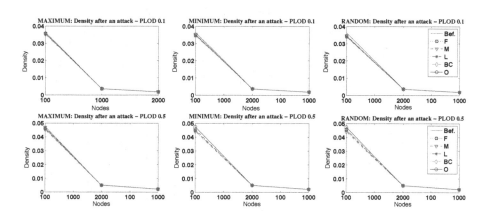

Fig. 5. Global density after attack low-exponent power-law networks

5 Conclusions

In this paper we have analysed the robustness of power-dominating sets (PDS) determining the controllability of a network on a number of network topologies including elementary *Erdös-Renyi* random graphs as well as the small-world *Watts-Strogatz* models and several scale-free networks including the *Barabási-Albert* model and particularly power-law networks which approximate structures e.g. found in power networks [25]. We have studied the effects of several non-interactive attack types on the PDS and underlying graphs, showing even limited *targeted* attacks to be highly disruptive in connectivity terms in power-law and small-world networks, or in observability terms in scale-free networks. Ongoing and future work extends this analysis to *interactive* and *concurrent attacks* and the development of efficient stabilisation mechanisms preserv-

Table 2. Diameter and observation rate for a varied exponentiation of PLOD

	Diameter						CC						Observation Rate					
	PLOD $\alpha \simeq 0.1$			PLOD $\alpha \simeq 0.5$			PLOD $\alpha \simeq 0.1$			PLOD $\alpha \simeq 0.5$			PLOD $\alpha \simeq 0.1$			PLOD $\alpha \simeq 0.5$		
	100	1000	2000	100	1000	2000	100	1000	2000	100	1000	2000	100	1000	2000	100	1000	2000
AM_1																		
N_D^{max}	10	36	36	14	25	46	0.0152	0.0028	0.0013	0.0192	0.0036	0.0007	99.0	99.7	99.9	98.0	99.7	100.0
N_D^{min}	10	36	36	14	25	46	0.0162	0.0028	0.0013	0.0169	0.0039	0.0007	100.0	99.8	99.85	100.0	99.8	100.0
N_D^{rand}	9	36	36	14	23	46	0.0180	0.0028	0.0013	0.0176	0.0036	0.0007	100.0	99.9	99.9	100.0	99.8	100.0
AM_2																		
N_D^{max}	10	36	36	14	25	46	0.0136	0.0028	0.0013	0.0198	0.0039	0.0007	99.0	99.7	99.9	98.0	99.9	100.0
N_D^{min}	10	36	36	14	25	46	0.0153	0.0028	0.0013	0.0195	0.0039	0.0007	100.0	99.8	99.85	100.0	99.8	100.0
N_D^{rand}	9	36	36	14	25	46	0.0155	0.0028	0.0013	0.0187	0.0039	0.0007	100.0	99.9	99.9	100.0	99.8	100.0
AM_3																		
N_D^{max}	10	36	36	14	25	46	0.0123	0.0028	0.0013	0.0179	0.0039	0.0007	99.9	99.7	99.9	98.0	99.9	100.0
N_D^{min}	12	36	36	14	25	46	0.0146	0.0028	0.0013	0.0181	0.0039	0.0007	100.0	99.8	99.85	100.0	99.8	100.0
N_D^{rand}	10	36	36	14	23	46	0.0158	0.0028	0.0013	0.0181	0.0039	0.0007	100.0	99.9	99.9	100.0	99.8	100.0
AM_4																		
N_D^{max}	12	36	38	11	26	51	0.0145	0.0028	0.0013	0.0162	0.0037	0.0007	99.0	99.7	99.9	97.0	99.9	100.0
N_D^{min}	12	36	38	11	26	51	0.0146	0.0028	0.0013	0.0151	0.0037	0.0007	100.0	99.8	99.85	100.0	99.8	100.0
N_D^{rand}	11	36	38	11	26	51	0.0148	0.0028	0.0013	0.0151	0.0037	0.0007	1000.0	99.9	99.9	100.0	99.8	100.0
AM_5																		
N_D^{max}	10	36	36	14	25	46	0.0153	0.0028	0.0013	0.0187	0.0039	0.0007	99.0	99.7	99.85	97.0	99.8	99.95
N_D^{min}	10	36	36	14	23	46	0.0155	0.0028	0.0013	0.0198	0.0039	0.0007	99.0	99.8	99.8	100.0	99.8	99.95
N_D^{rand}	10	36	36	14	23	46	0.0158	0.0028	0.0013	0.0198	0.0039	0.0007	99.0	99.8	99.85	100.0	99.7	99.95

Table 3. Observation rate after perturbation or attack

	ER					WS					BA with $\alpha \simeq 3$					PLOD with $\alpha \simeq 0.3$				
	50	100	500	1000	2000	50	100	500	1000	2000	50	100	500	1000	2000	50	100	500	1000	2000
AM_1																				
N_D^{max}	92.0	86.0	99.8	99.5	99.95	96.0	89.0	99.8	99.7	99.9	20.0	97.0	100.0	100.0	100.0	98.0	100.0	100.0	99.6	100.0
N_D^{min}	100.0	100.0	100.0	100.0	100.0	100.0	98.0	100.0	100.0	100.0	100.0	99.0	100.0	100.0	100.0	100.0	100.0	100.0	100.0	100.0
N_D^{rand}	92.0	96.0	98.4	99.5	99.8	96.0	98.0	96.2	97.8	97.85	94.0	96.0	99.8	99.8	99.9	100.0	100.0	100.0	100.0	100.0
AM_2																				
N_D^{max}	100.0	86.0	100.0	99.8	99.9	100.0	90.0	99.80	99.9	99.95	20.0	95.0	100.0	100.0	100.0	98.0	100.0	100.0	100.0	100.0
N_D^{min}	100.0	100.0	100.0	100.0	100.0	100.0	98.0	100.0	99.9	100.0	100.0	99.0	100.0	100.0	100.0	100.0	100.0	100.0	100.0	100.0
N_D^{rand}	88.0	98.0	98.4	99.3	99.85	96.0	98.0	96.2	97.8	97.85	94.0	96.0	99.8	99.8	99.9	100.0	100.0	100.0	100.0	100.0
AM_3																				
N_D^{max}	100.0	91.0	100.0	99.9	100.0	100.0	91.0	100.0	99.9	100.0	20.0	96.0	100.0	100.0	100.0	98.0	100.0	100.0	100.0	100.0
N_D^{min}	100.0	100.0	99.8	99.9	99.95	98.0	98.0	100.0	100.0	100.0	100.0	99.0	100.0	100.0	99.95	100.0	100.0	100.0	100.0	100.0
N_D^{rand}	86.0	96.0	98.0	99.3	99.8	96.0	98.0	96.2	97.8	97.85	92.0	96.0	99.8	99.8	99.9	100.0	100.0	100.0	100.0	100.0
AM_4																				
N_D^{max}	98.0	90.0	99.8	99.9	99.95	100.0	91.0	99.8	100.0	99.95	20.0	97.0	100.0	100.0	100.0	98.0	100.0	100.0	100.0	100.0
N_D^{min}	100.0	99.0	99.8	99.9	99.95	98.0	98.0	99.8	100.0	99.95	100.0	98.0	100.0	100.0	100.0	100.0	100.0	100.0	100.0	100.0
N_D^{rand}	90.0	97.0	98.2	99.3	99.75	96.0	98.0	96.2	97.8	97.85	92.0	95.0	99.8	99.8	99.9	100.0	100.0	100.0	100.0	100.0
AM_5																				
N_D^{max}	98.0	90.0	99.8	99.9	99.95	98.0	90.0	99.8	99.9	99.95	50.0	95.0	100.0	100.0	100.0	98.0	100.0	99.8	100.0	99.95
N_D^{min}	98.0	98.0	99.8	99.9	99.95	98.0	98.0	99.8	99.9	99.95	100.0	98.0	100.0	100.0	100.0	98.0	99.0	99.8	100.0	99.95
N_D^{rand}	90.0	96.0	98.4	99.3	99.8	96.0	97.0	96.2	97.8	97.85	96.0	96.0	99.6	99.8	99.85	100.0	100.0	99.8	100.0	99.95

ing domination properties and hence controllability for the types of graph studied here as little is presently known for these highly relevant classes [16].

Acknowledgements. The authors would like to acknowledge contributions by A. Baiocco to simulations. Research of C. Alcaraz was funded by the Marie Curie CO-FUND programme "U-Mobility" co-financed by University of Málaga and the EU 7th FP (GA 246550). Research by A. Baiocco and S. Wolthusen is based in part upon work supported by the 7th Framework Programme of the European Union Joint Technology Initiatives Collaborative Project ARTEMIS under Grant Agreement 269374 (Internet of Energy for Electric Mobility).

References

1. Kalman, R.E.: Mathematical description of linear dynamical systems. Journal of the Society of Industrial and Applied Mathematics Control Series A 1, 152–192 (1963)
2. Lin, C.-T.: Structual Controllability. IEEE Transactions on Automatic Control 19(3), 201–208 (1974)
3. Liu, Y.-Y., Slotine, J.-J., Barabási, A.-L.: Controllability of Complex Networks. Nature 473, 167–173 (2011)
4. Wang, W.-X., Ni, X., Lai, Y.-C., Grebogi, C.: Optimizing controllability of complex networks by minimum structural perturbations. Physical Review E 85(2), 026115 (2012)
5. Pu, C.-L., Pei, W.-J., Michaelson, A.: Robustness analysis of network controllability. Physica A: Statistical Mechanics and its Applications 391(18), 4420–4425 (2012)
6. Downey, R.G., Fellows, M.R.: Parameterized Complexity. Monographs in Computer Science. Springer, Heidelberg (1999)
7. Micali, S., Vazirani, V.V.: An $O(\sqrt{|V|}|E|)$ Algorithm for Finding Maximum Matching in General Graphs. In: Book, R.V. (ed.) Proceedings of the 21st Annual Symposium on Foundations of Computer Science (FOCS 1980), Syracuse, NY, USA, pp. 17–27. IEEE Press (October 1980)
8. Lovász, L., Plummer, M.D.: Matching Theory. American Mathematical Society, Providence (2009)
9. Pósfai, M., Liu, Y.-Y., Slotine, J.-J., Barabási, A.-L.: Effect of Correlations on Network Controllability. Nature Scientific Reports 3(1067), 1–7 (2013)
10. Bollobás, B., Riordan, O.: Robustness and Vulnerability of Scale-Free Random Graphs. Internet Mathematics 1(1), 1–35 (2003)
11. Sudakov, B., Vu, V.H.: Local Resilience of Graphs. Random Structures & Algorithms 33(4), 409–433 (2008)
12. Haynes, T.W., Mitchell Hedetniemi, S., Hedetniemi, S.T., Henning, M.A.: Domination in Graphs Applied to Electric Power Networks. SIAM Journal on Discrete Mathematics 15(4), 519–529 (2002)
13. Feige, U.: A Threshold of $\ln n$ for Approximating Set Cover. Journal of the ACM 45(4), 634–652 (1998)
14. Kneis, J., Mölle, D., Richter, S., Rossmanith, P.: Parameterized Power Domination Complexity. Information Processing Letters 98(4), 145–149 (2006)
15. Aazami, A., Stilp, K.: Approximation Algorithms and Hardness for Domination with Propagation. SIAM Journal on Discrete Mathematics 23(3), 1382–1399 (2009)
16. Guo, J., Niedermeier, R., Raible, D.: Improved Algorithms and Complexity Results for Power Domination in Graphs. Algorithmica 52(2), 177–202 (2008)
17. Binkele-Raible, D., Fernau, H.: An Exact Exponential Time Algorithm for POWER DOMINATING SET. Algorithmica 63(1-2), 323–346 (2012)
18. Pai, K.-J., Chang, J.-M., Wang, Y.-L.: Restricted Power Domination and Fault-Tolerant Power Domination on Grids. Discrete Applied Mathematics 158(10), 1079–1089 (2010)
19. Atkins, D., Haynes, T.W., Henning, M.A.: Placing Monitoring Devices in Electric Power Networks Modelled by Block Graphs. Ars Combinatorica 79(1) (April 2006)
20. Bollobás, B.: Random Graphs, 2nd edn. Cambridge Studies in Advanced Mathematics, vol. 73. Cambridge University Press, Cambridge (2001)
21. Watts, D.J., Strogatz, S.H.: Collective Dynamics of 'Small-World' Networks. Nature 393, 440–442 (1998)
22. Albert, R., Barabási, A.-L.: Statistical Mechanics of Complex Networks. Reviews of Modern Physics 74(1), 47–97 (2002)

23. Cohen, R., Havlin, S., Ben Avraham, D.: Structural Properties of Scale-Free Networks. In: Bornholdt, S., Schuster, H.-G. (eds.) Handbook of Graphs and Networks: From the Genome to the Internet, Wiley-VCH, Weinheim (2005)
24. Palmer, C.R., Steffan, J.G.: Generating Network Topologies That Obey Power Laws. In: Proceedings of the 2000 IEEE Global Telecommunications Conference (GLOBECOM 2000), vol. 1, pp. 434–438. IEEE Press, San Francisco (2000)
25. Pagani, G.A., Aiello, M.: The Power Grid as a Complex Network: A Survey. Physica A: Statistical Mechanics and its Applications 392(11), 2688–2700 (2013)

Real Time Threat Prediction, Identification and Mitigation for Critical Infrastructure Protection Using Semantics, Event Processing and Sequential Analysis

Dimitris Kostopoulos[1], Vasilis Tsoulkas[1], George Leventakis[1,2],
Prokopios Drogkaris[1,2], and Vasiliki Politopoulou[1,2]

[1] Center for Security Studies (KEMEA), Ministry of Public Order and Citizen Protection,
Athens, GR-10177, Greece
[2] Department of Information and Communication Systems Engineering,
University of the Aegean, Samos, GR-83200, Greece
{dimkostopoulos,tsoulkas.kemea,george.leventakis,
prokopis.drogkaris,v.politopoulou}@gmail.com

Abstract. Seamless and faultless operational conditions of multi stakeholder Critical Infrastructures (CIs) are of high importance for today's societies on a global scale. Due to their population impact, attacks against their interconnected components can create serious damages and performance degradation which eventually can result in a societal crisis. Therefore it is crucial to effectively and timely protect these high performance - critical systems against any type of malicious cyber-physical intrusions. This can be realized by protecting CIs against threat consequences or by blocking threats to take place at an early stage and preventing further escalation or predicting threat occurrences and have the ability to rapidly react by eliminating its roots. In this paper a novel architecture is proposed in which these three ways of confronting with cyber – physical threats are combined using a novel semantics based risk methodology that relies on real time behavioral analysis. The final prototype provides the CI operator with a decision tool (DST) that imprints the proposed approach and which is capable of alerting on new unknown threats, generate suggestions of the required counter-actions and alert of probable threat existence. The implemented architecture has been tested and validated in a proof of concept scenario of an airport CI with simulated monitoring data.

Keywords: Real Time Threat Detection, Critical Infrastructures, Semantics, Event Processing, Sequential Analysis, CUSUM Statistic.

1   Introduction

The growing number of security risks, potential vulnerabilities and constant expo-sure to internal or external security incidents has increased the need for rapid, accurate and low false alarm rate (LFAR) threat detection and risk analysis for Critical Infrastructure Protection (CIP). Especially cyber-attacks against interconnected information and communication channels do not only disrupt exchanged data flow and data integrity

E. Luiijf and P. Hartel (Eds.): CRITIS 2013, LNCS 8328, pp. 133–141, 2013.
© Springer International Publishing Switzerland 2013

but also generate cascaded risks due to the coupling and dependencies of data and networks.

Most well-established risk management methodologies are based on an *a priori* analysis of information security risks for a given fixed system design and configuration. During the analysis phase, system vulnerabilities are identified and a taxonomy of the associated risks is quantified. Following the time period where the system has gone into service, risk management must be monitored and reviewed to keep any alteration under control, which may result in re-evaluation of risk levels and system modifications. In order to enhance and robustify this static approach we deploy semantic modeling at design time and machine reasoning at run-time to construct and analyze a model of the running system, allowing dynamic changes to be taken into account, including dynamic variations in the likelihood of specific classes of threats being active.

In this paper we address the issue of threat generated risks and induced behaviors of unknown dynamic composition and present an innovative architecture integrating real time threat prediction, identification, detection and mitigation using statistical sequential analysis with semantic monitoring and reasoning components[1]. The architecture has been implemented and validated in the proof of concept scenario (PoC) of an airport with simulated data that uses an Airport – based Collaborative Decision Making scenario (A-CDM) defined by Eurocontrol for the optimization of airport operations on a European level. The rest of the paper is structured as follows; Section 2 provides an overview of some existing novel approaches for the protection of large complex critical infrastructures (CIs), Section 3 discusses the proposed architecture capable of alerting CI operators for possible existence of new threats based on sequential statistical analysis and stream reasoning techniques. Finally, Section 4 concludes the paper and provides discussion on future planned activities in the field of Intrusion Detection Systems (IDS) for CIP within the Greek Cybercrime Center of Excellence[2].

2   Related Work

Several research and development efforts have been realized in the past few years on an international level for the protection of complex and interconnected CIs. Interesting efforts and methodologies have been proposed in [3] [4] where the basic focus is on threat-attack models and taxonomies, vulnerabilities and societal impact of SCADA systems failures and modeling of power transmission and distribution networks. The methodologies developed are centered heavily on formal and semi-formal mathematical modeling techniques and tools. It is mentioned that the developed solutions are complementary and similar in spirit to our work. A notable difference is the

[1] With the financial support of the Prevention of and Fight against Crime Programme European Commission – Directorate-General Home Affairs. This project has been funded with support from the European Commission, under grant agreement No. HOME/2011/ISEC/AG/INT/4000002166. This publication reflects the views only of the author, and the European Commission cannot be held responsible for any use which may be made of the information contained therein.

[2] Greek Cybercrime Center: http://www.cybercc.gr/

strict application of these methodologies to specific hardware and metering components of power transmission, voltage generation and distribution networks. Additionally, the adopted point of view is very effective and proven for this type of
well-defined and concrete CIs but much less flexible and effective for heterogeneous
and multi-stakeholder service oriented environments where mathematical modeling
techniques are not applicable and the requirements for real time processing of large
volumes of data are high.

Additional efforts have been proposed in [5] [6] [7]. The authors' objective is to
develop and establish a CI warning information network capable of identifying and
alerting on threats induced by undesired events in real time. These models take into
account the interdependencies between CIs and the development of risk analysis and
assessment tools taking into account the complex inter-couplings between a multitude
of components. The approaches involve the application of mature state space control
concepts and Input – Output Inoperability Sate Space Modeling formalisms for real
time risk prediction.

3   Implemented Semantic Driven Architecture

In this section we present the architecture of an implemented run-time monitoring and
decision support framework that takes into account system monitored data, the dynamically evolving CI model composition and it's dominating semantic rules [2]. In
effect the CI operators are supported with real time situational awareness of threat
occurrence and escalation, threat estimation and their probable consequences. The
overall architecture is presented in Fig. 1. Our framework consists of three modular
core blocks;

- the Semantic Monitoring Block which is responsible for converting raw monitoring and management data into semantic time stamped induced system behaviors,
- the Reasoning Block which combines induced behaviors with the system semantic model and its rules for further classification and estimation of the involved threats and
- the Decision Support Tool User Interface which is the final stage between the
  human in the loop decision maker and the machine reasoning process.

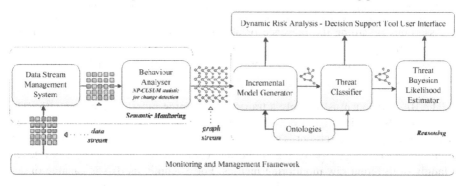

Fig. 1. The Semantics Driven Architecture

3.1   Semantic Monitoring Block

The Semantic Monitoring Block integrates two modular components, the Data Stream Management System and the Behaviour Analyzer.

Data Stream Management System (DSMS)
The Data Stream Management System (DSMS) component is used to manage the event data streams that arrive from the monitoring and management framework. In that manner data are merged and continuously analyzed by the semantic monitoring, modeling and reasoning process chain. It is noted that the run time tools are connected to the monitoring interfaces of the airport simulator receiving input raw data for different flight scenarios under different service performance conditions. Data from registered streams in the DSMS are processed or queried on the fly without being saved into a persistent storage. On the input side, the DSMS keeps unbounded data streams from the runtime framework, i.e. data arriving continuously. On the output side, queries are registered with the DSMS to perform simple selection queries or complex data processing, e.g. aggregating data from multiple data streams or filtering noisy data. This mechanism provides the necessary inputs to the Behaviour Analyser component presented below. Rather than being on-time request-responses, a query is only registered with the DSMS once and stays forever. Additionally, queries can be window-based, making them ideal for capturing violations and abnormal sequences based on recent behaviors. For the DSMS engine we use an open-source complex event processor written in Java, named ESPER [8]. ESPER works as a real-time engine that triggers listeners or subscribers when certain conditions, expressed using a tailored Event Processing language (EPL), occur among data streams.

Behaviour Analyser
The Behaviour Analyser (BA) is the central component that acts as an "Observer" and listens to answers with interesting events which are evaluated by the registered query statement against the sequential data streams. The BA decides how to convert the incoming streams of the monitoring data generated from the DSMS block into semantic assertions relevant to the presence of assets and to the relevant behaviors. The runtime framework is dedicated to generate two types of time-stamped RDF assertions:

1. Assertions regarding the presence or absence of assets such as assets joining or leaving the system and
2. Assertions concerning the measurability, presence or absence of adverse behaviors of those assets.

The BA component is not only a transcoder mapping monitoring events into RDF graphs but also an intelligent decision making mechanism capable to decide which behaviors are present or absent. This is realized by taking into account past events up to present discrete time *(where $n \geq 0$)* relevant to a particular asset which may refer to a family of different raw monitoring metrics. For example, the BA is capable of determining if an asset is overloaded or underperforming using monitoring data for the load and performance of a specific asset. Other threat induced behavior states include loss of confidentiality generating 'indiscreet" behaviors or loss of trustworthiness leading to "unauthentic" or "unaccountable" asset behaviors. Additionally, a sequential algorithmic scheme is introduced to detect changes in streams of monitoring data in order to assert the previously mentioned states of presence and absence of threat – induced behaviors relevant to particular classes of monitored assets.

We have implemented the Non-Parametric CUSUM (NP-CUSUM) scheme to detect an abrupt change at an unknown point in time with the objective to detect the change and react "as soon as possible" [1] [11] [13]. The observer (BA) detects the changes in the mean value (cumulative effect of changes) of the random sequence of data. Thus we are able to monitor the streaming random variable data sequentially. The detection problem then amounts to detect abrupt changes generated from unwanted intrusions in the random sequence of the form:

$$Z_n = \mathbf{a} + \xi_n I(n < m) + (\mathbf{h} + \eta_n) I(n \geq m) \tag{1}$$

Where $\mathbf{a} < 0$ is the negative mean of the random sequence and $-\mathbf{a} < h$ where $\{h\}$ is defined as the minimum distance (incremental increase) of the mean value during malicious attacks. Moreover $\xi = \{\xi_n\}_{n=1}^{\infty}, \eta = \{\eta_n\}_{n=1}^{\infty}$, are zero mean stationary random sequences and $I(H)$ is the standard Indicator function. $\{m\}$ is the unknown point in time of attack initiation. Our test statistic is of the recurrent form:

$$\begin{aligned} y_n &= (y_{n-1} + Z_n)^+ \\ y_0 &= 0 : initial\ condition\,. \\ &with\ X^+ = max\ (0\,,x)\,. \end{aligned} \tag{2}$$

The above set up basically means that a large value of the test statistic y_n will imply an indication of attack and so the mean value of Z_n will be positive. Successive values of the random sequence in a finite horizon will gradually keep increasing. From the previous definition and for practical reasons the test statistic will reset to zero thus avoiding accumulation in time. We also define the following decision rule:

$$d_N(y_n) = \begin{cases} 0\ if\ y_n \leq N \\ 1\ if\ y_n > N \end{cases} \tag{3}$$

where N represents the attack detection threshold.

It is important to note that the stopping rule or detection time τ_N is defined as $\tau_N = \inf\ \{n: d_N(y_n) = 1\}$ and is the alarm time of our application. For clarity we state the following well known definition from sequential statistics that is implicitly used for our detection rule.

Definition: Let $\mathbf{Z} = \{Z_n : n \geq 0\}$ be a random process. A stopping time with respect to $\mathbf{Z}$ is a random time such that for each $n \geq 0$, the event $\{\tau = n\}$ is completely determined by (at most) the total information known up to time n, $\{Z_0, ... Z_n\}$.

Thus our decision to stop and raise an alarm (or not) is based on our sequential observations on the values of $\{y_0, y_1, y_2, ...\}$. The detection time τ is a random time which is a discrete random variable [1] [11].

3.2 Reasoning Block

In this subsection we briefly provide a description of the Reasoning Block of the implemented architecture. An analytical description is beyond the scope of this article and can be found in the relevant references [15] [16] [17]. The Reasoning Block consists of the Incremental Model Generator, the Threat Classifier and the Threat Likelihood Estimator.

Incremental Model Generator
The Incremental Model Generator creates and incrementally updates a concrete model of assets, behaviors and controls (threat counteractions), based on the behavioral RDF triples issued by the BA combined with the semantic system model. The infrastructure model is constructed in a manner that allows its application in any possible type of critical infrastructure. This is achieved by organizing its structure into four different levels of abstraction [16]. The concrete model is then used as input for the threat classification and activity estimation tools.

Threat Classifier
The Threat Classifier categorizes threats as mitigated or blocked, based mainly on the presence of adequate controls and decides which threats are making the system vulnerable. The classification is accomplished using semantic stream reasoning techniques [18]. Currently we use the Hermit Reasoner [15]. The output is the updated concrete model which is fed into the Threat Likelihood Estimator and the DST User Interface.

Threat Likelihood Estimator
The Threat Likelihood Estimator updates the current threat likelihood for all threats and decides how likely it is that a threat is active or not active. The estimation phase is based on classical Bayesian estimation [17]. The output is the updated concrete model which is fed into the DST User Interface.

3.3 Decision Support Tool User Interface

The Decision Support Tool (DST) interface includes a schematic representation of the test bed to provide context for information generated from the Behaviour Analyser, Threat Classifier and Threat Activity Estimator. A screenshot of the DST is presented in Fig. 2 where a global physical system assets view is provided with information color coding for the associated risk levels and assets on the right column window. The DST represents risks (threats) to users in a way that conforms to conventional risk management methodologies. Threats are classified as i) Low, Medium or High [9], [10] according to their potential impact; ii) Blocked, Mitigated or Vulnerabilities depending on how well they are addressed by controls and iii) Primary or Secondary depending on whether the causes are evident in the status of system assets. Additionally, it can be used to assess in real-time the security configuration of the CI based on monitoring information in a time window. The monitoring data is used to dynamically calculate varying risk levels. The DST refreshes the model (fetching new configuration and monitoring data) and dynamically deduces the involved risk factors. Finally, it provides explanations of threats, including reasoning for the classification of: Blocked or Mitigated categories. This capability is very helpful to the CI operator for enhanced supervision and understanding the system evolution and for deciding what actions are required when confronted by a similar threat.

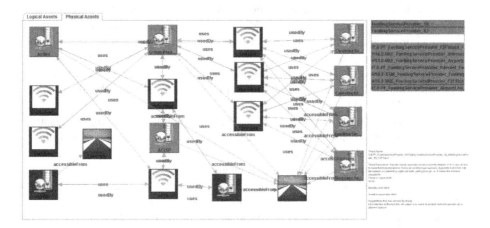

Fig. 2. CI global view of Decision Support Tool User Interface

4 Conclusions and Future Work

In this paper we presented a novel threat management architecture that in real time assesses cyber physical threats in dynamically evolving multi stakeholder critical infrastructures. The main advantages of this approach are:

- flexible architecture which can be implemented for any type of critical infrastructures (including the Gas-Oil, Transportation, Port and Air-traffic sectors),
- enhanced situational awareness in real time as the infrastructure assets are under continuous evolution, and
- assessment capability of the state of the infrastructure in a dynamic fashion in contrast to static ones [19] in terms of risk analytics.

The final Decision Support Tool prototype addresses the challenge of real time decision making for the supervision operators utilizing machine reasoning over the CI system model for the interpretation of run-time monitoring data. It is proven that the approach which uses a blend of semantics modeling, event processing and sequential analysis techniques significantly enhances the situational awareness and decision making stages of the man - in the - loop operators.

Next envisioned steps include targeted actions such as:

- Applying and integrating, decentralized detection algorithms for point change detection and distributed hypothesis testing concerning parallel and distributed cyber threats [1] [13] [14]. A family of different non-parametric / parametric anomaly detection algorithms exists which are valid candidates for a wide class of network intrusions (DoS/DDoS attacks) which occur randomly at unknown points in time leading to changes of the statistical properties of event observables.

- Optimization of the performance accounting for the well-known trade-off between performance measures such as: Average Detection Delay (ADD) and frequency of false alarms is an additional central issue. Furthermore an attack can produce abrupt or gradual and linear increase of the hostile traffic in the overall network traffic. Two competitive detection techniques exist for this type of problems: Page's CUSUM detection and the Shiryaev-Roberts- Pollak procedure which are based on different motivations and probabilistic arguments [11] [13] [14] [20].

Another relevant direction includes the introduction and testing of adaptive methods for activity monitoring of the streaming data which are based on Recursive Least Squares type algorithms (RLS, RLS with forgetting factor), or Kalman type algorithms for streaming data outliers and change point detection. We also plan to test other than Hermit stream reasoners such as Pellet [21] in order to increase the performance of the reasoning process in terms of time and memory requirements. For the time being the reasoning process consumes the most resources from all system components. The infrastructure model and its accompanying semantic rules (SWRL rules) consists of huge data volumes and as such novel cloud techniques can be used for the performance upgrading of the stream reasoning process as well as of the event data processing [22].

References

1. Polunchenko, A., Tartakovsky, A.: State-of-the-Art in Sequential Change-Point Detection. Methodology and Computing in Applied Probability Journal 14(3), 649–684 (2012)
2. Kostopoulos, D., Leventakis, G., Tsoulkas, V., Nikitakos, N.: An Intelligent Fault Monitoring and Risk Management Tool for Complex Critical Infrastructures: The SERSCIS Approach in Air-Traffic Surface Control. In: 14th International Conference on Computer Modelling and Simulation (UKSim 2012), pp. 205–210. IEEE Xplore (2012)
3. Teixeira, A., Dán, G., Sandberg, H., Johansson, K.H.: A Cyber Security Study of a SCADA Energy Management System: Stealthy Deception Attacks on the State Estimator. In: 18th IFAC World Congress, Milan, Italy, IFAC (2011)
4. Sandberg, H., Teixeira, A., Johansson, K.H.: On security indices for state estimators in power networks. In: 1st Workshop on Secure Control Systems, CPS Week, Stockholm, Sweden (2010)

5. Schaberreiter, T., Aubert, J., Khadraoui, D.: Critical infrastructure security modeling and resci-monitor: A risk based critical infrastructure model. In: IST-Africa Conference Proceedings, pp. 1–9 (2011)
6. Aubert, J., Schaberreiter, T., Incoul, C., Khadraoui, D., Gateau, B.: Risk-Based Methodology for Real-Time Security Monitoring of Interdependent Services in Critical Infrastructures. In: International Conference on Availability, Reliability and Security (ARES 2010), pp. 262–267 (2010)
7. Oliva, G., Panzieri, S., Setola, R.: Agent-based input–output interdependency model. International Journal of Critical Infrastructure Protection 3(2), 76–82 (2010)
8. Esper - Complex Event Processing, http://esper.codehaus.org
9. Adar, E., Wuchner, A.: Risk management for critical infrastructure protection (CIP) challenges, best practices & tools. In: First IEEE International Workshop on Critical Infrastructure Protection, pp. 8–16 (2005)
10. Garvey, P.R.: Analytical Methods for Risk Management: A Systems Engineering Perspective Analytical Methods for Risk Management: A Systems Engineering Perspective. Chapman and Hall/CRC, Boca Raton (2009)
11. Basseville, M., Nikiforov, I.V.: Detection of abrupt changes: theory and application. Prentice-Hall, Inc., Upper Saddle River (1993)
12. Vaculín, R.: Semantic Monitoring of Service-Oriented Business Processes. In: Handbook of Research on E-Business Standards and Protocols: Documents, Data and Advanced Web Technologies, pp. 467–494. IGI Global (2012)
13. Moustakides, G.: Optimal procedures for detecting changes in distributions. Ann. Statist. 14(4), 1379–1387 (1986)
14. Moustakides, G.V.: Decentralized CUSUM Change Detection. In: 9th International Conference on Information Fusion, pp. 1–6 (2006)
15. Hermit OWL Reasoner, http://www.hermit-reasoner.com
16. Surridge, M., Chakravarthy, A., Hall-May, M., Chen, X., Nasser, B., Nossal, R.: SERSCIS: Semantic Modelling of Dynamic, Multi-Stakeholder Systems. In: 2nd SESAR Innovations Days, Braunschweig (2012)
17. Chakravarthy, A., Surridge, M., Hall-May, M., Nasser, B., Chen, W., Leonard, T.: System modelling tools: Full Prototype Implementation. SERSCIS Deliverable D2.2 v1.5 (2013)
18. Della Valle, E., Ceri, S., Barbieri, D.F., Braga, D., Campi, A.: A First Step Towards Stream Reasoning. In: Domingue, J., Fensel, D., Traverso, P. (eds.) FIS 2008. LNCS, vol. 5468, pp. 72–81. Springer, Heidelberg (2009)
19. Touzeau, J., Hamon, E., Krempel, M., Gölz, B., Madarasz, R., Alemany, J.: SESAR DEL16.02.01-D03: SESAR ATM Preliminary Security Risk Assessment Method (2011)
20. Pollak, M.: Optimal Detection of a Change in Distribution. The Annals of Statistics 13, 206–227 (1985)
21. Pellet: OWL 2 Reasoner for Java, http://clarkparsia.com/pellet/
22. Malini, S., Poobalan, A.: Semantic Web Standard in Cloud Computing. International Journal of Soft Computing and Engineering (IJSCE) 1, 1–5 (2012)

Determining Risks from Advanced Multi-step Attacks to Critical Information Infrastructures

Zhendong Ma and Paul Smith

Safety & Security Department
Austrian Institute of Technology
2444 Seibersdorf, Austria
{zhendong.ma,paul.smith}@ait.ac.at

Abstract. Industrial Control Systems (ICS) monitor and control industrial processes, and enable automation in industry facilities. Many of these facilities are regarded as Critical Infrastructures (CIs). Due to the increasing use of Commercial-Off-The-Shelf (COTS) IT products and connectivity offerings, CIs have become an attractive target for cyber-attacks. A successful attack could have significant consequences. An important step in securing Critical Information Infrastructures (CIIs) against cyber-attacks is risk analysis – understanding security risks, based on a systematic analysis of information on vulnerabilities, cyber threats, and the impacts related to the targeted system. Existing risk analysis approaches have various limitations, such as scalability and practicability problems. In contrast to previous work, we propose a practical and *vulnerability-centric* risk analysis approach for determining security risks associated with advanced, multi-step cyber-attacks. In order to examine multi-step attacks that exploit chains of vulnerabilities, we map vulnerabilities into *preconditions* and *effects*, and use *rule-based reasoning* for identifying advanced attacks and their path through a CII.

Keywords: Risk analysis, critical infrastructure, vulnerability.

1 Introduction

Critical Information Infrastructures (CIIs) are the networked computer systems that support the operation of critical infrastructures, such as gas and electricity grids. They consist of different sub-systems and networks, such as enterprise, Industrial Control Systems (ICS)/Supervisory Control and Data Acquisition (SCADA) systems, and field networks that connect Remote Terminal Units (RTUs). Traditionally, the SCADA and field networks of a CII were not connected to other networks. However, there are increasing organisational and commercial reasons to allow greater access to the data and systems from these previously isolated (or "air-gapped") networks. With this greater degree of inter-connectivity the risk of cyber-attacks dramatically increases. To make matters worse, PC-based devices using commodity software are widely used in CIIs to replace special-purpose hardware, which facilitates cyber-attacks previously plaguing conventional IT systems. In recent years, CIIs are becoming an

E. Luiijf and P. Hartel (Eds.): CRITIS 2013, LNCS 8328, pp. 142–154, 2013.

attractive target for cyber-attackers, from individual hackers to organizations that have significant financial budgets and man power [14,8]. Consequently, critical infrastructure (CI) owners and operators are facing an increasing number of network-based attacks [19,34] with higher level of sophistication [16].

In this context, it is important to carry out information security risk analysis on CIIs – understanding security risks based on systematic analysis of information on vulnerabilities and potential exploits related to targeted system and information assets. A particularly challenging activity is understanding risks associated with new forms of advanced malware that target CIIs using a number of intermediate attack stages. The canonical example of this is the Advanced Persistent Threat (APT) Stuxnet [9], which targeted a very specific type of Programmable Logic Controller (PLC). We foresee understanding the risks associated with these forms of malware becoming increasingly important, given the potential for them to be more readily generated via malware toolkits. For example, shortly after Stuxnet, malware such as Duqu [7] and Flame [31] have been discovered, pointing to the potential for this trend.

A multitude of approaches to analysing the vulnerabilities and threats to networked IT systems exist to date. For several reasons their applicability to risk analysis for CIIs is limited. First, most approaches have severe scalability problems, which makes them impractical to analysis large networks. Second, many approaches take an attacker's perspective to check the security of a system. Since extensive information regarding attacks is difficult to obtain or not totally known to the public, attack-centric approaches suffer from incomplete information when performing risk analysis. Third, most CIIs consist of large scale, heterogeneous, and complex systems. Some approaches do not support automatic processing of information, which makes it difficult to develop tools for promoting practical usage in industry.

In this paper, we propose a systematic approach to analysing risks associated with advanced cyber-attacks targeting CIIs, with a focus on identifying and analysing vulnerabilities and threats. The main contributions of our approach include the following: *(i)* we tackle the scalability problem by building our system model on the information of hosts and their connectivity, as opposed to state space enumeration, which is typically applied; *(ii)*we shift the focus from analysing attack behaviour, which is challenging to reason about, to the vulnerabilities of a system, i.e., we analyse risks based on common vulnerability information that is readily available; and *(iii)*we adopt a simple rule-based reasoning process, which enables automatic information processing during risk analysis.

The rest of the paper is organized as follows: Sec. 2 reviews related work and points out its limitations. Following on from this, Sec. 3 describes the system model considered in the paper. Sec. 4 describes our approach in detail, which is then applied in a case study for analysing a Stuxnet-like attack in Sec. 5.

2   Related Work

Risk analysis is an integral part of the risk management process for identifying, assessing, and monitoring risks to information security and business operation. A number of industry standards exist [5,32,15], which describe basics and provide guiding procedures for establishing and conducting risk analysis on Information and Communication Technology (ICT) systems in an organization.

Many academic work on risk analysis of network attacks are built on the attack graph approach [24,28,23,26,30], which are rooted in model-checking methods [25]. The network is modelled as a finite state machine. Nodes represent network states with respect to security properties, edges represent attack actions that cause the transition of states. An attack graph can be generated by using vulnerability information and network connectivity. Each path in the graph indicates a series of exploits which starts from an initial secure state to an unsecured (attacker's) goal state. Different reasoning and graph processing techniques are proposed to analysis the generated graph. The attack graph expands exponentially with the size of the network. Despite efforts to reduce computation complexity [22], attack graph approaches have scalability problems, thus are impractical for analysing large networks [17].

Attack trees are another prominent approach to threat analysis [20,12,10,36]. The philosophy behind attack trees is to think like an attacker, in order to prevent attacks. Attack trees consist of nodes and edges, whereby nodes in an attack tree represent an attacker's actions. Attack trees use a root node to specify an attacker's goal and systematically expand the tree with leaf nodes to enumerate possible attacks that contribute to reach the goal. The leaf nodes are grouped by logical AND and OR relations. Attack trees provide a structured way of security analysis and have the potential to identify hidden risks. However, for each attack goal, a new tree needs to be constructed. Although it is possible to reuse a part of an attack tree, this form of analysis remains labour intensive, hence it is difficult to scale to large networks. Furthermore, since extensive information regarding attacks is difficult to obtain, it is also difficult to construct attack trees that contain enough details for meaningful analysis.

Commercial products, such as Tenable Attack Path Analytics [37], combine manual and automatic analysis to detect attack paths. The vulnerability data are collected by active (i.e., Nessus) and passive scanners. Based on the data, an experienced user (e.g., a network administrator) filters over the itemized vulnerabilities with self-defined classification criteria to correlate the data and detect attack paths. The tool offers a practical approach, but it depends largely on the user's capability to derive information from raw vulnerability data.

3   System Model

In this paper, we assume a typical ICS system model, as shown in Fig. 1. The system model is an adaptation from the architectures described in [33] and [29]. Our system model has a three-zone architecture separated by firewalls. The

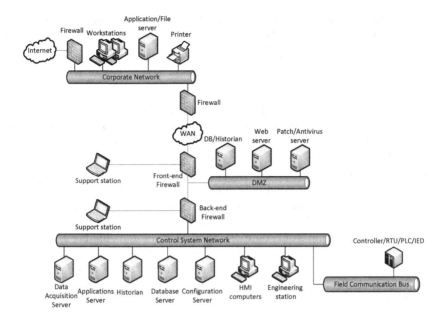

Fig. 1. ICS system model

corporate network consists of workstations, server, and printer to support an organization's daily business. It is connected to the Internet through a firewall for necessary IT activities such as browsing and emails. The second zone is the demilitarized zone (DMZ), established by two front/back-end firewalls. The DMZ is created for a "defence-in-depth" protection of the control system network. The firewalls avoid direct connectivity between the corporate network, which is considered less critical, and the highly critical control system network. By placing a historian in the DMZ, a user in the corporate network can access control data without making a direct connection to the control system network. The DMZ also includes other applications and services such as the Web server for a user to access the historian by Web technologies, as well as the security server for patch and anti-virus management for the control network. A large-scale industry facility often has multiple control systems installed at different field sites. A Wide Area Network (WAN) is used to connect the field sites over a large geographic area. The control system network is the third zone that includes field devices, SCADA servers and other core functions of the control system. The field devices (e.g., controller, Remote Terminal Unit, Programmable Logic Controller (PLC), and Intelligent Electronic Device) are connected to the control system network to form control loops for monitoring and controlling local processes.

Based on the communication protocols in use, devices within the same zone can connect to each other. Communication between different zones is controlled by firewalls. Occasionally, external support stations from vendors or trusted third-parties are allowed to connect to the ICS zones for maintenance or diagnosis purposes. Note that the system model presents a high degree of security according to the "state-of-the-practice".

4   Risk Analysis

Our approach to risk analysis follows a *global-local-global* paradigm to identify attacks that exploits vulnerabilities on a single host and attacks that take advantage of inter-networking to exploit a series of vulnerabilities on multiple hosts. First, we identify the *global* connectivity among the networked hosts (i.e., any computer device connected to the network) and model the system with a conditional connectivity graph. Second, common vulnerabilities related to each of the hosts are collected and enumerated (*local*). The identified vulnerabilities provide a basis for the analysis of potential threats and impacts to the host. Third, we extract useful information from common vulnerabilities and enhance the vulnerability description, such that we can define rules to automatically reason about the inter-dependencies among chains of vulnerabilities. Finally, based on the understanding of chains of vulnerabilities, we identify possible multi-step attacks paths (*global*) in the system.

4.1   Host and Connectivity Identification

Network connectivity is the main enabler for malware propagation and network-based remote attacks. Identifying connectivity at the host level allows us to discover potential ingress points of attacks to the system. To identify hosts and their connectivity, we use a *conditional connectivity graph* to capture and model permanent, transient, and indirect connections among the hosts in the system. A connectivity exists if two hosts engage in any form of data exchange. Therefore, a connectivity might exist even when two hosts are not connected to the same network. For example, a standalone engineering station and a PLC might have a connectivity relationship if the PLC performs program updates occasionally on the engineering station; a vendor's support station might have a connectivity to a host in the control system network through a logged VPN connection; or a host on the corporate network might have a connectivity with an external computer if it transfers files from the computer using USB flash drive.

The key to capturing and modelling these occasional and indirect connections in ICS with partitioned networks is to introduce the concept of conditional connectivity. We define a conditional connectivity model adapted from the firewall model in [35]. As illustrated in Fig. 2, data flows uni- or bi-directionally between A to B, if and only if one of the rules (Rule 1, Rule 2, ..., Rule$_n$) are fulfilled. Rules can be specified in accordance with those in the firewalls, for example, blocking all communications by default and making exceptions based on the protocol, source and destination IP addresses, ports, and services. The conditional connectivity model can also be used to model occasional connections, such as a VPN connection from an external support station to the ICS, or an external computer to an internal host through a USB flash drive.

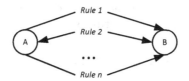

Fig. 2. Conditional connectivity model

4.2   Common Vulnerability Enumeration

A vulnerability is a weakness in the system exploitable by attacks. Vulnerabilities might originate from design and implementation flaws or misconfigurations. During the last decade, a significant number of vulnerabilities have been discovered. A number of community-based initiatives exist with the goal of collecting, organizing, maintaining, and communicating publicly known vulnerabilities. The most prominent is the Common Vulnerabilities and Exposures (CVE) system [1]. CVE uses a standardized and unified naming scheme, called the CVE identifier, to uniquely identify each of the publicly known information security vulnerabilities or exposures. The complementary Common Vulnerability Scoring System (CVSS) [2] uses a score range from 0 to 10 to assess the severity of each of the CVE vulnerabilities. The National Vulnerability Database (NVD) [21] is a public repository for CVE vulnerability data and corresponding impact metrics. NVD has become the primary database for common vulnerabilities since the data are from multiple sources, such as Bugtraq [27], US-CERT [38] and other community and industry sources. In addition, many open source and commercial vulnerability scanners have been developed to automate vulnerability discovery on a computer, network, or system based on CVE data [3].

CVE vulnerabilities are related to a specific product or vendor. For example, an engineering station (ES) that configures process control systems in an ICS might have a number of vulnerabilities, such as CVE-2006-3448 that allows "remote attackers to execute arbitrary code via a long Syllabus string in crafted bookmark link files" due to running Windows 2000 Professional SP2, or CVE-2012-3015 that allows "local users to gain privileges via a Trojan horse DLL" due to the installation of Siemens PCS 7 software.

Since most exploits are bound to a specific host [6], the entries in the vulnerability database are often host-based, which means the easiest way to collect vulnerabilities is to enumerate them according to each of the hosts. Given a host's software installation information, including types and versions, running protocols and services, and open ports, manual look-ups are able to discover and enumerate the most common vulnerabilities. This can also be done by automatic vulnerability scanners. However, a significant challenge in risk analysis is to obtain a higher level of understanding of the inter-dependency among the vulnerabilities in the context of network-based, multi-step attacks – advanced attacks that exploit several vulnerabilities across multiple hosts in the system before reaching their target. As a result, systematic risk analysis should consider not only attacks from adjacent ingress points, but also attacks that exploit multiple vulnerabilities in multiple stages.

4.3 Vulnerability Modelling and Chaining

To put vulnerabilities into context and have a higher level of understanding during risk analysis, we need a way to chain seemingly unrelated vulnerabilities from different hosts. However, the problem is that the current textual CVE vulnerability description is mainly intended for human consumption. A different way of representing these vulnerabilities will be necessary if we want to process the vulnerability data automatically for risk analysis of large scale systems.

A set of conditions must be met before an attacker can exploit a vulnerability on a host, e.g., the presence of a vulnerability, an attacker's level of privilege, network connections, or a certain running service on the host. Prior art on network attack analysis [18,28,23,11] emphasize the specification of *preconditions* that are necessary for an attack to succeed, and *post-conditions* that describe the system state or the effect after the attack. Since existing vulnerability data lack machine-readable descriptions, the authors of [18] proposed to extend the XML-based vulnerability description language to include preconditions and post-conditions to allow automatic reasoning for determining chains of exploits.

Adopting these approaches, we enhance the vulnerability description by modelling a vulnerability to include a set of preconditions and effects (i.e., post-conditions). The details of the preconditions and effects are mapped from the structured CVE data. A CVE entry includes the description of the "Access Vector", "Access Complexity", and "Authentication" from CVSS. These are the factors, in addition to the presence of a vulnerability, that are prerequisite for an attack. According to [4], all CVE vulnerabilities can be classified as one or more of thirteen types. Since a successful exploit leads to a new set of conditions in the system, usually in terms of the attacker's knowledge and capability, the vulnerability types give us a hint to describe the effects of an attack.

Fig. 3 illustrates some of the CVE data that are candidates for mapping to the preconditions and effects. The entries on the left side describe the access vector, access complexity, and authentication requirements to exploit a vulnerability. According to CVSS, a local access means a vulnerability is exploitable with physical access or a local account; an adjacent network access means a vulnerability is exploitable with local networks or hosts in the same broadcast or collision domain; a network access means a vulnerability is exploitable remotely. For a high access complexity, specialized access conditions are needed, e.g., an attacker must have elevated privileges or spoof additional systems; a medium complexity requires an attack to have somewhat specialized access conditions, e.g., some level of authorization, possibly untrusted; a low complexity requires no specialized access conditions. For multiple authentication, an attacker must authenticate two or more times; a single authentication indicates that an attacker needs to log into the system once; none means authentication is not required. On the right side of Fig. 3, we have all the vulnerability types. As we are interested in chains of vulnerabilities, we need only to include those effects that allow an attack to launch further attacks that exploit other vulnerabilities. Consequently, the effects that meet this criterion are "Code execution" and "Elevation of privileges". Thus, we can describe a vulnerability by extracting the data from sources like [4] and map them to preconditions and effects. For example, a CVE-2012-3032 vulnerability is a "SQL injection vulnerability in Siemens WinCC software that allows remote attackers to execute arbitrary SQL commands". Its preconditions are "network exploitable", "low complexity", and "no authentication". The effects are "SQL injection" and "Code execution". Since the vulnerability includes "Code execution", it is able to induce further attacks.

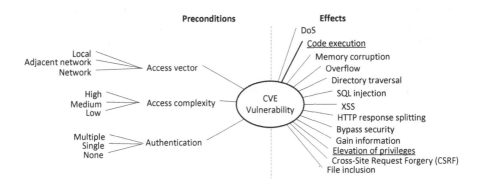

Fig. 3. Possible CVE vulnerability description for mapping to preconditions and effects

After the aforementioned steps, we can chain vulnerabilities on different hosts to discover multi-step attacks. To be able to conduct risk analysis on large systems, we propose to use rule-based reasoning. Rules are expressed using IF-THEN statements. The IF part of the rule contains the conditions, and the THEN part of the rule contains the conclusion or a new set of inferred facts. Rule-based reasoning is more practical and lightweight compared to other logical reasoning processes. The IF-THEN rules are close to natural language. Thus they are easier to create, maintain, and use in inference.

The rule-based reasoning engine, which is used to chain vulnerabilities, is based on the information from the conditional network connectivity and the vulnerability descriptions. Recall that a host might be associated with a list of vulnerabilities. Our reasoning engine takes one vulnerability at a time and use the following rules to decide whether the host can be used as an intermediate step to induce further attacks.

RULE 1: IF $(c_1 \wedge c_2 \ldots) \wedge (p_1 \wedge p_2 \ldots) \wedge$ threat.agent THEN $e_1, e_2, \ldots$
RULE 2: IF code.execution $\vee$ privilege.escalation THEN step.stone

We define the rule elements (e.g., c_1, p_1, code.execution) to be Boolean. The left-hand-side part of RULE 1 contains the conjunction of the system conditions captured in the conditional connectivity graph, i.e., (c_1, c_2), the preconditions for the vulnerability, i.e., (p_1, p_2), and threat.agent that indicates the host is accessed by a host controlled by an attacker. The right-hand-side part of RULE 1 is the enumeration of one or more of the thirteen effects listed in Fig. 3, i.e., (e_1, e_2). RULE 2 simply decides whether a host becomes an intermediate node if a successful exploit causes the effects of code execution or elevation of privileges. If step.stone is **true**, a host can be used to launch further attacks on other hosts.

An automatic way to construct the vulnerability chains is to augment the conditional connectivity graph, and use the rule-based reasoning for deciding whether there is an edge between two vulnerabilities on adjacent hosts. We use the example in Fig. 4 to explain the technique. Imagine Host A and B are connected, as indicated by the straight line. Due to the presence and the effects of the vulnerabilities V_m and V_n, Host A becomes a step stone once an attacker successfully exploits them. By using rule-based reasoning, we can decide whether the vulnerabilities V_x, V_y, and V_z on Host B can be exploited by attacks from Host A, as a consequence of exploiting V_m and/or V_n. If the answer is yes, we draw an edge between the two vulnerabilities. We can repeat the process for all vulnerabilities on adjacent hosts.

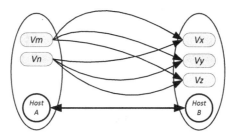

Fig. 4. Determining edges for vulnerability chaining

4.4   Attack Path Identification

Based on the graph augmented with the vulnerability chains, we can identify potential attack paths in the system. To identify the attack paths to an arbitrary host, we select the host as the root node and use a Breadth-first Search (BFS) to find all edges to it. Informally, BFS initially creates a queue Q and enqueues the root node v_i onto Q. BFS repeats the following steps: 1) dequeue a node v from Q; 2) visit all neighbouring nodes of v; 3) if a neighbouring node w has not been discovered before, enqueue the node w onto Q; until the queue becomes empty. The result of BFS gives all one-hop and multi-hop nodes connected to v_i. Since the computational complexity for running BFS on a single vertex is $O(n)$, where n is the number of nodes in the analysis, the complexity of considering all vulnerabilities on all hosts will only incur a linear growth.

5   Case Study

In this section, we use a simple case study to demonstrate the risk analysis approach. The setting of the case study is a hypothetical ICS that is similar to the system model in Sec. 3. We consider a Stuxnet-like attack targeting the programs on a PLC. The attacker uses a malware to infect several hosts and propagate itself in the system towards its ultimate target. Researchers have identified that Stuxnet has multiple ways of infecting and penetrating an ICS [9,13]. In this case study, we only consider a subset of the complex capabilities of Stuxnet-like attacks, in which an attack starts from the sub-network with low security level to the critical part of the system.

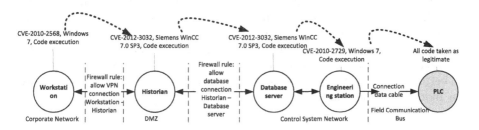

Fig. 5. Case study: risk analysis of Stuxnet-like attack in ICS

Fig. 5 illustrates the system components and the attack path. We identify several hosts and their interconnections. The hosts include a workstation in the corporate network, a historian in the DMZ, a database server for process data management and an engineering station for configuring logic functions on control devices in the control system network, and the target PLC. The workstation is allowed by the firewall to communicate with the historian. The historian has a database connection with the database server, which is similarly allowed by the firewall. The database server and the engineering station is in the same sub-network within the trust boundary. The engineering station accesses the PLC occasionally by direct data cable connection. For each of the hosts, a number of vulnerabilities are discovered. For simplicity, we are only interested in the relevant ones, which are shown in Fig. 5, with a CVE identifier, a possible software or protocol as the cause, and the effect of a successful exploit. Note that the vulnerability associated with the PLC is not explicitly listed in CVE.

Based on the CVE descriptions, we extracted the useful information and mapped them to preconditions and effects, which are then used by the rule-based reasoning process. The result is the attack path shown in Fig. 5 as arrow curves that chain the vulnerabilities and the underlying hosts. The attack path shows clearly how an attack can infect and penetrate the system to inject malicious code into a critical component, despite layers of defence. This analysis can help CI owners and operators to deploy appropriate technical and organizational measures to reduce or mitigate the risks from advanced attacks. We envision that an automated tool with a link to existing vulnerability repositories can greatly increase the efficiency of the risk analysis process.

6   Conclusion

In this paper, we introduced a practical risk analysis approach for determining security risks associated with Stuxnet-like, multi-step, advanced cyber-attacks to CIIs. We use a conditional connectivity graph to model network connections, and host-based vulnerability enumeration to collect CVE data. The vulnerability data are then mapped into preconditions and effects to facilitate rule-based reasoning for vulnerability chaining. We demonstrate the application of the approach via a case study within a realistic ICS setting. Future work will investigate the feasibility of our approach in an ongoing critical infrastructure protection project with our industry partners. A supporting tool will be developed to automate parts of the analysis. A large amount of common vulnerability data has been accumulated over the years; how to mine and analyse these data to better utilize the existing information in current risk analysis frameworks will be another undertaking.

Acknowledgements. This work has been supported by the "PRECYSE – Protection, prevention and reaction to cyber-attacks to critical infrastructures" project, funded by the European Commission with contract FP7-SEC-2012-1-285181 (`www.precyse.eu`).

References

1. Common vulnerabilities and exposures, `http://cve.mitre.org/`
2. Common vulnerability scoring system, `http://www.first.org/cvss`
3. CVE-compatible products and services,
   `http://cve.mitre.org/compatible/compatible.html`
4. CVE Details, `http://www.cvedetails.com/`
5. ISO/IEC 27000-series Information Security Management System Family of Standards
6. Ammann, P., Pamula, J., Street, J., Ritchey, R.: A host-based approach to network attack chaining analysis. In: 21st Annual Computer Security Applications Conference (2005)
7. Bencsáth, B., Pék, G., Buttyán, L., Felegyhazi, M.: Duqu: A Stuxnet-like malware found in the wild Technical report (October 2011),
   `http://www.crysys.hu/publications/files/bencsathPBF11duqu.pdf`
8. Brundle, M., Naedele, M.: Security for Process Control Systems: An Overview. IEEE Security & Privacy 6(6), 24–29 (2008)
9. Byres, E., Ginter, A., Langill, J.: How Stuxnet Spreads A Study of Infection Paths in Best Practice Systems, White paper (February 2011)
10. Çamtepe, S.A., Yener, B.: Modeling and detection of complex attacks. In: SecureComm., pp. 234–243 (2007)

11. Cheminod, M., et al.: Detecting chains of vulnerabilities in industrial networks. IEEE Transactions on Industrial Informatics 5(2), 181–193 (2009)
12. Daley, K., Larson, R., Dawkins, J.: A structural framework for modeling multi-stage network attacks. In: ICPP Workshops, pp. 5–10 (2002)
13. Falliere, N., Murchu, L.O., Chien, E.: W32.Stuxnet dossier. Symantec white paper (September 2010)
14. Igure, V.M., Laughter, S.A., Williams, R.D.: Security issues in SCADA networks. Computers & Security 25(7), 498–506 (2006)
15. International Society of Automation: ANSI/ISA-99.00.01-2007 Security for Industrial Automation and Control Systems (2007)
16. Langner, R.: Stuxnet: Dissecting a cyberwarfare weapon. IEEE Security & Privacy 9(3), 49–51 (2011)
17. Lippmann, R.P., Ingols, K.W.: An annotated review of past papers on attck graphs. Lincoln Laboratory Technical Report ESC-TR-2005-054 (March 2005)
18. Maggi, P., Pozza, D., Sisto, R.: Vulnerability modelling for the analysis of network attacks. In: Third International Conference on Dependability of Computer Systems, DepCos-RELCOMEX 2008, pp. 15–22 (2008)
19. McAfee: In the Dark: Crucial Industries Confront Cyberattacks (2011)
20. Moore, A.P., Ellison, R.J., Linger, R.C.: Attack modeling for information security and survivability (2001)
21. NIST: National vulnerability database, http://nvd.nist.gov/
22. Ou, X., Boyer, W.F., McQueen, M.A.: A scalable approach to attack graph generation. In: Proceedings of the 13th ACM Conference on Computer and Communications Security, CCS 2006, pp. 336–345. ACM, New York (2006)
23. Ou, X., Govindavajhala, S., Appel, A.W.: MulVAL: a logic-based network security analyzer. In: 14th Conference on USENIX Security Symposium (2005)
24. Phillips, C., Swiler, L.P.: A graph-based system for network-vulnerability analysis. In: Proceedings of the 1998 Workshop on New Security Paradigms (1998)
25. Ritchey, R.W., Ammann, P.: Using model checking to analyze network vulnerabilities. In: IEEE Symposium on Security and Privacy (2000)
26. Sawilla, R.E., Ou, X.: Identifying critical attack assets in dependency attack graphs. In: Proceedings of the 13th European Symposium on Research in Computer Security: Computer Security (2008)
27. SecurityFocus: Bugtraq, http://www.securityfocus.com/
28. Sheyner, O., et al.: Automated generation and analysis of attack graphs. In: Proceedings of the 2002 IEEE Symposium on Security and Privacy (2002)
29. SIEMENS: Security concept PCS 7 and WinCC - Basic document, white paper (August 2008)
30. Singhal, A., Ou, X.: Security risk analysis analysis of enterprise networks using probabilistic attack graphs. NIST Interagency Report 7788 (August 2011)
31. sKyWIper Analysis Team: sKyWIper (a.k.a. Flame a.k.a. Flamer): A complex malware for targeted attacks Technical report (May 2012), http://www.crysys.hu/skywiper/skywiper.pdf
32. Stoneburner, G., Goguen, A., Feringa, A.: NIST special publication 800-30 risk management guide for information technology systems (2002)
33. Stouffer, K., Falco, J., Kent, K.: Guide to Industrial Control Systems (ICS) Security. NIST SP 800-82 (June 2011)
34. Symantec: Symantec Critical Infrastrucutrre Protection Survey (2011)

35. Ten, C.W., Manimaran, G., Liu, C.C.: Vulnerability Assessment of Cybersecurity for SCADA Systems. IEEE Trans. on Power Systems 23(4), 1836–1846 (2008)
36. Ten, C.W., Manimaran, G., Liu, C.C.: Cybersecurity for critical infrastructures: attack and defense modeling. Trans. Sys. Man Cyber. Part A 40(4), 853–865 (2010)
37. Tenable Network Security, Inc.: Boosting your network defenses with Tenable's integral attack path analytics, white paper, www.tenable.com
38. US-CERT: Security bulletins, http://www.us-cert.gov/ncas/bulletins/

On the Feasibility of Device Fingerprinting in Industrial Control Systems

Marco Caselli[1], Dina Hadžiosmanović[1],
Emmanuele Zambon[1], and Frank Kargl[1,2]

[1] Distributed and Embedded Security Group, University of Twente, The Netherlands
{m.caselli,d.hadziosmanovic,e.zambon,f.kargl}@utwente.nl
[2] University of Ulm, Germany
frank.kargl@uni-ulm.de

Abstract. As Industrial Control Systems (ICS) and standard IT networks are becoming one heterogeneous entity, there has been an increasing effort in adjusting common security tools and methodologies to fit the industrial environment. Fingerprinting of industrial devices is still an unexplored research field. In this paper we provide an overview of standard device fingerprinting techniques and an assessment on the application feasibility in ICS infrastructures. We identify challenges that fingerprinting has to face and mechanisms to be used to obtain reliable results. Finally, we provide guidelines for implementing reliable ICS fingerprinters.

Keywords: Fingerprinting, Critical Infrastructure, ICS, SCADA, PLC.

1 Introduction

Power plants and industrial facilities have used industrial control systems for a long time and, until few decades ago, ICS has not significantly changed its architecture and protocols. In the last decade, ICS infrastructure increasingly opened up to standard IT networks. The advantage of this decision is twofold. First, a complex infrastructure previously running only on-site became easily accessible from remote premises by engineers. Second, the possibility to use the TCP/IP protocol suite and COTS (Commercial Off-the-Shelf) components reduces design time and costs [1]. However, this change has resulted in an increase of cyber-threats for ICS infrastructures. The situation endangers both the security of the ICS system and of the supervised physical process [1] [2]. For example, Stuxent and Flame malwares exploit Windows vulnerabilities to damage or steal information from industrial systems.

ICS and standard IT networks nowadays resemble more as they are using common protocols and devices. Researchers have been working on adapting security methodologies and tools previously used only in standard IT. Some of the applications include: firewalls, IDS (Intrusion Detection Systems), IPS (Intrusion Prevention Systems) as well as forensics, system discovery and vulnerability assessment applications.

E. Luiijf and P. Hartel (Eds.): CRITIS 2013, LNCS 8328, pp. 155–166, 2013.

In the IT field, *fingerprinting* is a set of activities for automatic system discovery. Fingerprinting tools exploit different information to identify devices, software and processes inside a computer network. Fingerprinting is an important building block of many security related activities and it is often used in unknown IT environments. For example, penetration testing methodologies state that system discovery, including device fingerprinting, is often the first step towards vulnerability identification [3]. Moreover, fingerprinting is used to support security systems in order to increase the accuracy of the assessments (i.e. together with intrusion prevention or detection systems).

For the ICS context, a reliable technique to recognize devices can be useful to improve industrial penetration testing techniques and security checks. Fingerprinting tools can be used to measure the level of knowledge about ICS components that can be obtained by the attackers from the network. Moreover, ICS operators can use fingerprinting to check their network verifying the absence of deviations from its standard configuration.

Problem. Fingerprinting techniques are not commonly supported in ICS environments. Comprehensive studies on ICS fingerprinting still do not exist. This is mainly because ICS environments experience different operational conditions compared from traditional IT networks (e.g. operate on proprietary protocols, specific embedded devices, etc.).

Contribution. In this paper we analyze challenges and opportunities for performing network-based device fingerprinting in ICS. In particular, our contributions are:

1. we perform a comprehensive analysis of traditional fingerprinting techniques to identify steps that are common to all approaches.
2. we analyze the applicability of common fingerprinting techniques in the ICS domain.
3. we build a reference model that highlights which ICS features can be used to build reliable network fingerprints.

2   Background

In this section we present concepts and terminology that will be used in the remaining of the paper.

2.1   ICS Overview

ICS is a term generally used to indicate several types of control systems used in industrial production and aimed at monitoring and controlling physical processes. ICSs include "Distributed Control Systems" (DCS) and "Supervisory Control And Data Acquisition" (SCADA). DCSs are locally deployed systems with the only purpose of gathering information and presenting it to control engineers. On the other hand, SCADA systems are usually extended to geographical scale and collect data from different locations implementing complex mechanisms of process control.

ICS networks are often divided in two main sub-networks: the *Field Network* and the *Process Network*. The first hosts devices close to the physical process. As outlined in [4], such devices are: Sensors, Actuators, Programmable Logic Controllers (PLCs) and Remote Terminal Units (RTUs).

The Process Network contains the servers used to manage industrial processes. According to [5], it typically hosts: SCADA Servers, Distributed Control Servers (DCS Servers), the Human Machine Interface (HMI), the Engineer's Workstation, Historian Servers.

Industry and critical infrastructures have used serial communications for years. Today, TCP and IP are becoming increasingly important and involved in ICSs. This change has three main advantages both at business and network management level. First, the two systems can share network infrastructures reducing costs for communication lines and exploit cheaper TCP/IP-based components. Second, common elements such as network, database, and security can be managed by the same trained experts [6]. Finally, there is a much easier communication and information flow between corporate offices and plants personnel [7]. On the other hand, there are also disadvantages. Several IT threats now affect also ICS systems. Stuxnet and Flame are two main examples. Both malwares exploit Windows vulnerabilities to attack or steal information from industrial systems. More generally, works as [8] identify how Internet worms are now concrete threats for ICSs.

2.2   Device Fingerprinting

Device fingerprinting is a set of activities aimed at describing hardware and software components on a computer network. There are two type of fingerprinting techniques: active and passive. Active fingerprinting actively queries the system to obtain a set of information required to define the fingerprint. Passive fingerprinting acquires information in a less intrusive way by only observing the existing communication. An active fingerprinter can collect all the information necessary for describing a fingerprint therefore, this approach has higher chances to succeed.

There are two main scenarios in which fingerprinting plays an important role: penetration testing and infrastructure protection. Penetration testing methodologies always present such activities as the first step towards vulnerability identification [3] (e.g. tools like Nmap [9], P0f [10], or XProbe2++ [11] are widely used for this purpose). Also Nessus [12] implements several fingerprinting methods. Fingerprinting tools provide different information regarding operating systems and applications running on network hosts (e.g. OS and services versions). The analysis allows pentesters to organize and tune following attacks. The literature proposes also to use fingerprinting together with common security systems (e.g. IPSs, IDSs, and spam filters) to improve their effectiveness and accuracy. For example, CISCO IPSs can leverage passive OS fingerprinting and OS mappings on a host to determine the relevance of a specific attack signature [13].

Within an IDS, fingerprinting could be an additional method to resolve cases where the alerted anomaly has a high probability to be a false positive. The approach described in [14] uses the passively detected OS fingerprint of the end host to correctly resolve ambiguities between different network stack implementations. In this work, the authors provide to IDS sensors additional knowledge about the network stack implementation of the end host and thus improve the chances of detecting the attacker. Finally, fingerprinting techniques are used to mitigate specific sets of cyber-attacks. This is the case of the work described in [15]. In their paper, the authors propose a preliminary architecture that applies spam detection filtering at the router-level using light-weight signatures for spam senders. Such signatures can be used to identify spamming hosts based on the specific operating system and version from which the email is sent.

The most widely adopted fingerprinting technique uses the following information of the TCP/IP protocol headers: *initial packet size, initial TTL, windows size, max segment size, windows scaling value, "don't fragment" flag, "sackOK" flag*, and *"nop" flag*. Together these fields form a 67-bits signature capable to identify an operating system working in a standard network. Common operating systems implement TCP/IP protocols with, at least, a difference in one of the characteristics listed above. Fingerprinting tools leverage this information to identify the specific operating system.

A large part of the research on TCP/IP stack fingerprinting focuses on optimizing the standard methodology. This is usually performed by refining stored information about connection negotiation and similar mechanisms implemented by the TCP/IP protocols [16]. In [14] the authors succeed in increasing the level of confidence in TCP/IP standard fingerprinting by looking at several specific characteristic of protocol implementations. The work is mostly focused on the SYN/SYN-ACK phase of the TCP three-way handshake. Several authors present works on exploiting implementation differences of other protocols to define fingerprints. A practical work on this topic is [17] in which application-level features of protocols like HTTP, FTP, SMTP are used to improve the recognition of software installed on standard PCs. This is the approach used by Shodan [18]. Shodan is search engine that, instead of indexing web page content, analyzes banner information. This feature allows it to scan the Internet and identify machines with specific characteristics. On the other hand, there are several works that try to take advantage of hardware properties to define suitable signatures for IT systems. In [19] authors show that Ethernet devices can be uniquely identified and tracked using as few as 25 Ethernet frames. An alternative approach implies recording small deviations called clock skews in devices hardware [20]. Works like [21] explain in detail how it is possible to build a highly-reliable classification technique based on packet payload inspection. In [22] authors present an operating system detection method based on temporal response analysis. Moreover, there are fingerprinting approaches based on port scanning. Some works as [23] exploits the use of standard network ports by known services to recognize systems and applications. Finally, the creation and maintenance of the fingerprints is one of the major problem of fingerprinting. Machine learning is one of

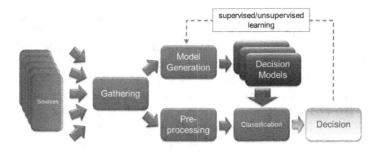

Fig. 1. Fingerprinting tools' reference architecture

the solution used to improve these two activities. For example, in [24] the authors propose probabilistic learning to develop a Naïve Bayesian classifier that passively infers a host operating system from packet headers.

3   A Reference Model for Device Fingerprinting

Despite different purposes and information sources, device fingerprinting activities have several common tasks. Due to this reason, it is possible to summarize such activities into few logical modules (or components) which can be found in all fingerprinting tools. A reference model allows to abstract details from specific solutions and makes them easier to compare. Each component of the model receives an input from the previous component, elaborates the provided data and forward the information. Our proposal for a fingerprinting reference architecture is provided in Fig. 1.

Every fingerprinting tool depends on one or more information *Sources*. A source can be uniform or heterogeneous, depending on the target of the analysis or the overall tool complexity. As already described in Sec. 2.2, fingerprinters usually exploit TCP/IP protocol information. Furthermore, some tools try to fingerprint different levels of the ISO/OSI stack (e.g. application headers, Ethernet headers, etc.). Finally, network topologies, time patterns, or also network ports usage can be potentially valuable sources as well.

The *Gathering* module implements the techniques used to collect the required data. This module relies directly on the information source and works capturing the valuable data and discarding the useless ones. Gathering module implementations differ according to the choice to do active or passive fingerprinting. During the active fingerprinting, the Gathering module manages the probing activity of the tool (i.e. by creating suitable packets and sending them to a device in order to study the responses). This is the case of Nmap and XProbe2++. The information collected, once labeled and organized, will form the dataset used by the tool for the analyses. Not all the traffic always contains valuable sources of information. Because of this, the Gathering module has to filter out useless or unknown communication and bad traffic.

The *Model Generation* performs data organization and storing. Data provided by the Gathering module is sometimes labeled by humans. For example, in the device fingerprinting training, fingerprints captured by tools are linked to information regarding the system that has generated them. Also, some tools automatically refine the dataset using machine learning techniques as in [17], [24]. Models generated by fingerprinting tools must be consistent and unambiguous. Exploiting few characteristics in generating models can cause overlaps in the dataset. Avoiding identical signatures or ambiguous data structures is the key element for fingerprinting reliability. For example, P0f provides a command for a signature collision check.

The *Decision Models* are the outputs of the Model Generation phase. The models represent the knowledge of a fingerprinter. A fingerprinter uses such knowledge as an input in the classification process. Usually, models are organized in signatures and stored in files. Both Nmap and P0f have a signature for each operating system. More advanced tools exploit different kinds of signature at the same time. This is the case of XProbe2++ and SinFP. The former has a variable number of signature items per OS, related to several tests it can perform [11]. The latter exploits two different datasets keeping active and passive signatures separated [25].

The *Pre-processing* component organizes information to be a suitable input for the analysis. Most of the times, fingerprinters exploit the Model Generation module to create temporary Decision Model of the system under examination. In few cases, such as XProbe2++, the Pre-processing component selects one by one the information needed for the comparison.

The *Classification* module implements the analysis of the collected information with respect to the dataset. This is the last component of the architecture. The classification may imply different kinds of actions. For example, P0f performs simple comparisons among signatures. Nmap and XProbe2++ exploit different methods like fuzzy signature matching. Moreover, XProbe2++ refines its classification by using decision trees. Most advanced tools add awareness about fingerprinting mitigation techniques to Classification modules. This is used to detect information artificially manipulated against fingerprinting. In particular, a software called "scrubber" is often used to confuse fingerprinting. As explained in [26] a scrubber is an active mechanism that converts heterogeneous network flows into well-behaved flows that cannot be equivocally interpreted. XProbe2++ implements systems to avoid such problem [11].

Finally, the *Decision* made by the Classification module gives the input for the manual or automatic refinement process of the dataset. Numerous tools calculate percentages of uncertainty for the provided results.

4   Fingerprinting Applicability on ICS

4.1   Overview

Fingerprinting a standard LAN works for a number of reasons. First of all, these networks often contain similar devices (e.g. personal computers) running common operating systems. Such software is widely studied and all fingerprinting tools provide comprehensive fingerprints about it. Communications usually implement open protocols like HTTP, SMTP, etc. Some of these already provide information about the systems they are working on. Moreover, PCs working on a network continuously open and close communications making connection setup information (SYN, SYN-ACK and RST packets) largely available.

To the best of our knowledge, there are only few examples of applying standard techniques to the industrial environment. This is because, there are few applicable solutions. In [27], authors argue that using already available information (as opposed to actively querying for it) is always preferable to minimize any risk to interfere with industrial operations. On the other hand, existing passive fingerprinting tools rely on the presence of Decision Models with already-known system and device fingerprints. None of such fingerprinting tools today provides such Decision Models (e.g. signatures of industrial devices) per se.

To the best of our knowledge, there is still no evidence that standard TCP/IP fingerprinting methodologies would work also for PLCs and RTUs.

4.2   Tests

We conducted preliminary tests to study how standard fingerprinting tools behave in an ICS environment. The tests involved different kinds of tools and PLCs (Siemens SIMATIC S7-1200 and ABB 800M). Our tests show that passive tool P0f working on real PCAP traces recognized only standard components like windows machines (SCADA servers or HMI) but was not able to provide any information about PLCs. Even probing devices, Nmap, Xprobe2++ and SinFP were not able to correctly identify any industrial device. Exploiting Siemens PLC's web server running on port 80, Nmap succeeded in recognizing its version and labeling it as "Siemens Simatic S7-1200 PLC httpd". Despite that, the tool fingerprinted the device as a QEMU showing its limitations in solving ambiguities related to industrial devices. It is worth noting that these tests were also useful to evaluate how feasible standard signatures' structures are for ICSs. For example, we set up a signature for the Siemens PLC and we added it to the Xprobe2++ database. Despite this new information, the tool was not able to recognize the same device. Further analyses showed that the field "icmp_echo_tos_bits" was filled in randomly by the PLC invalidating the signature enough to be discarded in favor of a different one (in this specific case an "HP JetDirect" printer).

4.3   IT/ICS Comparison

The tests were useful to identify several characteristics of ICSs that makes device fingerprinting more challenging compared to regular Internet or company LAN settings.

- **Device heterogeneity** while standard fingerprinting mostly focuses on PCs and their operating systems, in an industrial environment we deal with many different embedded devices.

– **Proprietary protocol** related to device heterogeneity, it makes difficult to exploit application layer information.
– **Device computational power** industrial devices do not have the capabilities to deal with massive network traffic and can not set up as many connections as standard PCs. This makes it difficult to use active fingerprinting.
– **Long-running TCP sessions** standard fingerprinting mostly use specific network packets (e.g. SYN, SYN-ACK, etc.). Typically, once a PLC and a control server set up a connection, the TCP session remains open for a very long time (days or even weeks) making it impossible to see those packets.

On the other hand, there are a few characteristics that fingerprinting tools can exploit in industrial environments.

– **Long life-cycle of devices** devices' working period without updates is usually long enough to guarantee a fingerprint to remain valid for years
– **Predictable behavior of components and Stable topology** once established, the process control remains the same and components behave accordingly by continuously performing stable instructions and communications [28]. This property can be exploited to create signatures based on traffic and communications patterns.
– **Protocol specification** some ICS protocols, like Modbus and Profinet, provide a way to query components in order to have information about their hardware and software.

It is worth noting that exploiting protocol specifications to query a device still has to deal with its computational power constraints. Also in this case, there is no guarantee to not interfere with process control.

5   ICS Fingerprinting Based on the Reference Model

To the best of our knowledge, there are only few examples of ICS fingerprinters. PLCscan and Modbuspatrol [29] exploit the "Read Device Identification" function in Modbus allowing users to query a device for information. However, the tools are biased to a specific protocol, exploiting the last characteristic described in Sec. 4. Furthermore, Shodan has been proven to be effective with ICS systems [30]. Several banners used by PLCs contains special keywords (e.g. brand names) that often allow an easy recognition. Standard tools provide still insufficient support for ICS environments (e.g. Nmap provides only a few scripts to be used with Siemens components and Shodan works just with well-known application protocols).

A comprehensive approach to the development of ICS fingerprinters has to face all the challenges outlined in Sec. 4. For this reason, we use the reference architecture defined in Sec. 3 to structure the discussion about ICS fingerprinting and to describe the properties required for an industrial environment.

Sources: In ICS environments, there is no guarantee to see any information useful to exploit standard TCP/IP signatures due to long TCP sessions and consequently few useful packets. The only way to avoid such constraint is to set up a new connection with the target. Application layer protocols might show useful fingerprinting data especially if we deal with protocols that already provide instruments to facilitate fingerprinting (e.g. Modbus and Profinet). In several cases there still is the problem of unknown protocols. We believe that using temporal, traffic and communication patterns can be a viable solution to implement ICS fingerprinting. The use of this information does not suffer from any of the problems listed before. Moreover, we suggest to exploit the substantial stability and regularity of ICS networks' communication to identify component roles inside the system.

Gathering: with respect to standard fingerprinting we propose to reverse the balance in using active and passive techniques. We argue to exploit passive fingerprinting more than active to avoid any interference with the system under analysis. ICS often monitor or control processes in systems where a component failure may have disastrous consequences (or may be otherwise very undesirable). Because of this, a generic active probing of systems (like scanning for open ports and then opening arbitrary TCP connections), may have undesired consequences, such as network delays or unexpected component behaviors [31]. However, we know that PLCScan and Modbuspatrol actively query devices for information. It is worth noting that, in this case, Modbus provides the function to perform such query thus it is unlikely to cause problems to the infrastructure. Most preferably, the sniffer used to capture network traffic has to be transparent to ICS components. without injecting any kind of traffic in the network and sending responses to any incoming message. This often guarantees no interferences with ICS operations. Collected information regarding traffic flows has a strong constraint as it relies on the position the sniffer has in the network. For instance, two traffic captures taken from the Field Network and the Process Network are hardly comparable. Thus, the Gathering module has to provide some general information about its position and accordingly label captured data. Fingerprinting based on packets' information does not suffer such problem and allows a simpler and more performing implementation of the module.

Model Generation: signatures are the most widely adopted structures to organize fingerprinting information. However, creating signatures (e.g. the standard TCP/IP) works well only with a fingerprinting methodology that relies on several precise properties. In Sec 4.3 we show that this is not always possible in ICS environments. Querying devices for information usually provides a structured and detailed list of data that does not need any further specification. In other cases, fingerprinters involving temporal, traffic and communication patterns deal with one comprehensive set of characteristics about an ICS infrastructure that cannot be reduced to a simple signature. For example, we may want to describe a communication between two ICS components with respect to the behavior that other devices have in the same network. In this case, the purpose of our analysis is to spot the differences that make such communication unique in an

ICS system (e.g. amount of packets sent, transferred bytes, etc.) and look for the same behavior in another networks. To extract and store this information we need a comprehensive data structure that outlines architecture, properties, and trends of an ICS infrastructure.

For this reason, a *Decision Model* can be either a simple signature or a more complex set of heterogeneous information. In the second case data can be related to both the component and the system within it is deployed.

Pre-processing: after the gathering phase, communication information undergoes a further refinement process. This process depends on the structure of the Decision Model and on the classification algorithms used by the ICS fingerprinter.

Classification: without precise signatures it is difficult to make ICS fingerprinters deal with operating systems and services profiling. When ICS protocols provide a way to query devices for information, a comprehensive fingerprinting analysis is possible. In this case, we argue that the primary target of ICS fingerprinting is to recognize component's vendor, hardware (e.g. device model), and software. If it is not possible to query the device for that data, the information we can obtain is usually not complete enough to detail the component. Consequently, other possible targets in ICS fingerprinting are: component type identification (e.g differentiate between SCADA servers and PLCs), component role identification (e.g. differentiate between main PLCs and normal PLCs), network topology identification (e.g. differentiate situations in which PLCs communicate only with a SCADA server or schemas in which PLC coordinate with each other), and gathering general information about the process (e.g. ICS working on energy systems perform updates and send messages often than in water infrastructures). We can achieve the first three targets by looking at communication patterns while the last one can be the result of a temporal analysis on the observed traffic.

Decision: the Decision is the output of the ICS fingerprinter. Depending on the exploited information or the complexity of the Decision Model it can be difficult to reliably update the dataset in an automatic way. Adding unverified information into the Decision Models increases the risk of false positive and break the integrity of the dataset. However, due the heterogeneity of ICS environments, the amount of information owned is a key element toward finding matches to unknown devices. Storing new Decision Models and keeping them distinct from the original dataset can be a solution. This method allows the fingerprinter to use new models only in specific cases (e.g. solving ambiguities if the main dataset does not give reliable results).

6   Conclusions and Future Works

In this paper we analyzed the concept of device fingerprinting for ICS networks and discussed feasibility and requirements fingerprinters need to work in an industrial environment.

We started our research testing widely used fingerprinting tools with industrial devices. These tests showed that current tools are not yet tuned on such components. Consequently, our study focused on understanding how we can modify already in place fingerprinting schemes and methodologies to be effective with ICS.

The value of this work is twofold. First, we analyzed specific features of ICS systems and the challenges they pose to traditional fingerprinting. This study describes main differences and analogies with IT networks and lays the foundation for further comparative analyses. Second, we created a fingerprinting reference model by generalizing the operations performed by state of the art fingerprinting techniques. This reference model allowed us to propose and organize a guideline for the development of ICS-specific fingerprinting techniques.

We are currently working on the implementation of a proof-of-concept tool, based on the proposed reference architecture. Such fingerprinter will analyze communication patterns and will exploit a SCADA/ICS Context Model to elaborate and use information about traffic flows. This tool will take into account challenges imposed by the working environments and will implement a way to identify components types and roles inside an ICS infrastructure.

Acknowledgement. This work was conceived within the "CRitical Infrastructure Security AnaLysIS" (CRISALIS) FP7 European project [32]. CRISALIS aims at providing new means to secure critical infrastructure environments from targeted attacks, carried out by resourceful and motivated individuals.

References

1. Robles, R., Choi, M., Cho, E., Kim, S., Park, G., Yeo, S.: Vulnerabilities in SCADA and critical infrastructure systems. International J. of Future Generation and Networking (2008)
2. Ten, C., Liu, C., Manimaran, G.: Vulnerability assessment of cybersecurity for SCADA systems. IEEE Trans. Power Systems (2008)
3. Pfleeger, C., Pfleeger, S., Theofanos, M.: A methodology for penetration testing. Computers & Security (1989)
4. Endi, M., Elhalwagy, Y., Hashad, A.: Three-layer PLC/SCADA system architecture in process automation and data monitoring. In: Computer and Automation Engineering, ICCAE. IEEE (2010)
5. Fovino, I.N., Coletta, A., Masera, M.: Taxonomy of security solutions for the SCADA sector (2010)
6. Clark, R., Hakim, S., Ostfeld, A.: Handbook of Water and Wastewater Systems Protection. Springer (2011)
7. McClanahan, R.: The benefits of networked SCADA systems utilizing IP-enabled networks. In: Rural Electric Power Conference. IEEE (2002)
8. Munro, K.: Scada - a critical situation. Network Security (2008)
9. Lyon, G.: Nmap security scanner (February 2013), http://nmap.org/
10. Zalewski, M.: p0f: Passive OS fingerprinting tool (2006), http://lcamtuf.coredump.cx/p0f.shtml (February 1, 2002)
11. Yarochkin, F., Arkin, O., Kydyraliev, M., Dai, S., Huang, Y., Kuo, S.: Xprobe2++: Low volume remote network information gathering tool. In: Dependable Systems & Networks, DSN 2009. IEEE/IFIP (2009)

12. Deraison, R., Meer, H., Walt, C.V.D.: Nessus network auditing. Syngress Media Incorporated (2004)
13. Cisco Systems Inc. User guide for Cisco security manager 4.3 (2012)
14. Taleck, G.: Ambiguity resolution via passive os fingerprinting. In: Vigna, G., Kruegel, C., Jonsson, E. (eds.) RAID 2003. LNCS, vol. 2820, pp. 192–206. Springer, Heidelberg (2003)
15. Esquivel, H., Mori, T., Akella, A.: Router-level spam filtering using TCP fingerprints: Architecture and measurement-based evaluation. In: Proceedings of the Sixth Conference on Email and Anti-Spam (2009)
16. Paxson, V.: Automated packet trace analysis of TCP implementations. ACM SIGCOMM Computer Communication Review (1997)
17. Haffner, P., Sen, S., Spatscheck, O., Wang, D.: ACAS: automated construction of application signatures. In: Proceedings of the 2005 ACM SIGCOMM Workshop on Mining Network Data (2005)
18. Matherly, J.: Expose online devices (May 2013), http://www.shodanhq.com/
19. Gerdes, R., Daniels, T., Mina, M., Russell, S.: Device identification via analog signal fingerprinting: A matched filter approach. In: Network and Distributed System Security Symposium, NDSS (2006)
20. Kohno, T., Broido, A., Claffy, K.: Remote physical device fingerprinting. IEEE Trans. Dependable and Secure Computing (2005)
21. Moore, A., Papagiannaki, K.: Toward the accurate identification of network applications. Passive and Active Network Measurement (2005)
22. Veysset, F., Courtay, O., Heen, O.: New tool and technique for remote operating system fingerprinting. Intranode Software Technologies (2002)
23. Moore, D., Keys, K., Koga, R., Lagache, E., Claffy, K.: The coralreef software suite as a tool for system and network administrators. In: Proceedings of the 15th USENIX Conference on System Administration (2001)
24. Beverly, R.: A robust classifier for passive TCP/IP fingerprinting. Passive and Active Network Measurement (2004)
25. Auffret, P.: Sinfp, unification of active and passive operating system fingerprinting. Journal in Computer Virology (2010)
26. Watson, D., Smart, M., Malan, G., Jahanian, F.: Protocol scrubbing: network security through transparent flow modification. IEEE/ACM Trans. on Networking, TON (2004)
27. Mahmood, A., Leckie, C., Hu, J., Tari, Z., Atiquzzaman, M.: Network traffic analysis and SCADA security. In: Handbook of Information and Communication Security (2010)
28. Hadziosmanovic, D., Bolzoni, D., Etalle, S., Hartel, P.: Challenges and opportunities in securing industrial control systems. In: Proceedings of the IEEE Workshop on Complexity in Engineering, COMPENG 2012, Aachen, Germany (2012)
29. Gordeychik, S.: SCADA strangelove or: How i learned to start worrying and love nuclear plants (February 2013)
30. ICS-CERT, ICS-ALERT-11-343-01 Control System Internet Accessibility, U.S. Department of Homeland Security (December 2011)
31. Duggan, D., Berg, M., Dillinger, J., Stamp, J.: Penetration testing of industrial control systems. Sandia National Laboratories (2005)
32. CRitical Infrastructure Security AnaLysIS (CRISALIS) (2012), http://www.crisalis-project.eu/

Bridging Dolev-Yao Adversaries and Control Systems with Time-Sensitive Channels

Bogdan Groza and Marius Minea

Politehnica University of Timişoara and Institute e-Austria Timişoara*
bogdan.groza@aut.upt.ro, marius@cs.upt.ro

Abstract. Defining security objectives for industrial control scenarios is a challenging task due to the subtle interactions between system components and because security goals are often far from obvious. Moreover, there is a persistent gap between formal models for channels and adversaries (usually, transition systems) and models for control systems (differential or recurrent equations). To bind these two realms, we translate control systems into transition systems by means of an abstraction with variable time granularity and compose them with a channel model that is controlled by Dolev-Yao adversaries. This opens the road for automatic reasoning about the formal model of a control system using model checkers in a context where the communication channel is tampered with. We address a security objective that has so far largely eluded in models, namely freshness, which is highly relevant for control systems. Beyond the traditional resilience to replay attacks, we point out several flavours of freshness which are often overlooked, e.g., ordering and bounded lifespan. We formalize these notions and show that their absence can lead to attacks that subvert the control system. Finally, we build a proof-of-concept implementation that we use to determine attacks on a simple model which clearly shows that real-world scenarios are within reach.

Keywords: control system, formal modelling, freshness.

1   Introduction

CONTEXT AND REALISM. The generic image of a control system is that of a closed loop in which a controller regulates the behaviour of a process (usually called plant) as shown in Figure 1. The design of such systems is commonly based on intricacies known only to producers and insiders that use them. However, an important aspect reconfirmed time and again by incidents such as Stuxnet that is that the internal details of a system are hard to be kept secret to well motivated outsiders (likely, the worm exploited specific system details). Relying on security through obscurity is a fatal flaw. Since for cryptographic protocols, modeling has proved to be a crucial tool to assess security, it is quite obvious that modeling industrial control systems in their relation to the communication channels and adversaries is much more relevant today as they become exposed as parts of Internet-like structures, e.g., Internet of Things (IoT) [1]. Indeed, there has been constant attention in the previous years on attack surfaces and countermeasures for control

---

* This work is supported in part by FP7-ICT-2009-5 project 257876, SPaCIoS: Secure Provision and Consumption in the Internet of Services.

E. Luiijf and P. Hartel (Eds.): CRITIS 2013, LNCS 8328, pp. 167–178, 2013.

systems [3,14], but these lines of work are not based on Dolev-Yao adversary models. While several related cases of modeling industrial communication channels exist, for example Modbus [6] or Fieldbus [4], (the former using tools from the AVISPA project, a precursory of the tools that we employ here) we are unaware of any related work that tries to combine the behaviour of the control system with the communication channel and the adversary abilities.

FRESHNESS. The sparsity of work combining control systems and formal adversary models is compounded by the marginal interest toward certain objectives such as freshness. So far, freshness in security protocols has been interpreted mostly in the traditional sense that disallows the same message to be accepted twice by a principal, e.g., prevention of replay attacks. Clearly, cryptography provides tools to do more than this: nonces, counters and timestamps, carefully embedded in the protocol can all be used to assure ordering (establishing the order in which messages are issued) or limit lifespan (decide if a particular message is still valid). Syverson [12] presents a taxonomy of replay attacks in which the classical sense is extended to more than the mere replay of a message. The taxonomy considers not only classic replays, but also attacks in which a message (or part of it) is used in a context for which it was not intended, e.g., interleaving, reflection or deflection attacks. Indeed, this taxonomy evades the traditional interpretation of replay attacks as used by BAN logic [2]. However, in general, interleavings, reflections or deflections are treated as violations of non-injective agreement [9] and they are not necessarily related to freshness. Besides Syverson's taxonomy [12] there is little interest to use freshness for more than uniqueness. While all tools employed for automatic formal protocol verification are able to detect replay attacks, to the best of our knowledge there is no support to check for objectives such as ordering or limited lifespan. Efforts to model time-sensitive security goals exist [5] but appear to be rather isolated. While in security protocols there seems to be a limited interest in freshness compared to other security objectives that have been extensively studied (e.g., secrecy, authenticity, etc.), this objective can be critical in control scenarios.

METHODOLOGY AND RESULTS. While disrupting standard security goals such as confidentiality or authenticity is within reach for the adversary modelled here, we are not specifically interested in such goals since there is consistent related work on how to model and assure them. Even if a channel is secure in this sense, freshness is not necessarily guaranteed. Here we address three flavours of freshness: uniqueness, which is the usual meaning, that a message cannot be subject to replay; ordering, if a principal does not accept messages out of order, and bounded lifespan, referring to the delay within which messages are accepted. To model control systems, we translate the state model of a process into a transition system based on a Δ-grain abstraction, resulting in a model that can interact with the adversary of the communication channel. This formal model allows us to assess whether in the presence (or absence) of the previously mentioned freshness flavours an adversary can subvert the control law at will. This opens the road to employ model checkers commonly used to verify security protocols in order to assess the security of a control system in this context. Using a model checker, we analyze the composition of the adversary, the channel model, and the system model to obtain an attack trace. Future work may include testing these attacks on real-world industrial communication channels, here we focus mostly on the theoretical foundations.

2   System Model and Abstraction

2.1   State Space Model

Bridging control engineering and computer science is a challenging task since the former usually models systems by differential (continuous-time) or recurrent (discrete-time) equations while the latter uses finite state automata, transition systems, etc. Still, there is significant interest to bridge the two. The problem of extracting a transition system from a generic discrete (or continuous) time system was studied by Pappas [10]. Further refinements of the methodology can be found in later works by Girard and Pappas [7,8], where metrics are introduced to characterize the degree to which two systems are (bi)similar. The same framework can be extended to non-linear systems, preoccupation for this can be found in the work of Tazaki and Imura [13].

Definition 1 (Discrete Time System). *A discrete-time system is a tuple of three spaces* $\mathbb{X}, \mathbb{U}, \mathbb{Y}$ *(domain of state, input and output), and two functions* $\mathcal{F}, \mathcal{G}$ *(mapping the current state and input to the next state and output, respectively), i.e.,* $DTS(\mathbb{X}, \mathbb{U}, \mathbb{Y}, \mathcal{F}, \mathcal{G})$:
$$\begin{cases} x(t+1) = \mathcal{F}(x(t), u(t)) \\ y(t) = \mathcal{G}(x(t), u(t)) \end{cases}, \text{ where } x(0) = x_0 \text{ is some fixed initial state.}$$

This model is called the state space model since it accounts for the state of the system and is the preferred way to model control systems.

EXAMPLE: A WATER TANK SYSTEM. Consider a mechanical-fluid system where a simple on/off controller tries to preserve a given reference level (r) of fluid in the tank as shown in Figure 1. The controller receives the error $e(t)$ computed as difference between the reference level and the output of the system $y(t)$ (which is the height of fluid in the tank), then outputs the command $u(t)$. A zero-order hold (ZOH) on the feedback loop preserves the value from the current time interval for the next, i.e., the output of the plant at step $t-1$ is the input of the controller at step t. To model the tank we use the equations from [11] which are straightforward from Bernoulli's equations. The physical system parameters are: g gravitational acceleration ($9.8\,m/s^2$), A_1 tank area (m^2), A_2 orifice area (m^2), h_1 height of water in the tank (m), h_2 height of orifice (m) and water inflow $f_1 = 0.004$ (m^3/s). The physical system behaviour is governed by Torricelli's law, that is: $\frac{d}{dt}h_1(t) + A_2\sqrt{2g(h_1(t) - h_2)} = f_1(t)$. This continuous time differential equation can be turned into a discrete time recurrent equation by replacing the differential with a finite difference, e.g., $\frac{d}{dt}h_1(t) = \frac{h_1((n+1)T_s) - h_1(nT_s)}{T_s}$ where T_s is the discretization step. By equating the finite difference with the differential the following discrete input-output model of the system is obtained [11]: $h_1(n) = \frac{1}{A_1}\left[T_s f_1[n-1] + A_1 h_1[n-1] - A_2 T_s \sqrt{2g(h_1(n) - h_2)}\right]$. The discrete input-output model is accurate enough for small values of T_s (in the order of seconds or hundreds of seconds) given that this mechanical-fluid system is not a fast process.

2.2 Δ-Grain Abstractions

INTUITION. Clearly, the recurrent equations that define a discrete system can be directly transposed into a transition system. But the state space will likely be very large (even

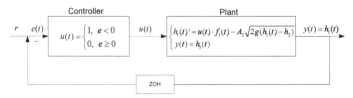

Fig. 1. Flow control system

infinite in case when the state of the system is a real number, e.g., the water level) and the complexity of this model will become prohibitive for our tools. The intention behind the Δ-grain abstraction is to simplify the model of the system in terms of input, output and state spaces as well as transitions between states. This is needed in order to make the model approachable by the formalism of the employed tools, and nevertheless usable (by selecting an abstraction which is just precise enough to check the desired property). The Δ-grain abstraction is flexible in the sense that it doesn't require describing the behaviour of the system at equidistant steps in time. In the Δ-grain abstraction we are merely interested in the fact that the trajectory of the discrete system is eventually (after k steps) in relation with that of the abstraction. Such an abstraction is not unique, for any real system there exist multiple Δ-grain abstractions. Our minimal prescription for designing it, is to select the states of the process that trigger an output change from the controller as well as the states that are the target of the control rule or of the adversary, then to describe the transitions between them. Choosing more abstract states leads to a more accurate model, but which is harder to verify, resulting in a trade-off.

Definition 2 (Δ-grain abstraction). *A discrete time system $DTS^\natural(\mathbb{X}^\natural, \mathbb{U}^\natural, \mathbb{Y}^\natural, \mathcal{F}^\natural, \mathcal{G}^\natural)$ is a Δ-grain abstraction of a discrete time system $DTS(\mathbb{X}, \mathbb{U}, \mathbb{Y}, \mathcal{F}, \mathcal{G})$ under relations $\mathcal{R}_x$, $\mathcal{R}_u$, $\mathcal{R}_y$ for states, inputs and outputs iff: i) for any $x \in \mathbb{X}, y \in \mathbb{Y}, u \in \mathbb{U}$ there exist $x^\natural \in \mathbb{X}^\natural, y^\natural \in \mathbb{Y}^\natural, u^\natural \in \mathbb{U}^\natural$ with $(x, x^\natural) \in \mathcal{R}_x$, $(y, y^\natural) \in \mathcal{R}_y$ and $(u, u^\natural) \in \mathcal{R}_u$, ii) for any $x_0 \in \mathbb{X}, u_0 \in \mathbb{U}, x_0^\natural \in \mathbb{X}^\natural, u_0^\natural \in \mathbb{U}^\natural$ with $(x_0, x_0^\natural) \in \mathcal{R}_x$, $(u_0, u_0^\natural) \in \mathcal{R}_u$ there exists $0 < k \le \Delta$ such that $(x(k), x^\natural(1)) \in \mathcal{R}_x$ and $(y(k), y^\natural(1)) \in \mathcal{R}_y$ if the input is constant for k steps, i.e., $u(i) = u_0, i \in [0, k-1]$, and iii) for any $k' < k$, $(x(k'), x^\natural(0)) \in \mathcal{R}_x$ and $(y(k'), y^\natural(0)) \in \mathcal{R}_y$ (all intermediary states and outputs have the same abstraction).*

According to the definition of a discrete time system, for the abstraction we have $x^\natural(1) = \mathcal{F}^\natural(x^\natural(0), u^\natural(0))$ while for the discrete system $x(k) = \mathcal{F}(x(k-1), u(k-1))$ is computed similarly by recurrence from x_0, u_0.

Proposition 1 (Step-or-hold). *Let $DTS^\natural$ be a Δ-grain abstraction of a discrete time system DTS and $(x^\natural, u^\natural)$ an abstract state and input pair. For any state and input of the real system DTS that is related to this pair the next state of DTS is uniquely related either to the current state or to the next state of the abstract system, i.e., $\forall x, u, (x, x^\natural) \in \mathcal{R}_x, (u, u^\natural) \in \mathcal{R}_u \Rightarrow (\mathcal{F}(x, u), \chi^\natural) \in \mathcal{R}_x, \chi^\natural \in \{x^\natural, \mathcal{F}^\natural(x^\natural, u^\natural)\}.$*

Proof. Condition ii) of Definition 2 requires that after some number k of steps the state of the real system is related to the state of the abstraction. If $k = 1$ then we have $(\mathcal{F}(x, u), \mathcal{F}^\natural(x^\natural, u^\natural)) \in \mathcal{R}_x$. Otherwise, if $k > 1$ then by condition iii) all intermediary states are part of the same abstraction which means $(\mathcal{F}(x, u), x^\natural) \in \mathcal{R}_x$.

EXAMPLE OF Δ-GRAIN ABSTRACTION. We build a Δ-grain abstraction for the previous water tank model. This model does not account explicitly for a state of the system and we apply the previous definition on its output, i.e., the state plays the role of the output. Assume the controller reference value r is set to 20. Naturally, one abstract state must be associated to the values above the reference and one to the values below it. Let these states be med^- and med^+. These states along with similar states for the adversary target, e.g., $high^-$ and $high^+$, are enough in a minimalistic model. But for better granularity, let us refine the state space of the abstraction (which represents the height of fluid and the output of the system) as $\mathbb{X}^\natural = \mathbb{Y}^\natural = \{vlow^-, vlow^+, low^-, low^+, med^-, med^+, high^-, high^+, vhigh^-, vhigh^+\}$. We set the input space of the abstraction as $\mathbb{U}^\natural = \{off, on\}$ according to the valve close and open commands. We define the relations between the abstract states and the real valued states as shown in Table 1 which summarizes the abstraction so far. Let functions $prec$ and $succ$ return the value that precedes or succeeds another value in the set, e.g., $vlow^+ \leftarrow prec(low^-)$, $high^+ \leftarrow succ(high^-)$, with the extremes as fixed points, $vlow^- \leftarrow prec(vlow^-)$ and $vhigh^+ \leftarrow succ(vhigh^+)$. At each step n we define the output of the plant according to $\mathcal{G}_\mathcal{P}^\natural(off, y^\natural(n-1)) = prec(y^\natural(n-1))$ and $\mathcal{G}_\mathcal{P}^\natural(on, y^\natural(n-1)) = succ(y^\natural(n-1))$ (this is in fact the value of $y^\natural(n)$). We use the same abstractions as in the case of the plant for the input and output spaces of the controller. Similarly, we define the output of the controller as $\mathcal{G}_\mathcal{C}^\natural(u^\natural(n-1)) = off$ iff $lower(u^\natural(n-1), med^-)$ or $u^\natural(n-1) = med^-$ and $\mathcal{G}_\mathcal{C}^\natural(u^\natural(n-1)) = on$ iff $higher(u^\natural(n-1), med^-)$. Predicates $lower$ and $higher$ can be inferred from the already defined $prec$ and $succ$. We now show that these form a Δ-grained abstraction (the exact value of Δ is not relevant for this example as it is merely an upper bound). Relation i) of Definition 2 is clearly satisfied for both the plant and controller: for any state we have defined an abstract state. Relations ii) and iii) are proved as follows. For the plant, in any abstract state the next state will be the predecessor or successor of the current state according to the value of the abstract input: off or on. In the case of the real plant, the input will be either 0 or 1 and given that this input is preserved constant eventually the water level will decrease or increase to a state that is related to the successor of the abstract state that is related to the current state. Since whenever the input of the real plant is preserved constant, the output is a monotonic function, relation iii) is satisfied as well for the plant and until the next abstract state is reached all states are in relation to the current state. For the controller, if the input (which is the water level) is preserved constant, there is no change in the output and the same happens in the real system which proves relation ii). Since the output does not change unless the input changes, relation iii) holds as well for the controller.

Table 1. Abstraction sets and relations with the real system

Abstraction sets	Relations between abstract and real values
$\mathbb{U}^\natural = \{off, on\}$	$\forall x \in [0, 5) : (x, vlow^-) \in \mathcal{R}_x, \forall x \in [5, 10) : (x, vlow^+) \in \mathcal{R}_x$
$\mathbb{X}^\natural = \mathbb{Y}^\natural = \{vlow^-, vlow^+,$	$\forall x \in [10, 15) : (x, low^-) \in \mathcal{R}_x, \forall x \in [15, 20) : (x, low^+) \in \mathcal{R}_x$
$low^-, low^+, med^-, med^+,$	$\forall x \in [20, 25) : (x, med^-) \in \mathcal{R}_x, \forall x \in [25, 30) : (x, med^+) \in \mathcal{R}_x$
$high^-, high^+, vhigh^-, vhigh^+\}$	$\forall x \in [30, 35) : (x, high^-) \in \mathcal{R}_x, \forall x \in [35, 40) : (x, high^+) \in \mathcal{R}_x$
	$\forall x \in [40, 45) : (x, vhigh^+) \in \mathcal{R}_x, \forall x \in [45, 50) : (x, vhigh^+) \in \mathcal{R}_x$
	$(0, off) \in \mathcal{R}_u \ (1, on) \in \mathcal{R}_u$

The next proposition establishes that for any behaviour of the abstraction there exists a behaviour of the real system. This property is important since otherwise an attack over the abstraction may simply be a false-positive alarm.

Proposition 2 (Realizability of the abstract trajectory). *Let $DTS^\natural$ be a Δ-grain abstraction of some real system DTS and consider an initial state x_0 with its corresponding abstraction $x_0^\natural$. For any trajectory of the abstraction $\Sigma^\natural = \{(x^\natural(0), u^\natural(0)), (x^\natural(1), u^\natural(1)), \ldots, (x^\natural(\ell), u^\natural(\ell))\}$ there exists a trajectory of the real system:*

$$
\begin{aligned}
\Sigma = \{ & (x(0), u_0), (x(1), u_0), \ldots, (x(n_1 - 1), u_0), \\
& (x(n_1), u_1), (x(n_1 + 1), u_1) \ldots, (x(n_1 + n_2 - 1), u_1), \\
& \ldots, \\
& (x(n_1 + n_2 + \ldots + n_{\ell-1}), u_{\ell-1})), \ldots, (x(n_1 + n_2 + \ldots + n_\ell - 1), u_{\ell-1} \}
\end{aligned}
$$

for which it holds that $(x(n_1+n_2+\ldots+n_{i-1}), x^\natural(i)) \in \mathcal{R}_x, \forall i \in \{1..\ell\}$, provided that $(u_i, u^\natural(i)) \in \mathcal{R}_u, \forall i \in \{0..\ell - 1\}$.

Proof sketch. We prove the statement by induction over ℓ. Let x_0 be the initial state of the system and u_0 the input. Then the abstractions $x_0^\natural$ and $u_0^\natural$ exist by property i) of Definition 2. Thus for $\ell = 0$, the trajectory $\Sigma^\natural = \{(x^\natural(0), u^\natural(0))\}$ exists and there is nothing else to prove. Assume the statement holds for $\ell \geq 0$ and prove it for $\ell + 1$. Let $N_\ell = n_1 + \ldots + n_{\ell-1}$ and let $\mathcal{F}^n(x)$ be the n-fold application of $\mathcal{F}$ to x, preserving u: $\mathcal{F}^k(x, u) = \mathcal{F}(\ldots(\mathcal{F}(x, u)\ldots), u)$. Since $(u_\ell, u^\natural(\ell)) \in \mathcal{R}_u$ by property ii) of Definition 2 there exists an integer k such that $(\mathcal{F}^k(x(N_\ell), u_\ell), \mathcal{F}^\natural(x^\natural(\ell), u^\natural(\ell))) \in \mathcal{R}_x$, since the input is kept at $u(\ell)$. Choosing $n_l = k$, we clearly have $\mathcal{F}^k(x(N_\ell), u_\ell) = x(N_\ell + n_\ell)$ and thus $(x(n_1 + \ldots + n_\ell), x^\natural(\ell+1)) \in \mathcal{R}_x$. Moreover, $\mathcal{F}^j(x(N_\ell), u_\ell) = x(N_\ell)$ for any $j < k$, by property iii), thus the state does not change from $x(N_\ell)$ to $x(N_\ell + n_\ell - 1)$. Thus, the inductive step holds.

While the previous proposition addresses the state trajectory, it trivially extends to the output trajectory since the output directly results from applying $\mathcal{G}$ to state and input.

We next couple an abstraction (playing the role of the plant) with another system (playing the role of a controller). We establish under which circumstances for each trajectory of the coupled abstraction there exists a trajectory of the coupled real system.

Proposition 3. *Let DTS_α and DTS_β be discrete time systems associated to a controller and plant with $DTS_\alpha^\natural$ and $DTS_\beta^\natural$ their Δ-grain abstractions. Let $DTS_{\alpha \rightleftarrows \beta}$ denote the control system that results from the input-output coupling of DTS_α with DTS_β. To avoid a circular dependency, we assume that now the input of DTS_α at step t is the output of DTS_β from step $t - 1$ (i.e., they are connected via a zero-order hold on the feedback loop as shown in Figure 1). For any abstract trajectory of $DTS_\beta^\natural$ given as state-input pairs (note that its input is the output of $DTS_\alpha^\natural$):*

$$
\Sigma_\beta^\natural = \{(x_\beta^\natural(0), u_\beta^\natural(0)), (x_\beta^\natural(1), u_\beta^\natural(1)), \ldots, (x_\beta^\natural(n), u_\beta^\natural(n))\}
$$

where $\forall i \in [1..n]$, $x_\beta^\natural(i) = \mathcal{F}_\beta^\natural(x_\beta^\natural(i-1), u_\beta^\natural(i-1))$, $u_\beta^\natural(i) = \mathcal{F}_\alpha^\natural(y_\beta^\natural(i), x_\alpha^\natural(i))$, there exists a trajectory of the real system $DTS_{\alpha \rightleftarrows \beta}$ if the following relation exists between *the behaviour of the real and abstract systems: at any step t at which the output of DTS_α changes it holds that i) its input at step t is part of a distinct abstraction than its input at step $t - 1$, i.e., $(u_\alpha(t), u^\natural) \in \mathcal{R}_u, (u_\alpha(t-1), v^\natural) \in \mathcal{R}_u, u^\natural \neq v^\natural$, and, due to the delay on the feedback loop ii) the current output of DTS_β and the previous one are part of the same abstraction, i.e., $(y_\beta(t), y_\beta^\natural) \in \mathcal{R}_y$ and $(y_\beta(t-1), y_\beta^\natural) \in \mathcal{R}_y$.*

Proof sketch. We show that for any $t < n$, a trajectory of the real system between t and $t + 1$ exists and this is $\Sigma_\beta = \{(x_\beta(t'), u_{\beta,t-1}), (x_\beta(t'+1), u_{\beta,t}),..., (x_\beta(t'+k), u_{\beta,t})\}$ where t' denotes the time in the real system at step t in the abstract system. This is explained as follows. The first pair $(x_\beta(t'), u_{\beta,t-1})$ is built with the input from the previous step denoted as $u_{\beta,t-1}$ and this is due to the one-step delay at which the output of DTS_β becomes the input of DTS_α. Condition ii) requires that $(x_\beta(t'), x_\beta^\natural(t)) \in \mathcal{R}_x$ and $(x_\beta(t'+1), x_\beta^\natural(t)) \in \mathcal{R}_x$ (when the input changes the current and previous state are part of the same abstraction). By definition of the Δ-grained abstraction a k exists such that $(x_\beta(t'+k), x_\beta^\natural(t+1)) \in \mathcal{R}_x$ provided that the input remains constant and this is precisely the case from step $t'+1$ onward since condition i) requires that DTS_α remains unchanged unless its input (which is the output of DTS_β) does not switch to a distinct abstraction. This is assured by condition iii) from the definition of the Δ-grained abstraction as all intermediary states have the same abstraction.

3 Protocol Model and Adversary Goals

3.1 Protocol Syntax and Properties: Freshness, Ordering and Bounded Lifespan

We assume a standard Dolev-Yao adversary that tampers with the communication channel, including the ability to reorder messages. To express the intruder's ability to delay messages we also need to model time on the communication channel. Consequently we formalize the protocol model as a labeled transition system where each transition corresponds to a tick of a global abstract clock. We begin with a simple framework for protocol execution that allows to define time sensitive properties, then we augment this model with system states. Our framework is different from the usual transitions systems associated to protocol specifications. Usually, a transition system associated to a protocol performs a transition whenever a principal receives a message that fits the expected format and content (as far as the receiver can verify), this is naturally followed by the receiver issuing its response. In our model, a protocol agent may update its state at each step, regardless of a receive action taking place (this is needed as agents will be associated to system abstractions). Moreover, each transition can happen with or without a send event and at each clock tick, several agents may transition. For simplicity, we consider that all agents transition synchronously, possibly without changing their state.

Let $\mathcal{A} = \{A_1, \ldots, A_n\}$ be a set of agent names, $\mathcal{M}$ be a set of messages, and $\mathcal{T} = (\mathcal{A} \times \mathcal{M}) \cup \{\epsilon\}$ be the set of actions, where ϵ is the special empty action.

Definition 3 (Agent model). *A protocol agent (principal) is a state-transition system $\mathcal{P}_i = (\mathcal{S}_i, \mathcal{R}_i, \mathcal{I}_i)$, where $\mathcal{S}_i$ is a set of states, $\mathcal{I}_i \subseteq \mathcal{S}_i$ is a set of initial states, and $\mathcal{R}_i \subseteq \mathcal{S}_i \times \mathcal{T} \times \mathcal{T} \times \mathcal{S}_i$ is the transition relation.*

We also write $(\sigma, r_i, s_i, \sigma') \in \mathcal{R}_i$ as $\sigma \xrightarrow{r_i, s_i} \sigma'$, denoting a transition from state σ to σ', triggered in principal A_i by receive action r_i and executing send action s_i. Each of the two actions is either empty (ϵ) or a pair (A_j, m) representing communication (receive/send) of message $m \in \mathcal{M}$ with principal A_j ($j \neq i$).

For the case of n agents, let $\mathcal{S} = \mathcal{S}_1 \times \ldots \times \mathcal{S}_n$ and $\mathcal{I} = \mathcal{I}_1 \times \ldots \times \mathcal{I}_n$ be the overall and initial state space. For a state $\sigma \in \mathcal{S}$ we denote by σ_i its projection on $\mathcal{S}_i$, likewise, for vectors $\bar{r}, \bar{s} \in \mathcal{T}^n$ we denote by r_i, s_i the individual actions in agent A_i.

Definition 4 (Protocol execution). *A sequence $\rho = \sigma^0 \xrightarrow{\bar{r}^1, \bar{s}^1} \sigma^1 \ldots \xrightarrow{\bar{r}^t, \bar{s}^t} \sigma^t$ is a protocol execution by agents $\mathcal{P}_i = (\mathcal{S}_i, \mathcal{R}_i, \mathcal{I}_i)$ if: i) σ^0 is part of the initial state state space, i.e., $\sigma^0 \in \mathcal{I}$, and ii) the projections of a transition corresponds to a valid transition in each principal, i.e., $\forall j \in 1 \ .. \ t, i \in 1 \ .. \ n$ it holds $(\sigma_i^{j-1}, r_i^j, s_i^j, \sigma_i^j) \in \mathcal{R}_i$.*

Let $\mathsf{recv}_i(m, j, t)$ be a predicate which is true if A_i receives message m from A_j at time t, and if so, let $\mathsf{sndtime}_j(m)$ be the time at which m was sent by A_j.

Definition 5 (Freshness, ordering and bounded lifespan). *Consider two principals A_{i_0} and A_{i_1} of a protocol specification. We say that for any execution ρ the (bidirectional) communication channel between A_{i_0} and A_{i_1} ensures: i) uniqueness (the traditional sense of freshness), if a message is accepted only once by any principal, i.e., $\mathsf{recv}_{i_b}(m, i_{\neg b}, t_1) \wedge \mathsf{recv}_{i_b}(m, i_{\neg b}, t_2) \Rightarrow t_1 = t_2, \forall b \in \{0, 1\}$, ii) ordering, if in addition to uniqueness, once a message is accepted, only messages sent after it are subsequently accepted, i.e., $\mathsf{recv}_{i_b}(m_1, i_{\neg b}, t_1) \wedge \mathsf{recv}_{i_b}(m_2, i_{\neg b}, t_2) \wedge t_1 < t_2 \Rightarrow \mathsf{sndtime}_{i_{\neg b}}(m_1) < \mathsf{sndtime}_{i_{\neg b}}(m_2), \forall b \in \{0, 1\}$, iii) δ-bounded lifespan, if in addition to uniqueness, messages are accepted no later than a delay δ after the time they were issued, i.e., $\mathsf{recv}_{i_b}(m, i_{\neg b}, t) \Rightarrow t \leq \mathsf{sndtime}_{i_{\neg b}}(m) + \delta, \forall b \in \{0, 1\}$.*

If the channel is not symmetric between A_{i_0} and A_{i_1} and a particular goal is to be assured only from one side to another but not vice-versa, the definition can be easily modified by setting b to either 0 or 1 accordingly.

The case when the sender needs to send a message more than once is addressed in protocol design by adding distinct time variant parameters to each message (to avoid replay), thus two identical messages should never occur (unless this is intended).

3.2 Merging Δ-Grained Abstractions and Adversary Goals

We now simply add system states (via Δ-grained abstractions) to the protocol execution. Then we formulate the goal of the adversary and give a proposition which establishes under which circumstances the abstract attack trace has a real world instantiation.

Definition 6 (Protocol execution with system states and inputs). *A protocol agent $\mathcal{P}_j = (\mathcal{S}_j, \mathcal{R}_j, \mathcal{I}_j)$ can instantiate the abstraction $DTS_j^\natural$ of a discrete system DTS_j if its state and output evolve according to the Δ-grain abstraction of DTS_j having as input the message in the receive action and as output the message in the send action.*

If one or more such agents exist in protocol execution $\rho^\natural = \sigma^0 \xrightarrow{\bar{r}^1, \bar{s}^1} \sigma^1 \ldots \xrightarrow{\bar{r}^t, \bar{s}^t} \sigma^t$ we call this a protocol execution with system states and inputs and we denote by $X^i = \{x_1^i, .., x_n^i\}$, $U^i = \{u_1^i, .., u_n^i\}$ the system states and inputs of all agents at step i (for agents that do not instantiate a $DTS^\natural$ all system states x_j^i and inputs u_j^i are empty ϵ).

The adversary's goal is a set of target states for the plant (which consequently leads to a particular output). In many practical scenarios, including the examples in the following section, the adversary may force the process to go to any value of its choice. Still, this does not mean that the adversary is in control of the system, since the adversary might be able to take the system to a state only for a brief time instance. Our definition of λ-step subversion requires the adversary to gain complete control over the plant for at least λ steps. If subversion can be proved for any value of λ, then it means that the adversary has full control over the system.

Definition 7 (λ-step subversion). *Let the execution with system states and outputs* $\rho^\natural = \sigma^0 \xrightarrow{\bar{r}^1, \bar{s}^1} \sigma^1 \ldots \xrightarrow{\bar{r}^t, \bar{s}^t} \sigma^t$ *of protocol specification* $(\mathcal{S}, \mathcal{R}, \mathcal{I})$ *and let* $\mathcal{G}_{adv} = \{X_{adv}^0, X_{adv}^1, ..., X_{adv}^\lambda\}$ *the goal of the adversary defined over* λ *transitions. We say that an adversary can perform a* λ-step subversion w.r.t. $\mathcal{G}_{adv}$ *over the control system if the states in the goal of the adversary hold during all of the last* λ *steps of the execution, i.e.,* $\forall i \in [0, \lambda) : X^{t-i} = X_{adv}^{\lambda-i}$.

To avoid trivial attacks we assume that the adversary goal is distinct from the target of the controller, i.e., the protocol execution in the absence of the adversary.

For concurrent executions of two or more control systems, the abstract attack trace might not have a real world instantiation because one abstract step does not necessarily correspond to the same number of real steps in the systems. Clearly, one way to fix this would be do define an abstraction with the same number of steps, whenever a concurrent execution is needed. To keep the abstractions flexible, in the next proposition we define under what circumstances the attack trace has a real world instantiation.

Proposition 4 (Realizability of the execution). *Let* $\rho^\natural = \sigma^0 \xrightarrow{\bar{r}^1, \bar{s}^1} \sigma^1 \ldots \xrightarrow{\bar{r}^t, \bar{s}^t} \sigma^t$ *a protocol execution with systems states and inputs in the presence of a Dolev-Yao adversary that has access to the input of each plant (i.e., the output of each controller). Denote by* $T_p(i)$ *the real time step associated to principal p at transition i (due to the Δ-grained abstraction the number of steps in each system is different). Given that the abstract trajectory of each controller-plant ensemble has a real-world counterpart, the execution has a real world instantiation if either: i) the adversary acts independently on each system without using any input from one to build the input for the other, or ii) for any input that is given at step i to the Dolev-Yao adversary, given α, β the minimum integers at which $U^{i-\alpha} \neq U^i, U^{i+\beta} \neq U^i$ and any two principals p, q it holds $T_p(i) > T_q(i - \alpha)$ and $T_p(i) < T_q(i + \beta)$ (this enforces that at the real step associated to transition i the input is the same in all systems).*

Proof. Case i) is straightforward. If the adversary acts independently on the systems, there always exists a real world instantiation due to Proposition 1. Otherwise, if the adversary subverts inputs from one system to another (i.e., Dolev-Yao behaviour) since the Δ-grained abstraction requires variable number of steps, it may be that at the same step of the abstraction, the number of steps in the real systems is different. But case ii) requires that even if this is the case, the input of the system is unchanged at the time of the subversion, i.e., step i, and therefore whatever the intruder learns at step i of the abstraction, it will be able to learn the same from the real-world instantiation.

In the case of δ-bounded lifespan, one additional issue is to decide whether an input from a previous transition step of the abstraction can still be accepted in the current step. This can be done in two ways. The easiest and more accurate way is to associate each transition of the abstraction with an exact real-world delay (the number of steps needed by the real system). A message issued in the previous abstract time step is accepted only if its lifetime is greater than this value. Otherwise, one could use a globally fixed number of steps for the abstraction (which would be similar to a new discretization), but this will result in a more rigid model that will likely increase the state-space and make the search harder. A rule that can be used is that if $\delta < \Delta$ then a message received by the plant from the controller is either immediately used or will be dropped in the next step (as the maximum possible number of steps in the real system exceeds the message lifespan). If no attack is found, this may be a false negative since Δ is merely a maximum. In contrary, if the message is accepted, the attack may be a false positive. We defer such details for more concrete examples in future work.

3.3   Models and Attacks

We build a minimal, yet meaningful toy model around the fluid-mechanical system from Section 2 and find attack traces on it using a model checker.

TRANSITIONS VS. HORN CLAUSE BASED MODELS. To model the plant and controller, two distinct approaches are possible within the formalism employed by the tools that we work with: transitions and Horn clauses. In the transition based model, a global clock transition allows the plant to move from one state to another and the controller to issue a new command. The state of each principal is updated via a transition as well. In the case of two plants, which makes the attacks more interesting to model, there are four possible transitions for the controller as well as for the plant. The controller can issue for kinds of commands: on for both valves (on, on), on for the first and off for the second (on, off), off for the first and on for the second (off, on) and off for both (off, off). The two tanks can receive the correct and most recent command or each of these commands can be deflected by the adversary making the tank preserve the most recent command. Horn clauses allow a more efficient approach as both the controller output and process state can be inferred from atomic Horn clauses at the end of each transition (this significantly reduces the state space). Consequently, the Horn based model can be reduced to a single transition conditioned by the current state of the plant and contoller and the rules (Horn clauses) that define the new state of the controller and plant.

UNIQUENESS AND ORDERING AS A MUST. When uniqueness and ordering are not assured, the attacks are not surprising, λ-step subversion is feasible for any goal. Without uniqueness, once both possible commands are issued, the intruder can reuse them at will to keep the process in the desired state. Without ordering, the intruder can get any number of positive or negative commands (clearly, if the intruder cuts communication to the plant, the controller will continuously issue the same command) and then use them at will to preserve the desired state. Finding attack traces for this case is easy and for brevity we focus on finding attacks for the more complex case with bounded lifespan, when the intruder cannot reuse old commands from the controller.

ATTACKS IN THE PRESENCE OF BOUNDED LIFESPAN AND DELAYS. When a single tank is present, all that the intruder can do is to take the level to any desired value by cutting communication when the currently issued command sets the output toward its target (though, he is not able to preserve the level there). The case of two tanks is more interesting. This significantly increases the power of the intruder if he can also change the destination of the messages, etc. Assume that the reference level of the two tanks is different, e.g., low^+ vs. $high^+$. Due to the on/off nature of the controller, the level of fluid in the tank will oscillate around the reference level (this is consistent with the transition model described here). In this case the attack trace shows that the intruder can perform a λ-step subversion for any level if for one tank the adversary target level is above the reference while for the other the level is below the reference. This is achievable since the intruder can subvert the command for one of the tanks and send it to the other and additionally it can add delays at will. We present the attack traces, found by the CL-Atse [15] model checker which is part of the AVANTSSAR toolset (www.avantssar.eu), for two distinct cases as outlined below.

Same-phase oscillation. The controller preserves the desired level and the tanks work synchronously, oscillating between $\{low^+, low^-\}$ and $\{high^+, high^-\}$ respectively. The initial states are low^+ for the first and $high^+$ for the second and the initial commands are both negative leading to a first transition to low^- and $high^-$ respectively. The adversary goal is set to $\{med^-, med^+\}$. The attack trace in Figure 2 has 7 steps which use several intruder abilities: *delays* (step i) in which the first tank preserves the previous command), *redirection* (step ii) in which the command for each of the tank is sent to the other) and *replay* (steps iii) to vii) when the command to one of the tanks is also sent to the other; this still respects uniqueness since the command is still freshly issued). In Figure 2, the arrows from the controller to the tank denote the command that is taken as input (or preserved in case when a delay is introduced).

Opposite oscillation. We set the same reference levels ($\{low^+, low^-\}$ and $\{high^+, high^-\}$) and the same attack goals ($\{med^-, med^+\}$). The initial states are low^- and $high^+$ while the initial commands $^+$ and $^-$ respectively that lead to a first transition to low^+ and $high^-$. In this case the two tanks are oscillating in opposite directions at the desired levels. Again 7 attack steps are needed, but the intruder actions are different. Interestingly, in steps i), iv) and vii) the regular commands of the controller are used. In steps ii) and vi) a *redirection* is done, while in step iii) a *delay* is added to both receivers.

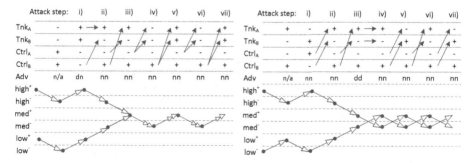

Fig. 2. Attack transition in the case of two synchronous (left) and asynchronous (right) tanks (based on the attack trace produced by CL-Atse)

4 Conclusion and Future Work

Bridging Dolev-Yao adversaries and control systems is an interesting and previously largely unaddressed topic. Freshness, ordering and bounded lifespan provide interesting goals for modelling system behaviour. We have shown that neglecting these objectives can lead an adversary to compromise the output of a control system by subverting it to desired target states at will. To the best of our knowledge, this work gives the first account of using formal verification tools to model time-sensitive channel goals in relation to control systems. We are concerned with making the first foundational steps for such analyses. There are several communication protocols widely employed in industrial systems; their investigation is out of scope here, but we see it as relevant future work. The adversary embedded in our practical examples can delay, delete or redirect messages, but he is also able to perform cryptographic operations if these are present in the protocol. Indeed, such operations are quite natural capabilities with the tools employed here. This opens the road to study a broader class of practical examples of more complex systems in the context of Dolev-Yao adversaries.

References

1. Alcaraz, C., Roman, R., Najera, P., Lopez, J.: Security of industrial sensor network-based remote substations in the context of the internet of things. Ad Hoc Networks 11(3), 1091–1104 (2013)
2. Burrows, M., Abadi, M., Needham, R.: A logic of authentication. Proc. Royal Society of London. Series A, Mathematical and Physical Sciences 426(1871), 233–271 (1989)
3. Cárdenas, A.A., Amin, S., Sastry, S.: Research challenges for the security of control systems. In: Proc. of the 3rd Conference on Hot Topics in Security, pp. 1–6. USENIX (2008)
4. Cheminod, M., Pironti, A., Sisto, R.: Formal vulnerability analysis of a security system for remote fieldbus access. IEEE Transactions on Industrial Informatics 7(1), 30–40 (2011)
5. Delzanno, G., Ganty, P.: Automatic verification of time sensitive cryptographic protocols. In: Jensen, K., Podelski, A. (eds.) TACAS 2004. LNCS, vol. 2988, pp. 342–356. Springer, Heidelberg (2004)
6. Edmonds, J., Papa, M., Shenoi, S.: Security analysis of multilayer SCADA protocols. In: Goetz, A.D.E., Shenoi, S. (eds.) Critical Infrastructure Protection. IFIP, vol. 253, pp. 205–221. Springer, Boston (2007)
7. Girard, A., Pappas, G.: Approximation metrics for discrete and continuous systems. IEEE Transactions on Automatic Control 52(5), 782–798 (2007)
8. Girard, A., Pappas, G.: Approximate bisimulation: A bridge between computer science and control theory. European Journal of Control 17(5), 568 (2011)
9. Lowe, G.: Casper: A compiler for the analysis of security protocols. In: 10th Computer Security Foundations Workshop, pp. 18–30. IEEE (1997)
10. Pappas, G.: Bisimilar linear systems. Automatica 39(12), 2035–2047 (2003)
11. Roberts, M.: Fundamentals of signals and systems. McGraw-Hill (2007)
12. Syverson, P.: A taxonomy of replay attacks. In: 7th Computer Security Foundations Workshop, pp. 187–191. IEEE (1994)
13. Tazaki, Y., Imura, J.: Discrete-state abstractions of nonlinear systems using multi-resolution quantizer. Hybrid Systems: Computation and Control, 351–365 (2009)
14. Teixeira, A., Pérez, D., Sandberg, H., Johansson, K.H.: Attack models and scenarios for networked control systems. In: Proc. of the 1st Conference on High Confidence Networked Systems, HiCoNS 2012, pp. 55–64. ACM (2012)
15. Turuani, M.: The CL-Atse protocol analyser. In: Pfenning, F. (ed.) RTA 2006. LNCS, vol. 4098, pp. 277–286. Springer, Heidelberg (2006)

An Indoor Contaminant Sensor Placement Toolbox for Critical Infrastructure Buildings

Demetrios G. Eliades[1,*], Michalis P. Michaelides[1,2], Marinos Christodoulou[1],
Marios Kyriakou[1], Christos G. Panayiotou[1], and Marios M. Polycarpou[1]

[1] KIOS Research Center for Intelligent Systems and Networks, and
Department of Electrical and Computer Engineering
University of Cyprus
75 Kallipoleos Ave., CY-1678 Nicosia, Cyprus
eldemet@ucy.ac.cy
[2] Department of Electrical Engineering and Information Technologies
Cyprus University of Technology
30 Archbishop Kyprianos Str., CY-3036 Lemesos, Cyprus

Abstract. In this work, we address the problem of airborne contaminant sensor placement in high-risk buildings where critical infrastructures are managed and operated, making them possible locations for terrorist attacks (such as governmental buildings and ministries, utilities, airports and hospitals). A new software is presented based on the "Matlab-CONTAM Toolbox" and the CONTAM multi-zone simulation software, to construct multiple scenarios of contamination events and to solve the multi-objective sensor placement problem for minimizing the average and maximum impact risk with respect to the contaminant mass inhaled impact metric. The use of the software is demonstrated in a case-study using the Holmes's House benchmark. The Toolbox is released under an open-source license at https://github.com/KIOS-Research/matlab-contam-toolbox.

Keywords: Sensor Placement, High-Risk Buildings, Critical Infrastructure Protection, Contamination, MATLAB-CONTAM Toolbox.

1 Introduction

According to the European Council Directive 2008/114/EC, Critical Infrastructures are defined as those systems which are essential for maintaining the societal and economic well-being of the people, and in case their operation would be disrupted or destroyed, the state would fail in maintaining those functions [8]. Infrastructures such as electricity, oil, gas, transportation, water and telecommunication systems are considered critical; this includes both cyber and physical layers as well as their associated facilities [7,8]. Critical infrastructures are susceptible to various types of faults which may be due to environmental conditions,

---

* Corresponding author.

E. Luiijf and P. Hartel (Eds.): CRITIS 2013, LNCS 8328, pp. 179–190, 2013.

human errors or malicious attacks. For this reason, Critical Infrastructure Protection has received significant interest by governments and researchers in the last decade, in order to identify risks leading to failure, study interdependencies between infrastructures, design tools for early detection of faults and software models, as well as protocols and controls for mitigating attacks [10].

In this work, we investigate the protection of buildings, which may be the operational or management centers of critical infrastructures, such as governmental buildings and ministries, utilities, airports and hospitals. In case of an attack in a critical infrastructure building, the overall operation of the corresponding infrastructure could be affected. A type of terrorist attack in buildings is through the release of some airborne chemical, biological or radiological agent, and such an event could affect the health and safety of the occupants in the different building zones dramatically [11]. In case a dangerous substance is released within a building zone, the substance would spread through the different parts of the building as a result of the air-flows between the different zones. Sensor information can be utilized to alert the occupants as well as the operators to take the appropriate measures in the case of a contaminant release. Ideally, it would be desirable to have sensors in every room of the building, measuring all different types of contaminants, but the cost and sophistication of most contaminant sensors today prohibits this. In practice, a small number of sensors will be available, with respect to the number of building zones which need to be covered. When solving this problem one should take into account the topology of the building, the significance of each zone as well as to consider uncertainties in the parameters considered. Determining where to install a limited number of sensors for contaminant detection is a non-trivial problem, as multiple and conflicting objectives need to be satisfied, such as coverage, detection time, number of people affected, installation costs etc.

The problem of selecting optimal sensor locations has also received significant interest in various fields, such as operational research [15], control systems [2] and water distribution systems security [13,6]. In [1], the optimal sensor locations were determined for detecting releases in a building by using a Computational Fluid Dynamics (CFD) tool to estimate the distribution of contaminants. In [19], CFD techniques were also applied to predict chemical and biological agent dispersion in an office complex for finding the best locations for sensors and for developing effective ventilation strategies. Multi-zone models have also been used, for instance, in [4], six attack scenarios for a small commercial building were simulated, and a genetic algorithm was applied for each attack scenario to optimize the sensor sensitivity, location, and number to achieve the best system behavior while minimizing system cost. In [3], the impact of zonal and multi-zone modeling techniques on indoor air protection systems was analyzed for a typical office environment and a large hall. The use of a systems engineering approach utilizing contamination attack scenarios, criteria for evaluating performance as well as the use of contaminant sensor technologies, has been advocated by [9]. Under these safety-critical situations, it becomes of paramount importance that the contaminant is promptly detected and localized so that appropriate control actions are taken to mitigate the damage and ensure the safety of the people [12]. A software tool for "smart buildings" was presented by [14], as a decision support tool for determining where to install contamination sensors, in order to reduce detection time. Probability distributions are considered for the different parameters, such as the release zone, the chemical agent quantity and the release duration.

The focus of this work is to present a new decision support tool for making recommendations regarding where to install a number of sensors for airborne contaminants. Compared to previous works, our approach differentiates in that it constructs multiple environmental and contamination scenarios based on sampling of the different probability distributions, taking into account building utilization and people distribution, for minimizing multiple impact-risk objectives. In our previous work [5], a methodology was presented for determining where to install a small number of contaminant sensors. First, a set of contamination scenarios is constructed, and each of the different scenarios is simulated using a multi-zone building simulation software. For assessing the damage caused by each scenario (e.g., number of people infected) we calculate an impact metric based on the total amount of contaminant inhaled and depending on the number of people, their age and type of their activity within the building. Finally, for deciding on where to place the sensors we solve an optimization problem that may involve multiple objectives, for instance to minimize (i) the average impact damage, (ii) the worst-case impact damage and (iii) the cost/number of sensors. In general, compared to existing simpler methods, this method allows better handling of more complex scenarios which involve many parameters and different optimization functions, as well as taking into account the building usage [5].

CONTAM [17] is a multi-zone simulation software developed by the US National Institute of Standards and Technology (NIST), with which the user can easily create the building outline and specify the zone volumes, the openings, the environmental conditions, as well as the contaminant sources present, to compute airflows and simulate contaminant concentrations in the different building zones. The computational engine of CONTAM has been used in various building security studies to simulate contaminant propagation [9,12,5].

Some of the key challenges in security research is to compare different methods through benchmarks as well as to implement usable software solutions so that these algorithms can be evaluated by the industry. This motivates the work presented in this paper, of a new software implemented in Matlab for computing sensor placement solutions based on the mathematical framework proposed in [5]. The software is based on the "Matlab-CONTAM Toolbox", a new development platform for researchers and the industry, which integrates a building simulation tool (CONTAM) as well as scenario construction and optimization algorithms, in order to be used as a benchmarking tool among the critical infrastructure protection community. Through the Toolbox, a large number of contamination scenarios under different conditions can be simulated, and these data can be used for further analysis by the different algorithms. In specific, the

Toolbox allows the creation of multiple contamination event scenarios by varying the different problem parameters (wind direction, wind speed, leakage path openings, source magnitude, evolution rate and onset time). The use of the Toolbox is illustrated through the use of a case study based on the Holmes's House benchmark [18]. The software is released under an open-source license and is available at `https://github.com/KIOS-Research/matlab-contam-toolbox`.

The remaining of this paper is organized as follows: In Section 2, the mathematical problem formulation is described as used in the developed software. In Section 3, the modular software architecture is presented. In Section 4, a case study is presented to illustrate the usage of the Toolbox and the Sensor Placement methodology. Finally, Section 5 concludes the paper and future work is discussed.

2   Problem Formulation

The indoor contaminant dispersion dynamics model and the sensor placement methodology, as utilized in the software, are described in this section. The goal is to solve a combinatorial problem for deciding where to install contamination sensors in a large high-risk building, in order to reduce the possibility of severe damage due to an airborne contaminant event which may affect the critical infrastructure operation.

In the following, the formulation used within the software is presented. Further details on the multi-zone model can be found in [12], along with the relation of the different model components and the mass-balance equations. The model used can represent both naturally and mechanically ventilated buildings. In addition, sources and sink elements can be incorporated in the model. Additional details in relation to the sensor placement methodology can be found in [5].

Let $\mathcal{R}$ represent the set of real numbers. The state-space equations for contaminant dispersion in an indoor building environment with N zones, as considered in this software, are described by

$$\dot{x} = A(p_x)x + \phi(p_x, p_\phi). \tag{1}$$

The vector $x \in \mathcal{R}^N$ represents the concentration of the contaminant in the building zones (measured in mass per volume). The state matrix $A \in \mathcal{R}^{N \times N}$ models the changes in the contaminant concentrations between the different building zones as a result of the airflows and is a function of vector p_x, which is comprised of the wind-direction and wind-speed, the ambient temperature, the volumes of all zones, the temperatures in all zones and the opening status of all doors, windows and fans. The term $\phi \in \mathcal{R}^N$ represents the contaminant mass release into the building due to an attack, and p_ϕ is a vector comprised of the locations where contaminants are released, their release duration, as well as their release rates.

To measure the damage caused during a contamination scenario at the k-th zone, an impact value z_k can be computed. This corresponds to the damage caused on the system measured through some impact metric. In this work, the contaminant mass inhaled is considered, which is given by

$$\dot{z}_k = f_z(x_k; p_z) \tag{2}$$

where $f_z(\cdot)$ is the function for computing the change rate of the impact z_k for an airborne contamination event at the k-th zone. This depends on the contaminant concentration x_k and the vector p_z, which is comprised of the average daily zone occupancy (proportional to the actual usage of some zone by people), the inhalation rate (which depends on the building/zone functionality), and the concentration threshold of the sensors.

In general, the parameter vectors p_x and p_ϕ may be partially/nominally known, and these uncertainties may influence the calculations of the sensor placement solutions. In this work, multiple scenarios with different parameter values are considered, to better capture the differences between the actual system and the model. Uniform bounds of each parameter are considered known, and the user can decide the number of samples within the range of each parameter.

A finite set $\mathcal{P}$ is constructed and is comprised of N_p elements corresponding to all the combinations of the different parameter sampled values considered. For each contamination scenario in $\mathcal{P}$, the indoor contaminant dispersion dynamics are simulated for a period of T hours. Let Ω be the overall-impact matrix

$$\Omega = \begin{bmatrix} \Omega_{1,1} & \cdots & \Omega_{1,N} \\ \vdots & \ddots & \vdots \\ \Omega_{N_p,1} & \cdots & \Omega_{N_p,N} \end{bmatrix}, \tag{3}$$

such that its (i,j)-th element, $\Omega_{i,j}$ corresponds to the total contaminant mass inhaled due to the i-th contamination scenario from $\mathcal{P}$, assuming a sensor is monitoring the j-th zone.

Finally, the optimization problem for contaminant sensor placement in high-risk buildings is formulated as a multi-objective risk-minimization problem, where the best solutions belong to a Pareto Front with respect to certain objectives. Specifically, in this software, the multi-objective optimization problem is formulated in the software as

$$Y = \operatorname*{argmin}_{\chi \in \{1,0\}^N} \{F_0(\chi), F_1(\chi; \Omega), F_2(\chi; \Omega)\}, \tag{4}$$

where χ is the zone index set for which $\chi_l = 1$ when a sensor is installed and $\chi_l = 0$ when there is no sensor installed at the l-th zone. Function F_0 corresponds to the number of sensors which depends on the user input, F_1 is the estimated average impact-risk and F_2 is the estimated worst-case impact-risk. For computing the best Pareto Front solutions, the selection of the algorithm depends on the problem size. For small problems, an exhaustive search may be computationally feasible, whereas for larger problem other methods such as multi-objective evolutionary optimization algorithms can be applied.

After solving the optimization problem and the Pareto Solutions set has been constructed, decision makers may use higher level reasoning to arrive at the final decision regarding which zones to install the contamination sensors.

3   Software Architecture

The Matlab-CONTAM Toolbox provides a programming interface for CON-TAM, a multizone airflow and contaminant transport analysis software. The goal of the Toolbox is to serve research and industry by facilitating the simulation of multiple contamination events under varying conditions as well as to store computed results in data structures so that they can be reused by different algorithms. An intuitive Graphical User Interface (GUI) has been designed to access the different functionalities of the Toolbox and the Sensor Placement algorithm. It is important to note that the architecture of the software allows for new modules to be added to the Toolbox. The Software Architecture is depicted in Fig. 1.

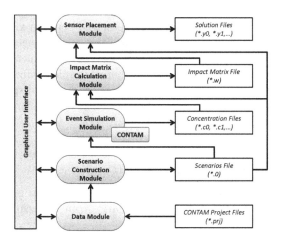

Fig. 1. The software architecture of the Matlab-CONTAM Toolbox and the Sensor Placement module

The software acquires the building information from CONTAM Project files, which are comprised of details regarding walls, floors, ceilings, air-handling systems, ducts, weather conditions etc. The "Data Module" opens CONTAM Project files (*.prj) and extracts the information which is related to the building parameters. In addition, the building zone schematics are extracted and this information is used by the GUI of the Toolbox to plot the building schematics.

The information from the "Data Module" is then used by the "Scenario Construction Module". This module assists for specifying, through the GUI, the building parameters for constructing a single or multiple simulation scenarios. The different contamination scenario parameters, along with structural and environmental information are stored in the Scenarios File (*.0).

The data stored in the Scenarios File is used by the "Event Simulation Module", which is responsible for communicating with the CONTAM engine to compute the path air-flows for different environmental conditions. When the flows have been computed, the module simulates the different contamination scenarios and computes the contaminant concentration at each building zone. The contaminant concentrations are then stored in one or more Concentration Files (*.c0, *.c1, ...).

The "Impact Matrix Calculation Module" utilizes the data from the scenarios and the simulation files, as well as data from the GUI (such as the average daily zone occupancy), to calculate the damage caused by some contamination event, until the time the contaminant exceeds some concentration at a certain zone. The matrix computed for all the possible scenarios and all the possible zones is stored in the Impact Matrix File (*.w).

Finally, the "Sensor Placement Module" is used to compute the final solutions, based on the computed impact matrices and the scenarios file. Through the GUI, the user specifies which method to use to solve the problem. For instance, exhaustive search methods would compute all the possible solution combinations, and calculate the Pareto Solutions. The solutions can be depicted graphically on the Interface, and are stored in a Solutions File (e.g. *.y0 for the exhaustive search method, *.y1 for the evolutionary computation method)

4   Case Study

In the following we present a case study for the high-risk building sensor placement software using a realistic benchmark based on the Holmes's House [18] which is depicted in Fig. 4. The building is comprised of 14 zones: a garage (Z1), a storage room (Z2), a utility room (Z3), a living room (Z4), a kitchen (Z5), two bathrooms (Z6 and Z13), a corridor (Z8), three bedrooms (Z7, Z9 and Z14) and three closets (Z10, Z11 and Z12). There are 30 path openings corresponding to windows and doors (P1–P30).

The first part of the sensor placement algorithm is the construction and simulation of multiple scenarios describing different environmental, structural and attack conditions. Figure 4 depicts the interface for selecting the scenario parameters: the simulation time and the time step for solving numerically the differential equations, the maximum number of simultaneous contamination sources, as well as the contaminant parameters and the environmental/structural parameters which affect flows. Where available, the building's nominal values are loaded (e.g. zone volumes, wind direction and speed, ambient and zone temperatures, path openings). However, the user can modify any of these parameters as required. The user can specify upper and lower bounds for each parameter using a percentage, for instance, for a wind speed 10 m/s, a 10% bound corresponds to a wind velocity within the range $[9, 11]$ m/s. Furthermore, the user can select how many samples to segment this range of values, for example, by taking 3 samples from the wind speed range $[9, 11]$ m/s, the set of wind speeds is $\{9, 10, 11\}$ m/s. In this work, grid-based parameter selection is considered.

In the following step, all the contamination scenarios are simulated in order to compute the time-series describing the contaminant concentrations in each zone, through the interface depicted in Fig. 4. The path air-flows are computed using

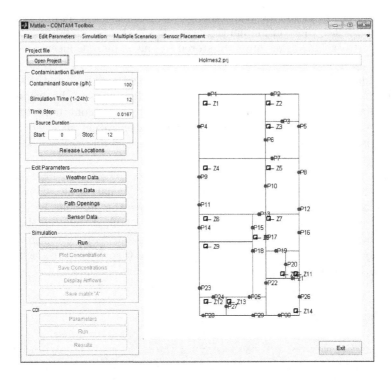

Fig. 2. The Matlab-CONTAM Toolbox with the Holmes's House project opened

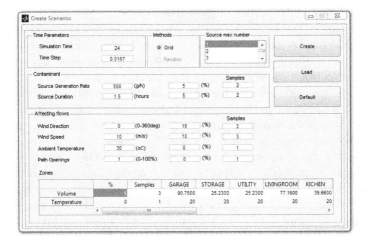

Fig. 3. The interface for selecting scenario parameters and constructing the scenarios set

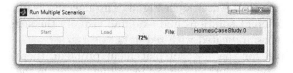

Fig. 4. The interface for running multiple scenarios

CONTAM, and these flows are used to construct matrix $A(p_x)$ which is used in (1) to solve the equation for the different contamination scenario parameters.

By using the computed contaminant concentration time-series for each zone, the impact matrix Ω can be constructed for solving the optimization problem. The (i, j)-th element of the impact matrix Ω corresponds to the damage caused due to the i-th contamination scenario with respect to having a sensor installed in the j-th zone. In this work, the contaminant mass inhaled metric is considered as a metric of the impact damage (2), however different metrics could be implemented as well. The interface for constructing the impact matrix is show in Fig. 4. For each zone, the user can specify an occupancy value, which corresponds to the average number of people residing within a certain zone within a day. For instance, if 10 people reside within a zone for 6 hours each day, the average daily occupancy of that zone would be $10(6/24) = 2.5$. The inhalation rate depends on the type of work which can be estimated using guidelines [16]. The sensor threshold corresponds to the concentration above which a certain sensor can detect the contaminant, according to its specifications.

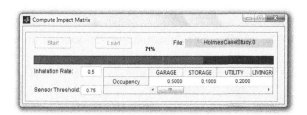

Fig. 5. The interface for constructing the impact matrix

The final step is to solve the optimization problem for sensor placement, using the interface depicted in Fig. 4. The user can select between two methods for constructing the solutions to evaluate the Pareto Front, using the Matlab's multi-objective evolutionary-based algorithm (*gamultiobj*) which is suitable for larger problems, and an exhaustive method which is suitable for smaller problems. The user can select different number of sensors to solve the optimization. The Pareto Solutions are computed for each different number of sensors, the final

solutions are shown to the user as in Fig. 4. Through the graphic interface, the
user can select different solutions and examine visually the suggested locations
for installing sensors, indicated with red dots.

In this example, for the 4-sensor placement problem, there are two Pareto
optimal solutions: both solutions suggest installing sensors in the living-room and
the two bedrooms, however the solution with the lowest mean risk impact suggest
to install the last sensor in a closet, and the solution with the lowest maximum
risk impact suggest to install the last sensor in the bath. It is important to note
that even though both solutions are Pareto optimal, i.e. one does not dominates
the other, the second solution has a significantly lower maximum risk impact
with only a moderate increase in the average risk impact objective, and thus a
decision maker might choose the second rather than the first solution.

Fig. 6. The interface for solving the sensor placement problem

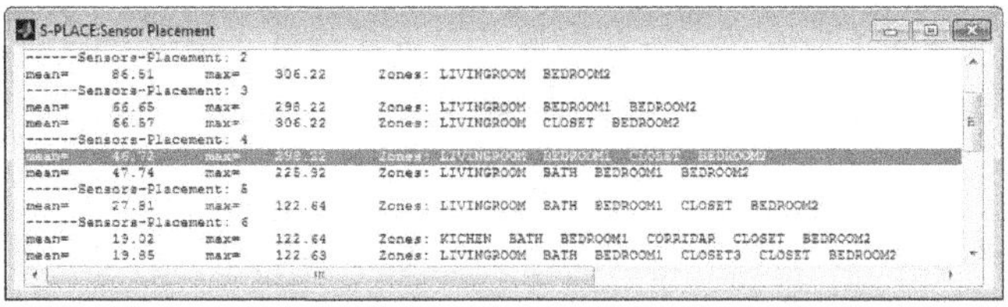

Fig. 7. The Sensor Placement solutions interface

5   Conclusions and Future Work

In this work, we examine the problem of improving security in high-risk critical infrastructure buildings from malicious airborne contaminations, by determining where to install a limited number of sensors, while taking into account the building usage and the uncertainty in the structural and environmental parameters. A new decision support software implemented in Matlab for computing sensor placement solutions is presented based on the mathematical framework proposed in [5] and the "Matlab-CONTAM Toolbox", a development platform for researchers and the industry, which integrates the building simulation software CONTAM as well as other scenario construction and optimization algorithms.

The software has been designed to be used both by the professional as well as by the academic community, making it easy to evaluate solutions under various scenarios, through an intuitive Graphical User Interface. The modular software architecture allows each part of the software data and algorithms to be accessed independently. New methods can be added to investigate the use of different metrics and optimization algorithms, or to solve new problems related with high-risk building security. In this paper, the use of the software is illustrated through the use of a case study based on the Holmes's House benchmark [18]. The Toolbox is released under an open-source license, and can be downloaded at https://github.com/KIOS-Research/matlab-contam-toolbox.

Future versions of the software will allow selecting different and more sophisticated methods for constructing the scenario parameters, allow the use of different impact metrics and response time-delays to construct multiple impact metrics as well as to allow different optimization methods for constructing the Pareto Solutions.

Acknowledgements. This research work has been partially funded by the European Research Council under the ERC Advanced Grant ERC-2011-ADG-291508 "Fault-Adaptive Monitoring and Control of Complex Distributed Dynamical Systems" (FAULT-ADAPTIVE) and by the EC project HOME/2011/CIPS/AG "online identification of Failure and Attack on interdependent Critical InfrastructurES" (FACIES).

References

1. Syverson, P.: A taxonomy of replay attacks. In: 7th Computer Security Foundations Workshop, pp. 187–191. IEEE (1994)
2. Basseville, M., Benveniste, A., Moustakides, G., Rougee, A.: Optimal sensor location for detecting changes in dynamical behavior. IEEE Transactions on Automatic Control 32(12), 1067–1075 (1987)
3. Chen, Y., Wen, J.: Application of zonal model on indoor air sensor network design. In: Proc. of SPIE (2007)
4. Chen, Y., Wen, J.: Sensor system design for building indoor air protection. Building and Environment 43(7), 1278–1285 (2008)

5. Eliades, D., Michaelides, M., Panayiotou, C., Polycarpou, M.: Security-oriented sensor placement in intelligent buildings. Building and Environment 63, 114–121 (2013)
6. Eliades, D., Polycarpou, M.: A fault diagnosis and security framework for water systems. IEEE Transactions on Control Systems Technology 18(6), 1254–1265 (2010)
7. European Commission: Critical infrastructure protection in the fight against terrorism. Communication, COM/2004/0702 (October 2004)
8. European Commission: Council directive 2008/114/ec of 8 december 2008 on the identification and designation of european critical infrastructures and the assessment of the need to improve their protection. Official Journal of the European Union L345(23) 12 (2008)
9. Ko, H.W.: Countermeasures against chemical/biological attacks in the built environment. Johns Hopkins APL Technical Digest 24(4), 360–367 (2003)
10. Lopez, J., Setola, R., Wolthusen, S.D.: Overview of critical information infrastructure protection. In: Lopez, J., Setola, R., Wolthusen, S.D. (eds.) Critical Infrastructure Protection. LNCS, vol. 7130, pp. 1–14. Springer, Heidelberg (2012)
11. Mead, K.R., Gressel, M.G.: Protecting building environments from airborne chemical, biological, or radiological attacks. Applied Occupational and Environmental Hygiene 17(10), 649–658 (2002); pMID: 12363204
12. Michaelides, M., Reppa, V., Panayiotou, C., Polycarpou, M.: Contaminant event monitoring in intelligent buildings using a multi-zone formulation. In: Proc. of SAFEPROCESS, Mexico City, Mexico (2012)
13. Ostfeld, A., Uber, J.G., Salomons, E., Berry, J.W., Hart, W.E., Phillips, C.A., Watson, J.P., Dorini, G., Jonkergouw, P., Kapelan, Z., di Pierro, F., Khu, S.T., Savic, D., Eliades, D., Polycarpou, M., Ghimire, S.R., Barkdoll, B.D., Gueli, R., Huang, J.J., McBean, E.A., James, W., Krause, A., Leskovec, J., Isovitsch, S., Xu, J., Guestrin, C., VanBriesen, J., Small, M., Fischbeck, P., Preis, A., Propato, M., Piller, O., Trachtman, G.B., Wu, Z.Y., Walski, T.: The battle of the water sensor networks (BWSN): A design challenge for engineers and algorithms. ASCE Journal of Water Resources Planning and Management 134(6), 556–568 (2008)
14. Schropp, D.: "smart building" technology for air safety monitoring: Sensor network design tool. Gases & Instrumentation, 24–28 (July/August 2008)
15. Toregas, C., ReVelle, C.: Optimal location under time or distance constraints. Papers in Regional Science 28(1), 131–143 (1972)
16. U.S. Environmental Protection Agency (EPA): Exposure factors handbook: 2011 edition. National Center for Environmental Assessment, Washington, DC, EPA/600/R-09/052F (September 2011)
17. Walton, G., Dols, W.: CONTAM 2.4 user guide and program documentation. National Institute of Standards and Technology, Gaithersburg, MD 20899-8633, 2.4c edn., nISTIR 7251 (2005)
18. Wang, L., Dols, W., Chen, Q.: Using CFD capabilities of CONTAM 3.0 for simulating airflow and contaminant transport in and around buildings. HVAC&R Research 16(6), 749–763 (2010)
19. Zhai, Z., Srebric, J., Chen, Q.: Application of CFD to predict and control chemical and biological agent dispersion in buildings. International Journal of Ventilation 2(3), 251–264 (2003)

Optimization Models in a Smart Tool
for the Railway Infrastructure Protection

Antonio Sforza[1], Claudio Sterle[1], Pasquale D'Amore[2], Annarita Tedesco[2],
Francesca De Cillis[3], and Roberto Setola[3]

[1] Department of Electrical Engineering and Information Technology,
University "Federico II" of Naples, Via Claudio, 80125, Naples, Italy
{sforza,claudio.sterle}@unina.it
[2] Ansaldo STS, Via delle Brecce, 80, Naples, Italy
{annarita.tedesco,pasquale.damore}@ansaldo-sts.com
[3] Università Campus Bio-Medico di Roma, Via Álvaro del Portillo, 21, 00128 Roma
{f.decillis,r.setola}@unicampus.it

Abstract. In this paper we describe a smart tool, developed for the European
project METRIP (MEthodological Tool for Railway Infrastructure Protection)
based on optimal covering integer programming models to be used in designing
the security system for a Railway Infrastructure. Two models are presented and
tested on a railway station scheme. The results highlight the role that the optimization models can fulfill in the design of an effective security system.

Keywords: railway infrastructure protection, security system, covering model.

1   Introduction

The great amount of incidents which have occurred worldwide illustrates that terror-
ists seek targets with emotional or symbolic value, such as widely recognizable icons
and targets whose destruction would significantly damage or disrupt the economy.
The economic impact of such attacks is indirect [1, 2]. A Railway Infrastructure System (RIS) has a great appeal on assailants, especially in urban areas, because of its
intrinsic value, vulnerability and difficulties in guaranteeing protection. This is due to
its nature, because it precludes passengers' screening and identification, and to specific features: open infrastructure; high levels of passenger density; hazardous materials
on the lines; extent of the infrastructures; economic and social relevance of the railway transportation service. So prevention and preparedness to risks in RIS requires:
proper analysis of the vulnerabilities of the system; clear awareness of criticalities and
possible countermeasures; adequate methods to design, scale and optimize the protection. METRIP (MEthodological Tools for Railway Infrastructure Protection) is a European Project focused on identifying the most critical and vulnerable assets, defining
the attack scenarios to be detected for each asset, designing the security system in
terms of type, number and position of the protection devices, and ultimately evaluating its effectiveness in terms of asset vulnerability to an attack.

In this paper we focus on optimal covering integer linear programming (ILP) models
implemented in METRIP project for the design of a RIS security system. In Section 2

E. Luiijf and P. Hartel (Eds.): CRITIS 2013, LNCS 8328, pp. 191–196, 2013.
© Springer International Publishing Switzerland 2013

we present the three level analysis of the RIS used in the METRIP tool and an overview of it; Section 3 is focused on some of the used optimization ILP models; finally results obtained by ILP models on a sample test case are presented in Section 4.

2   RIS, Attacks, Protection Devices and a Smart Tool

The smart tool developed for METRIP is based on a three level analysis of the RIS:

1. *Asset level.* The vulnerability of a RIS is directly associated to its main assets: trains, rail lines; depots; electric sub-systems; galleries; bridges; central management office; stations [3]. The analysis returns information about geometry, physical structure and relevance of main components.
2. *Attack level.* For each kind of attack the analysis returns information about: hit assets, used mean, main attack steps, effects on a single asset and on the RIS.
3. *Protection level.* The analysis returns the technological features of the devices composing a baseline security system (*BSS*), i.e. a system aimed at preventing malicious intrusions (e.g. video surveillance, access control and sound check devices).

The tool is composed by three main modules:

1. **Unified Modeling Language Module (*UMLM*),** devoted to develop the *UML* models representing all the components of the system under investigation: core assets, attacks and *BSS* protection devices.
2. **Optimization Module (*OM*),** devoted to find the optimal location of the *BSS* devices within the asset through ILP covering models solved by the optimization software Xpress-MP. The location of the devices is optimized with respect to the area of the asset and takes into account its specific geometry.
3. **Vulnerability Analysis Module (*VAM*),** devoted to the vulnerability evaluation of the asset in relation to the kind of attacks and protection devices.

In the following we will focus on the *OM*, highlighting its main steps and the operations performed to apply the covering models to the RIS context [4, 5].

3   The Optimization Module

The *OM* is devoted to manage a library of optimal covering ILP models to be used in the design of the security system. These models determine the number and the location of the control devices. Using the information provided by the *UMLM* about the asset to be protected by a specific set of attacks and about the specific kind of security device to be located, the *OM* performs the following operations: 1) asset discretization; 2) coverage analysis; 3) coverage model selection and solution by Xpress optimization software; 5) generation of the output for the *UMLM*.

Asset Discretization and Coverage Analysis
Given the information about the asset geometry (shape, width and length) provided by the *UMLM*, the area of the asset to be protected (region of interest) has to be made discrete, passing from the continuous two-dimensional representation to a discrete representation of the asset [4, 5]). This operation is performed building a grid with step k on the plant of the asset. The set of points of the grid is referred to as R.

In this phase we define also the set of points which are the potential locations of the devices, referred to as L. Generally L is constituted by the points sited on the edges and corners of the asset walls and of the obstacles present in the region of interest.

The *BSS* device activity can be schematized through a coverage area, i.e. the area protected/controlled by the device, defined by two main parameters:
— θ, coverage angle within which the device is active ($0° \leq \theta \leq 360°$);
— r, maximum distance to which the device is still effective (coverage ray).

Coverage analysis consists of determining which are the points of R that can be controlled by a device. In the following this sub-set of points will be referred to as S, $S \subseteq R$. The sub-set S for each potential location of a device is built with reference to angle θ and ray r of the coverage area. In case of the presence of an obstacle which can interdict the activity of the device, the sub-set S has to be filtered, so generating a set $S' \subseteq S$. In Fig. 1, the coverage area in the two cases is shown.
The result of the coverage analysis is a binary matrix of dimensions (L, R), named *Coverage Matrix* (*CM*), whose generic element c_{ij} is equal to 1, if point j, $j \in R$, belongs to the set S' of device i, $i \in L$, otherwise it is equal to 0.

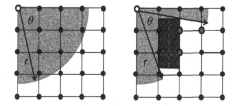

Fig. 1. Coverage areas and sub-sets S and S' without and with obstacles

3.1   Coverage Model Selection

Covering problems are NP hard [4] and consist in the placement of a set of facilities in points of a region with the aim of satisfying a real or virtual service demand. Their first usage for security purposes started with the *art gallery problem* [7]. In a security system design problem, we have to locate *BSS* devices, while the service demand to be satisfied is given by the covering of the set of points R of the region of interest. Covering problems can be classified in function of their objective in two main classes:
-    Minimization of number or total cost of control devices to be located,
-    Maximization of the region covered by the devices.

The first class arises when we have to cover all the points of the region of interest or a sub-set of them. These problems are based on the classification of the points in two main groups, *important* and *general* points, where the first ones have to be compulsorily controlled. If all the points have the same importance, then the problem is referred to as set covering problem (*SCP*), otherwise it is referred to as weighted demand covering problem (*WDCP*) [8]. The second class of covering problems arises when the number of available control devices is prefixed and we have to determine their position in order to maximize primary and/or secondary coverage of the region of interest (respectively maximal covering problem, MCP [9], and back-up covering problem, BCP, [9]). For the sake of brevity, we will present just the first class of ILP models.

Set Covering (*SCP*) and Weighted Demand Covering Problems (*WDCP*)
The ILP formulations for the set covering and the weighted demand covering problems, referred to respectively as *SCM* and *WDCM* are reported in Table 1.

Table 1. ILP formulations for SCP and WDCP

SCM		*WDCM*	
$Min\ z = \sum_{i \in L} h_i y_i$	(1)	$Min\ z = \sum_{i \in L} y_i - \alpha \sum_{j \in R} (1 - s_j) x_j$	(3)
$\sum_{i \in L} c_{ij} y_i \geq 1 \quad \forall j \in R$	(2)	$\sum_{i \in L} c_{ij} y_i \geq 1 \quad \forall j \in R \mid s_j = 1$	(4)
		$\sum_{i \in L} c_{ij} y_i \geq x_j \quad \forall j \in R \mid s_j = 0$	(5)

Concerning *SCM*, h_i is the installation cost at a potential device location i, $i \in L$, c_{ij} is the coverage matrix coefficient, y_i is a binary variable associated to each potential device location i, $i \in L$, which assumes value 1 if a device is installed at the location i, 0 otherwise. The objective function (1) minimizes the total installation cost of the devices. Constraints (2) impose that each point j, $j \in R$, has to be covered by at least one device. Note that, if the cost h_i is equal for all the potential locations i, $i \in L$, minimizing the installation cost is equivalent to minimizing the device number.

Concerning *WDCM*, y_j and c_{ij} assume the above described meaning, s_j is a flag value defined for each j, $j \in R$, equal to 1 if the point j has to be compulsorily controlled, 0 otherwise; x_j is a binary variable associated to each point j to be covered, $j \in R$, which assumes value 1 if the point j is covered, 0 otherwise; α is a parameter, between 0 and 1, weighting the installation of a new device with respect to the number of covered points. The objective function (3) is composed by two terms. The first term minimizes the number of devices to be located in order to cover all the important points of the region. The second term, instead, tries to locate an additional control device if its installation increases the number of controlled general points by a threshold value defined by the parameter α. Constraints (4), impose that each important point j, $j \in R$, has to be covered at least by one device i, $i \in L$. Constraints (5) impose that a general point is covered just in case a device, able to control it, has been installed.

The models have been solved by the optimization software FICO™ Xpress-MP 7.3 and run on an Intel® Core™ i7, 870, 2.93 GHz, 4GB RAM, Windows Vista™64 bit.

4   Application of the OM to a Railway Station

We present the results of the covering models on a railway station whose schemes are reported in Figures 2 and 3a. The station area has been discretized by 621 points, reduced to 526 points because of the presence of the obstacles. The potential locations for the cameras are 143 (black points in Fig. 3a). Important points are the white ones. We consider the case of designing the CCTV security system. Two kind of cameras have been taken into account: CCTV1 ($\theta = 90°$, $r = 25$) and CCTV2 ($\theta = 30°$, $r = 50$).

We solve the *SCM* and *WDCM* using two different settings: 1) CCTV1 with 8 orientations in the range $0° \div 360°$, with a 1144x621 coverage matrix; 2) CCTV1 with 8 orientations in the range $0° \div 360°$ and CCTV2 with 12 orientations in the range $0° \div 360°$, with a a 2860x621 coverage matrix.

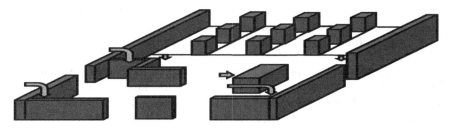

Fig. 2. 3D scheme of the station

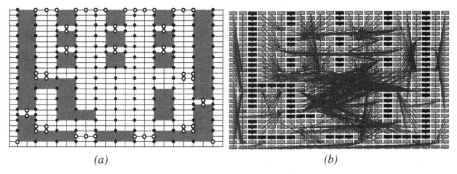

(a)   (b)

Fig. 3. a) 2D scheme of the station and grid with potential location of devices (in black). b) Solution of the SCM model

In *WDCM*, the parameter α has been set to 0.067. This means that the model will locate an additional camera if it covers at least 10 additional general points of the region of interest. Each grid point of Fig. 3a corresponds to a square of Fig. 3b. In Fig. 3b the solution obtained with *SCM* using both kinds of CCTV is reported. Computational results for the two settings are reported in Table 2. We can observe that both models are solved with very low computation time, despite the size of the coverage matrix. As expected, the *SCM* model provides a solution that covers all the points of the region of interest and the combined usage of the two kind of CCTVs allows to decrease the number of installed devices (from 45 to 39).

Table 2. Results of the SCM and WDCM models on the railway station scheme

SCM	# CCTV	Covered Points	Coverage %	CPU time (s)
CCTV1	45	526	100	0,5
CCTV1 + CCTV2	39	526	100	6,3
WDCM (α=0.067)	# CCTV	Covered Points	Coverage%	CPU time (s)
CCTV1	26	366	69,58	1,4
CCTV1 + CCTV2	28	449	85,36	5,5

5   Conclusions

In this work we presented an overview of a tool developed in the European project METRIP to design a security system for the protection of an asset of a railway infrastructure system. The tool is based on covering optimization ILP models tested on a railway station. Results show that the usage of optimization based methodologies can effectively support the designer in the definition of a RIS security system.

Acknowledgements. This work is partially supported by the European Commission, Directorate-General Home Affairs, within the Specific Programme on Prevention, Preparedness and Consequence Management of Terrorism and other Security-related risks, under Grant HOME/2010/CIPS/AG/035 METRIP - MEthodological Tools for Railway Infrastructure Protection.

References

1. Jenkins, B.M., Butterworth, B.R.: Explosives and incendiaries used in terrorist attacks on Public Surface Transportation: a preliminary empirical analysis. Mineta Transportation Institute (2010)
2. Butterworth, B.R.: Empirical Data to guide risk mitigation: examples from MTI database. Mineta Transportation Institute National Transportation Security Center (2011)
3. Wilson, J.M., Jackson, B.A., Eisman, M., Steinberg, P., Riley, K.J.: Securing America's Passenger-Rail Systems. Rand Corporation (2007)
4. Murray, A.T., Kim, K., Davis, J.W., Machiraju, R., Parent, R.: Coverage optimization to support security monitoring. Comp., Envir. Urb. Syst. 31(2), 133–147 (2007)
5. Yabuta, K., Kitazawa, H.: Optimum camera placement considering camera specification for security monitoring. In: IEEE Inter. Sym. on Circ. Syst., ISCAS 2008, pp. 2114–2117 (2008)
6. Cole, R., Sharir, M.: Visibility problems for polyhedral terrains. J. Symb. Comp. 7, 11–30 (1989)
7. O'Rourke, J.: Art gallery theorems and algorithms. Oxford University Press, New York (1987)
8. Toregas, C., ReVelle, C., Swain, R., Bergman, L.: The location of emergency service facilities. Oper. Res. 19, 1363–1373 (1971)
9. Church, R., ReVelle, C.: The maximal covering location problem. Papers of the Regional Science Association 32, 101–118 (1974)
10. Hogan, K., ReVelle, C.: Concepts and applications of backup coverage. Man. Scien. 32, 1434–1444 (1986)

Towards Automatic Critical Infrastructure Protection through Machine Learning

Lorena Cazorla, Cristina Alcaraz, and Javier Lopez

Network, Information and Computer Security (NICS) Lab,
University of Malaga, Spain
{lorena,alcaraz,jlm}@lcc.uma.es

Abstract. Critical Infrastructure Protection (CIP) faces increasing challenges in number and in sophistication, which makes vital to provide new forms of protection to face every day's threats. In order to make such protection holistic, covering all the needs of the systems from the point of view of security, prevention aspects and situational awareness should be considered. Researchers and Institutions stress the need of providing intelligent and automatic solutions for protection, calling our attention to the need of providing Intrusion Detection Systems (IDS) with intelligent active reaction capabilities. In this paper, we support the need of automating the processes implicated in the IDS solutions of the critical infrastructures and theorize that the introduction of Machine Learning (ML) techniques in IDS will be helpful for implementing automatic adaptable solutions capable of adjusting to new situations and timely reacting in the face of threats and anomalies. To this end, we study the different levels of automation that the IDS can implement, and outline a methodology to endow critical scenarios with preventive automation. Finally, we analyze current solutions presented in the literature and contrast them against the proposed methodology.

Keywords: Critical Infrastructure Protection, Machine Learning, Intrusion Detection.

1 Introduction

A control system (CS) is a device or set of devices that perform the management and the regulation of behavior of other devices or systems. Examples of such CS are supervisory control and data acquisition (SCADA) systems and distributed control systems (DCS). CS are deployed in multiple types of environments, but when they serve as assistance to infrastructures essential for the well being of the society, they are considered critical control systems, and their good functioning is of paramount importance. In order to protect these systems, different organizations have developed guidelines of protection for the *Critical Infrastructures* (CI)([1] [2]), that manifest the need of offering advanced defense solutions for the CIs in the prevention area. One of the main pillars in this research is the dynamic prevention solutions, such as Intrusion Detection Systems (IDS) [3], capable of complementing prevention with automated action in crisis scenarios.

Traditionally IDS were designed for general-purpose networks, and their application for CIP is not always adequate due to the presence of strict requirements and property

E. Luiijf and P. Hartel (Eds.): CRITIS 2013, LNCS 8328, pp. 197–203, 2013.

communication protocols in the CIs. However, the need of introducing such element in critical contexts has sound support of the scientific community [4] and the institutions [3]. What is more, according to [5] there is a great need for providing these IDS with intelligence and automatic capabilities, in order for them to respond rapidly and efficiently to emergency situations, especially in isolated scenarios. In this paper we therefore theorize that the application of ML techniques would help building the status of preparedness and response for the CIs, constructing intelligent protection systems that are capable of autonomously react against the threats posed to the CIs.

This paper is organized as follows: first we provide an introduction, in Section 2 the concept of automation in the field of detection for CIs is explained, discussing the main advantages of automation through ML. Section 3, provides an analysis of the state-of-the art solutions for IDS in CIP, classifying them according to the automation needs they cover. Finally, the conclusions of this study are provided and future work is outlined.

1.1 Machine Learning Techniques

Learning techniques are varied, and they originate from very different fields of knowledge (e.g. optimization, statistics, logic, etc.). It is interesting to study these methods taking into account characteristics that impose constraints to the underlying system and impact the possibility of introducing them in the context of CIP. It is important to discuss the *knowledge scheme* and the *level of supervision* of the system [6]. The knowledge scheme indicates the level of knowledge that is feed to the system prior to the training: *prior knowledge-based systems* are fed with the knowledge and experience of an expert, *prior knowledge free systems* are based on the knowledge extracted through an automatic (or semi-automatic) procedure of training, the *hybrid knowledge-based systems* add the knowledge of an expert to the model of the system obtained through training. The level of supervision of the system can be divided into: *supervised learning*, where the system has knowledge about the variables learned, and *unsupervised learning*, where no knowledge is provided to the system when training it [6].

According to the level of supervision or implication of the operator in the process of learning, it is possible to categorize the main ML techniques [7] that could result of use in the context of intrusion detection for CIP into *supervised* and *unsupervised* learning methods. In the first category, the main approaches are the *logic-based algorithms*, such as *decision trees*, *rule learners*; the *statistical learning algorithms*, such as the *Bayesian networks*, the *Naïve Bayes* and the *instance-based learners*; and the *artificial neural networks*, such as the *perceptron-based techniques*. Concerning the unsupervised learning methods, the main techniques are *association rule learning* (e.g. *Apriori* algorithm and *FP-growth* algorithm), *clustering* techniques (e.g. the *k-means*), and the *Markov chains*. In Section 3 we will study the IDS solutions available in the literature, and which of these techniques they implement.

2   Levels of Automation of an IDS in CIP

Automation is defined as the introduction of automatic equipment or processes within a system, to assist or replace human operators, mostly when the tasks involved are intensive in computations or the working conditions are extreme. In CIP, there are sub-systems that are usually deployed in distant and isolated locations, where the automation of the tasks is of paramount importance. In this context, there is a proven need [5] [8] of making certain processes automatic, and thus assisting the human operators in these complex tasks. Systems based on automatic methods will be capable of performing automatically, and will serve as powerful tools of *reaction*, providing methods of *prevention of cascading failures*, other than only detection of anomalies and intrusions.

When monitoring critical systems using ML techniques, the concept of automation can be split into four different dimensions: the *automation of the data collection and feeding*, the *automation of the learning process*, the *automation of the detection process*, and in several contexts [3], it is also vital to talk about the *automation of the reaction process*, when the IDS is capable of launching prevention mechanisms automatically as the first response against a detected threat or anomaly. Thus, we define the five levels of automation as a methodology to determine the degree of automation of an IDS:

- *Automation of the data collection*: the collection of the raw data is a process that is inherently automatic, since it involves capturing and recording vast amounts of data involving measurements, logs, etc. for later processing and training.
- *Automation of the data feeding*: comprises the preprocessing, normalizing and preparing the raw data to feed the inputs of the system. This process is difficult, costly and the majority of the real-life systems require the preprocessing of the data to be performed (semi-)manually. It is vital to provide automatic mechanisms with the object to adapt the functioning of ML-based system to face the real-life problems.
- *Automation of the learning process*: the learning process comprises three steps: *training*, *tuning* and *validation*. The training of the system is usually automatic, but the process of tuning and validation normally needs the participation of an operator in order to set the system to a correct functioning for a context. However, learning is performed before the deployment of the system, thus this kind of automation has less impact in the performance of the system.
- *Automation of the detection process*: is vital for the performance of the system, and it is usually referred to a deployed system that has to provide its services in real time. The need to tune the model in a later stage of the deployment of the system can impact negatively the performance of the system. In this case, the need of automation is vital, and the tuning of the models should be at least semi-automatic.
- *Automation of the reaction process*: after detecting any anomaly or intrusion, the system must take appropriate actions to avoid the problem to escalate. According to its nature, the reaction can be: *passive reaction* and *active reaction*. Passive responses are typical in current IDS and include actions such as raising alarms or logging off the system [8]; active responses are those implemented to react against the anomaly or the intrusion in order to avoid the system failure. In CIP, monitoring systems have traditionally implemented passive reaction processes based on sending warnings to the operators and making available the information for them to fix the system. These solutions are mostly semi-automatic and highly dependent on the presence and accuracy of the operators. The scientific community need to focus in

this dimension of the automation, to provide first response mechanisms to prevent failures to cascade through the critical systems in a rapid way [5].

Figure 1 shows the levels of automation of an IDS. For the sake of clarity it is represented as a line, but each step is a cycle of refinement itself. Here is stressed the need of online detection and reaction automation, understanding that preprocessing and learning processes can be performed offline without detriment to the IDS's behavior.

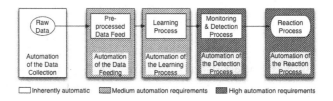

Fig. 1. The needs of online automation of a critical IDS system

3   Analysis of the Current Literature

Learning techniques can be applied to a variety of systems that provide protection for the CI, particularly to IDS solutions [9] [10]. We have surveyed the literature in the search of solutions that provide IDS solutions for CIP, reviewing the characteristics and the degree of automation of each solution. For each of these systems, we analyze the levels of automation provided according to the classification in Section 2. We have summarized our analysis in Table 1, where we can distinguish three different dimensions, namely: *prior-knowledge scheme*, *supervision* and *automation*, that categorize the reviewed systems according to the classification established in this paper.

Düssel et al. [9] present a payload-based anomaly-based network IDS for CIs, capable of monitoring the traffic in real time. The IDS makes use of different techniques, the system extracts the information in the form of vectors, calculates the distance measures of similarity and compares them to a previously learned model of normality, indicating the presence or absence of an anomaly by raising alarms. Roosta et al. [8] introduce an anomaly-based IDS for wireless process control systems. The IDS presented is theoretical, where the detection is based on expert-designed policy rules. Yang et al. [11] present and IDS based on pattern matching, capable of detecting anomalies by analyzing the deviation from normal behavior. They use autoassociative kernel regression models and a sequential probability ration test to discern an attack from the normal behavior. MELISSA [12] is a semantic-level IDS based on FP-Trees [7] that looks for undesirable user actions by processing logs in the SCADA control center. Carcano et al. [13] propose a state-based IDS that use rules to detect complex attack scenarios based on chains of illicit network packets. Autoscopy [14] is an IDS capable of detecting malware that tries to "hijack" pointers and routines of the system; first it learns the behavior of the system and during its operation, it uses statistics to discern anomalous behaviors and raise alarms. D'Antonio et al. present an IDS [10] that implements a rule learner to classify values into normal and attack data, it has a flow monitor component that extract statistical relations between different sessions to refine the learned model. Cheung et al. [15] propose a three-layer IDS that is based on models and patterns of the system designed by an expert. One of the layers implement a Bayesian learning module to detect changes in the availability of the surveilled system. Lin et al. [16] propose a specification-based IDS, that uses the formal specification of the system under surveillance to verify the correct use of the network packets. Raciti et al. present an IDS for Smart Grids [17] based on clustering techniques, for detecting anomalies in the cyber and the physical levels.

In Table 1 is interesting to observe that current systems implement only passive methods of reaction, they usually raise warnings to the operators, and they have to manually perform the inspections, repairs of the systems and help in crisis situations (e.g. voltage peaks in pylons, high pressures in dams, etc.). The main disadvantage of non-automatic systems is that help might arrive too late, and the failures of the system may cascade to other dependent systems, including other interdependent CIs, causing all kinds of havoc. Thus we find it vital that effective measures are taken, to avoid the possible social and economical harm derived from a cascading failure. There must be automatic active reaction processes, maybe based on ML techniques, that are capable of providing effective countermeasures in the face of any kind of anomaly or attack.

Table 1. Review of several systems according to the automation and knowledge dimensions

System	Method	Prior Knowledge	Automation					Technique
			Data Collection	Preprocessing	Learning	Detection	Reaction	
[9]	Sup.	Free	Auto	No	Auto	Auto	Passive	Statistics, ML and Rules
[8]	Sup.	Required	N/A	N/A	N/A	N/A	N/A	Rules
[11]	Sup.	Free	Auto	No	Auto	Auto	Passive	Statistics
[12]	Unsup.	Mixed	Auto	No	Auto	Auto	N/A	Pattern Discovery
[13]	Sup.	Required	N/A	N/A	N/A	Auto	Passive	Rules
[14]	Sup.	Required	Auto	N/A	N/A	Auto	Passive	Rules, Statistics
[10]	Unsup.	Free	Auto	Auto	Auto	Auto	N/A	Statistics, ML and Rules
[15]	Sup.	Required	N/A	N/A	N/A	Auto	Passive	Rules, ML
[16]	N/A	Required	N/A	N/A	N/A	Auto	Passive	Specifications
[17]	Unsup.	Free	Auto	No	Auto	Auto	Passive	Clustering

4 Conclusions

In this paper we support the need of implementing automatic and intelligent IDS in the CIs to create the state of readiness and prevention required by a CI. We defend that the introduction of ML for IDS can lead to autonomous systems capable of actively responding against the threats posed to a CI. To study the automation of IDS, we outline a methodology to evaluate the degree of automation of a given solution and stress the need of automation at the level of active reaction procedures against failures and intrusions. We discuss that the application of ML could be very beneficial to create IDS capable of reacting autonomously to threats. The need of automation has been contrasted with the current literature, describing the degree of automation of the reviewed solutions, and exposing the need of providing active reaction methods, intelligent enough to provide a safe layer of first response for CIs against threats. The methodology for automation and the revision of ML techniques for IDS in critical scenarios lays the foundations for future research and establishes the context for the design of IDS solutions that comply with the identified requirements of automation and intelligence.

Acknowledgments. This work has been partially supported by the EU FP7 project FACIES (HOME/2011/CIPS/AG/4000002115), by the Spanish Ministry of Science and Innovation and FEDER (European Regional Development Fund) through the project SPRINT (TIN 2009-09237), and by the Andalusian government through the project PISCIS (P10-TIC-06334). Additionally, the second author has received funding from the Marie Curie COFUND programme "U-Mobility" co-financed by Universidad de Malaga and the European Community 7th PF under Grant Agreement No. 246550.

References

1. European Commission: COM(2011) 163 Achievements and Next Steps: Towards Global Cyber-Security. Publications Office (2011)
2. European Commission: COM(2009) 149 Protecting Europe from Large Scale Cyber-Attacks and Disruptions: Enhancing Preparedness, Security and Resilience. Publications Office (2009)
3. Scarfone, K., Mell, P.: Guide to Intrusion Detection and Prevention Systems (IDPS). NIST Special Publication SP 800-94 (2012)
4. Chertoff, M.: National Infrastructure Protection Plan. Department of Homeland Security (DHS), Washington (2009)
5. Alcaraz, C., Lopez, J.: Wide-Area Situational Awareness for Critical Infrastructure Protection. IEEE Computer 46(4), 30–37 (2013),
   http://doi.ieeecomputersociety.org/10.1109/MC.2013.72
6. Burbeck, K., Nadjm-Tehrani, S.: Adaptive Real-Time Anomaly Detection with Incremental Clustering. Information Security Technical Report 12(1), 56–67 (2007)
7. Witten, I., Frank, E., Hall, M.: Data Mining: Practical Machine Learning Tools and Techniques. M. Kaufmann (2011)
8. Roosta, T., Nilsson, D., Lindqvist, U., Valdes, A.: An Intrusion Detection System for Wireless Process Control Systems. In: 5th IEEE International Conference on Mobile Ad Hoc and Sensor Systems, MASS 2008, pp. 866–872. IEEE (2008)
9. Düssel, P., Gehl, C., Laskov, P., Bußer, J., Störmann, C., Kästner, J.: Cyber-Critical Infrastructure Protection using Real-Time Payload-Based Anomaly Detection. Critical Information Infrastructures Security, 85–97 (2010)
10. D'Antonio, S., Oliviero, F., Setola, R.: High-Speed Intrusion Detection in Support of Critical Infrastructure Protection. Critical Information Infrastructures Security, 222–234 (2006)
11. Yang, D., Usynin, A., Hines, J.: Anomaly-based Intrusion Detection for SCADA Systems. In: 5th Intl. Topical Meeting on Nuclear Plant Instrumentation, Control and Human Machine Interface Technologies (NPIC&HMIT 2005), pp. 12–16 (2006)
12. Hadziosmanovic, D., Bolzoni, D., Hartel, P., Etalle, S.: MELISSA: Towards Automated Detection of Undesirable User Actions in Critical Infrastructures (2011)
13. Carcano, A., Fovino, I., Masera, M., Trombetta, A.: State-Based Network Intrusion Detection Systems for SCADA Protocols: a Proof of Concept. Critical Information Infrastructures Security, 138–150 (2010)
14. Reeves, J., Ramaswamy, A., Locasto, M., Bratus, S., Smith, S.: Intrusion Detection for Resource-Constrained Embedded Control Systems in the Power Grid. International Journal of Critical Infrastructure Protection (2012)

15. Cheung, S., Dutertre, B., Fong, M., Lindqvist, U., Skinner, K., Valdes, A.: Using Model-based Intrusion Detection for SCADA Networks. In: Proceedings of the SCADA Security Scientific Symposium, pp. 127–134 (2007)
16. Lin, H., Slagell, A., Martino, C.D., Kalbarczyk, Z., Iyer, R.: Adapting Bro into SCADA: Building a Specification-based Intrusion Detection System for the DNP3 Protocol (2012)
17. Raciti, M., Nadjm-Tehrani, S.: Embedded cyber-physical anomaly detection in smart meters. In: Hämmerli, B.M., Kalstad Svendsen, N., Lopez, J. (eds.) CRITIS 2012. LNCS, vol. 7722, pp. 34–45. Springer, Heidelberg (2013)

Using NATO Labelling to Support Controlled Information Sharing between Partners

Sander Oudkerk[1] and Konrad Wrona[2]

[1] Agent Sierra Consultancy Services, Amsterdam, Netherlands
sander.oudkerk@agentsierra.nl
[2] NATO Communications and Information Agency, The Hague, Netherlands
konrad.wrona@ncia.nato.int

Abstract. Protection of critical infrastructure requires collaboration between various stakeholders, including military, governmental and private organizations. The stakeholders are typically located in different information security domains or even different countries. We present a content labelling solution developed by NATO for the purpose of enabling information sharing between different communities of interest and coalition participants in NATO operations. We believe that the same solution can be used to support the enforcement of fine-grained access control for the protection of critical infrastructures. The focus of this paper is on the binding of sensitivity-marking metadata (i.e. 'labelling') to data objects, and the application of granular access control to labelled data objects. We provide an example of how access control can be efficiently enforced on portions of an XML document while preserving the essential parts of the XML structure of the document.

Keywords: Cross-domain information exchange, labelling, XML.

1 Introduction

Information sharing has been identified as an essential enabler for the protection of critical infrastructures, yet the realization of secure information sharing presents a substantial challenge [1]. Subsequent studies have identified the need to distinguish between different sensitivity levels of the shared information, and for trust enablers between the collaborating parties [2, 3]. Several approaches have been proposed for the negotiation of trust and security policies that enable fine-grained access control [4, 5]. Other work has focused on the development of standardized languages for the exchange of specific information [6]. All these approaches are based on the assumption that the required metadata and sensitivity markings are bound to the exchanged data objects. In this paper we present *NATO Labelling* (NL), a standardized approach to binding metadata to data objects that was developed by NATO in support of information sharing between different communities of interest (COIs) and coalition participants in NATO operations. In the context of critical infrastructure protection, COIs and coalitions can be seen as different groups of commercial and governmental partners collaborating towards common protection

E. Luiijf and P. Hartel (Eds.): CRITIS 2013, LNCS 8328, pp. 204–211, 2013.

goals. NL allows for the binding of any type of metadata to any type of data object and is therefore suitable for deployment between COIs that use different data (and metadata) formats and associated labelling solutions internally. Note that NL includes the definition of a syntax for a sensitivity label, however any kind of sensitivity label can be bound using the NL binding mechanism. Also, NL does not prescribe any specific label values (which are in fact defined by the COI involved). The application of NL is flexible in the sense that it does not require an existing label to be removed, and also allows for the inclusion of an alternative label (i.e. the 'local interpretation' of a label from a different COI). When enforcing release control as part of an information sharing solution it is essential to be able to exactly determine to which part of a data object a label pertains. To this purpose NL defines clear binding semantics for its binding mechanism. Because NL is flexible, in both its support for any type of label and data object as well its applicability, we believe that NL can be used to support the enforcement of fine-grained access control policies for critical infrastructure protection.

2   NL: A Standardized Approach to Labelling Data Objects

NATO Labelling (NL) is a standardized approach to labelling data objects that allows any type of (finite) data object to be labelled[1] with any type of metadata. If data objects are formatted in XML, granular access control becomes possible by labelling subsets of the XML tree. The development of NL was driven by the operational requirement to exchange information between different information domains and the need for a standardized cross-domain information exchange solution.

NL provides for a standardized sensitivity label format, a standardized binding mechanism and standardized binding semantics. NL is not intended to replace existing COI-specific labelling techniques when COIs have no requirement for cross-COI information sharing, however it was designed to provide a solution when interoperability between COIs is required with respect to the labelling of data and the interpretation of labels and binding. NL was designed to meet the following conditions:

- The use of NL must not imply a modification of existing data formats.
- The evolution of data formats must be independent of NL, e.g. a change in data format must not imply a change to the standardized sensitivity label format and vice versa.
- Various data formats must be accommodated (hence realizing a binding by embedding a sensitivity label in the data object is not a valid approach).
- The binding must be verifiable by an access control decision function (ACDF) without the ACDF having to support the data format or the application that generated the data.

---

[1] In this paper the verb 'to label' is understood to mean the process of selecting metadata, structuring the metadata in a label, and binding the label to a data object.

As a result, the sensitivity label and binding are defined as separate data elements, their format is independent of the format of the data object that is labelled, and the binding describes the relationship between the sensitivity label and the data object in a standardized way, independent of the data format and the application that generated the data. Having a standardized binding is important because in order to enforce access control it must be clear to which data object a sensitivity label applies.

Note that the method of NL is generic in the sense that it supports the binding of any type of metadata to any type of data object. Also, it is not required that an automated function that processes the label and binding provide support for the data format of the labelled data object or the information that it represents. However, in the case of granular access control, the ACDF must support the format of the data object in the sense that the ACDF must be able to select the portion of a data object to which the label pertains, and enforce an access control decision on this portion (e.g. remove a paragraph from a document).

In NL the sensitivity label and the binding are formatted in XML. This means that for data objects that are formatted in XML, it is possible to embed the sensitivity label and binding. Note that if the sensitivity label and binding are stored separately from the data object, e.g. in a central repository, the information management architecture must facilitate the retrieval of the sensitivity label and binding by an ACDF.

Note that in NL the term 'confidentiality label' is used in favour of 'sensitivity label'. In this paper 'confidentiality label' and 'sensitivity label' are interchangeable. NL is based on [7], and currently the description of NL is contained in two documents [8, 9] that contain profiles of the specifications in [7] and extend these specifications:

- The first document [8] contains a NATO profile for the XML confidentiality label syntax (XCLS) [7] that specifies the use of XML elements, attributes and their allowed values for use within NATO. The profile also extends the XCLS from [7] with additional elements.
- The second document [9] contains a NATO profile for the binding of metadata to data objects that specifies a method (and associated binding semantics) for labelling XML-formatted data objects to support granular access control while maximizing information sharing (called *top-down XML labelling*). [9] also specifies the semantics of the binding of metadata to XML nodes, and contains a NATO profile for the use of XMLDsig [10] for realizing a strong binding. Finally [9] introduces the notion of a Binding Information File (BIF) and considerations related to its management.

In NL a binding is realized by making the metadata and data object XML siblings (with parent called *MetadataBinding*). Metadata and data object can be included as separate nodes or as references identified by means of a Uniform Resource Identifier (URI). The binding is captured in a BIF. The use of a reference mechanism is common if metadata or data objects are not formatted in XML or if a deliberate choice is made not to include either or both in the BIF. A cryptographic binding is realized based on XMLDsig in which case the BIF also includes a *Signature* element. An example of a BIF is provided in **Fig. 1**. If a data object is formatted in XML it becomes possible to embed the BIF in the data object. An advantage of using a URI is that metadata can be bound to any data object that can be identified by a URI, but also to a directory on a file system or an entire web server.

XML data objects: For XML data objects the reference mechanism is extended to include the use of the XML Path (XPath) [11] and the XML Pointer (XPointer) [12] languages so that subsets of a data object's XML tree can be selected and metadata can be bound to portions of an XML data object (making granular access control possible).

In order to properly enforce access control there must be no ambiguity regarding the binding between confidentiality label and data object. For the purposes of this paper it is sufficient to state that when an XML node is labelled, the confidentiality label pertains to all nodes in the XPath node-set comprising the labelled XML node.

Note that an XML element node is always labelled explicitly by executing the NL binding mechanism and it never inherits its classification from one of its child nodes (i.e. the classification of a child node does not influence the classification of its parent). This is a deliberate choice that is based on the assumption that not all security policies identify a hierarchical relationship between classifications. This choice also allows a more efficient approach to granular access control, as illustrated by the method of *Top-down XML labelling* (see below).

Non-XML data objects: If the data object is not in XML format the sensitivity label applies to the information represented by the data object as well as the (file) structure of the data object. For example, if a PDF file is labelled, the access control decision is made for the PDF file and not only for its contents.

Other uses of the URI reference mechanism: Note that the binding semantics have to be defined for each distinct use of the URI reference mechanism. For example, if a sensitivity label is bound to a directory on a web server, it must be defined whether or not the sensitivity label applies to each individual data object that is stored in the directory, or only to the logical container the directory itself represents.

Traditional approach to labelling: The 'traditional approach' to labelling data objects is to apply the method that is followed when marking human-readable documents. This method determines the overall sensitivity marking of a document to be equal to the most restrictive sensitivity marking that is applied to any part of the document. Often, the overall sensitivity marking is a result of a recursive process in which sections are assigned a sensitivity marking equal to the most restrictive marking applied to any of its paragraphs, and chapters are assigned a sensitivity marking equal to the most restrictive marking applied to any of its sections. If the traditional approach to labelling is taken in labelling an XML-formatted data object, a parent element node is assumed to take on the most restrictive sensitivity marking of its children (recursively up to the root of the XML tree).

This traditional approach to labelling has the disadvantage that flexible granular access control (e.g. at the paragraph level) cannot easily be enforced without fully analyzing the document (which would be needed to determine which paragraphs are motivating the overall sensitivity marking).

Top-down XML labelling: This method of labelling supports granular access control and is based on the following rules:

- Rule 1: When a node is labelled, its descendant nodes (if any) inherit the label of the parent, i.e. they also become labelled.
- Rule 2: When an element node is labelled, the label will be inherited by its namespace and attribute nodes.
- Rule 3: When a labelled node is re-labelled, either directly or because one of its ancestors is (re-)labelled, it will keep all labels. In other words, a label is never replaced and such a node will have multiple labels associated to it. All labels will be evaluated independently by the ACDF. Access to the node is blocked when one of the labels is in conflict with the access control policy (ACP).
- Rule 4: Parent nodes that are required to preserve the structure of the XML document and of which the expanded name or (child) text nodes do not carry an explicit classification are labelled in such a way that the ACDF will apply the most relaxed ACP.

An immediate result of Rule 1 and Rule 3 is that if, based on the ACP, an ACDF cannot provide access to a parent node, it will also block access to its descendants regardless of their labels. Rule 2 is needed to cover XPath nodes that do not formally have a parent, i.e. attribute and namespace nodes (as opposed to requiring a separate assignment of a label to such nodes using XPath transformations. However a separate assignment can still be made in order to 're-label' these nodes if necessary.) In general the inheritance of labels (as formulated in Rule 1 and Rule 2) is required so that ACDFs that require all data to be labelled can enforce an ACP based on the label instead of blocking access by default.

The result of Rule 4 is that the XML tree is 'labelled from the root element node to the bottom nodes' starting with the most relaxed label (i.e. based on which an ACDF will apply the most relaxed policy). The underlying idea is that the XML structure should always be preserved (e.g. a child node cannot exist without its parent). Note that the target application that renders the actual file from the XML, and which presents the document to the end-user, must in fact determine the overall sensitivity marking (taking into account the hierarchy of classification levels if applicable). In the remainder of this document the method of XML labelling by which the XML tree is 'labelled from the root element node to the bottom nodes' starting with the most relaxed label is referred to as 'top-down XML labelling'.

The process of enforcing granular access control on an XML data object can be visualized as the ACDF descending down all branches in the XML tree (and providing access to its nodes) until it reaches a node that has a label that is in conflict with the ACP, to which it will consequently block access (by not descending further down the tree).

Fig. 1. shows an example of how shortname XPointers can be used to bind a confidentiality label 'MOCK RESTRICTED' to a portion of a file 'example.xml'[2]. In this example, the result of the binding mechanism is a separate BIF. Assume that only the first paragraph of example.xml is 'MOCK RESTRICTED' and that all other nodes are 'MOCK UNCLASSIFIED' or carry no explicit classification.

---

[2] The XML-formatted confidentiality labels that are used in the examples are not compliant with the NL XML confidentiality label syntax and only serve to illustrate the method of 'top-down XML labelling'.

```
<?xml version="1.0" encoding="UTF-8"?>
<Document>
  <Introduction>...</Introduction>
  <Chapter>
    <Section>
      <Paragraph Id="para-1">...</Paragraph>
      <Paragraph>...</Paragraph>
    </Section>
    <Section>...</Section>
  </Chapter>
</Document>
```

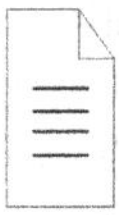

http://
www.someser
ver.net/
example.xml

```
<?xml version="1.0" encoding="UTF-8"?>
<BindingInformation>
  <MetadataBindingContainer>
    <MetadataBinding>
      <Metadata>
        <ConfidentialityLabel>
          <ConfidentialityInformation>
            <PolicyIdentifier>MOCK</PolicyIdentifier>
            <Classification>UNCLASSIFIED</Classification>
          </ConfidentialityInformation>
        </ConfidentialityLabel>
      </Metadata>
      <DataReference URI="http://www.someserver.net/
      example.xml"/>
    </MetadataBinding>
    <MetadataBinding>
      <Metadata>
        <ConfidentialityLabel>
          <ConfidentialityInformation>
            <PolicyIdentifier>MOCK</PolicyIdentifier>
            <Classification>RESTRICTED</Classification>
          </ConfidentialityInformation>
        </ConfidentialityLabel>
      </Metadata>
      <DataReference URI="http://www.someserver.net/
      example.xml#para-1"/>
    </MetadataBinding>
  </MetadataBindingContainer>
</BindingInformation>
```

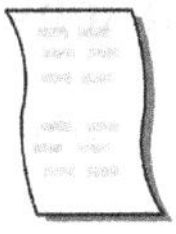

BIF

Fig. 1. XML instances of *example.xml* and the BIF

Top-down XML labelling is realized as follows:

- By Rule 4, the root element node is given the default label 'MOCK UNCLASSIFIED'.
- Then, by Rule 1, all child nodes of the root element node are now labelled 'MOCK UNCLASSIFIED' (and hence, recursively, the whole XML document).
- Then, by giving the restricted paragraph an XML Id value of 'para-1', a shortname XPointer can be used to select the paragraph node with Id="para-1" which is then bound to the label 'MOCK RESTRICTED' (i.e. it is re-labelled).

Note that if an element node with attribute Id="para-1" is selected it is assumed that the label is bound to all nodes in the XPath node-set comprising that element node (e.g. including attribute nodes). By Rule 3, the paragraph with XML Id="para-1" has two labels bound to it that are independently evaluated by an ACDF. An ACDF that enforces an ACP that blocks access to information that is labelled 'MOCK RESTRICTED' will therefore block access to the paragraph (e.g. a guard will remove this paragraph before releasing the associated document to the low domain).

XPath transformations can be used instead of or in addition to shortname XPointers and the principle of top-down XML labelling remains the same. As opposed to the use of shortname XPointers, XPath transformations do not depend on uniqueness of XML Id values and provide more control over the selection of XPath node-sets. For example, more than one node can be selected and selection is not limited to element nodes. In most cases however shortname XPointers will suffice.

3   Conclusions and Way Forward to Adopting NL

NATO Labelling (NL), a standardized approach to labelling data objects, allows for the binding of any type of metadata to any type of data object, and enables granular access control on XML data objects. NL includes the definition of a syntax for an XML-formatted sensitivity label, however any kind of sensitivity label can be bound using the NL binding mechanism. Also, NL does not prescribe specific label values (which are defined by the COI involved). When it is not possible to agree on common syntax and values for a sensitivity label, NL provides interoperability through the use of an alternative label. Based on bilateral agreements between COIs, an external COI label can be mapped into a local equivalent label and bound as an alternative label while retaining the original external COI label. The NL approach can be adopted by any community that has a requirement to label data objects or to bind a more elaborate mutually agreed ACP to data objects when exchanging information with collaborators. The NCI Agency has successfully deployed a cross-domain information exchange solution based on the use of NL in operational theatres. We believe that a similar solution can improve the protection of critical infrastructures.

For COIs that require a migration path to the use of NL, an intermediate solution can be realized in which an NL-compliant BIF can co-exist with COI-specific labels. This can be achieved for both XML and non-XML data objects. In certain information exchange scenarios it may also be possible to add the BIF to a higher layer in the protocol stack, e.g. for simple object access protocol (SOAP)-based information exchange [13]. For SOAP-based information exchange the BIF can be generated based on the COI-specific label, and then stored in the SOAP header. It is possible to choose which part of the (XML-formatted) SOAP message is covered by the binding: the original data object that is present in the SOAP body, or a bigger subset of the SOAP message. An approach to including an NL XML confidentiality label in the header of e-mail messages is detailed in [14].

The use of separate (detached) BIFs requires an information management infrastructure in which storage of and access to such BIFs is facilitated. A way of making detached BIFs accessible that is less dependent on the information management infrastructure is to package data object and associated BIF together in an Open Packaging Convention (OPC) container-file [15].

Labelling of data objects in support of granular access control in the current version of NL is defined for XML data objects only. The principle of the binding mechanism however can be extended to realize the labelling of subsets of other structured data formats such as JSON (see [16]). The NCI Agency is currently investigating the development of an NL OPC profile and the application of NL to JSON.

To facilitate the adoption of NATO Labelling, the NCI Agency designed the NATO Metadata Binding Service (NMBS, [17]), which can, on behalf of a user (or other entity), label data objects. The NMBS is designed to make metadata catalogues available to users, generate NL confidentiality labels on request and create (and sign) the BIF.

References

1. Gallagher, S., Neugebauer, M.: Critical Infrastructure Information Sharing. In: IEEE International Conference on Technologies for Homeland Security (2004)
2. The National Association of Regulatory Utility Commissioners: 2007 Information Sharing Practices in Regulated Critical Infrastructure States (2007)
3. Zhao, W., White, G.: A collaborative information sharing framework for Community Cyber Security. In: IEEE Conference on Technologies for Homeland Security (2012)
4. Ryutov, T., Kichkaylo, T., Neches, R., Orosz, M.: SFINKS: Secure focused information, news, and knowledge sharing. In: IEEE International Conference on Technologies for Homeland Security (2008)
5. Braghin, S., Fovino, I.N., Trombetta, A.: Advanced trust negotiation in critical infrastructures. In: 1st International Conference on Infrastructure Systems and Services (2008)
6. Flentge, F., Beyel, C., Rome, E.: Towards a standardised cross-sector information exchange on present risk factors. Critical Information Infrastructures Security (2008)
7. Oudkerk, S., Bryant, I., Eggen, A., Haakseth, R.: A Proposal for an XML Confidentiality Label Syntax and Binding of Metadata to Data Objects. In: NATO RTO Symposium on Information Assurance and Cyber Defence (2010)
8. Oudkerk, S., Lunt, G., Ross, A.: NATO Profile for the XML Confidentiality Label Syntax – Version 1.1, NCIA, The Hague, Netherlands (2013)
9. Oudkerk, S., Lunt, G., Ross, A.: NATO Profile for the Binding of Metadata to Data Objects – Version 1.1, NCIA, The Hague, Netherlands (2013)
10. W3C: XML Signature Syntax and Processing, 2nd edn., http://www.w3.org/TR/xmldsig-core/
11. W3C XSL Working Group and W3C XML Query Working Group: XML Path Language (XPath) 2.0, 2nd edn (2010)
12. W3C XML Linking Working Group: XPointer Framework (2003)
13. Oudkerk, S.: NATO Cross-Domain Web Services Experiment at CWID 2007, NC3A, The Hague, Netherlands (2008)
14. Zeilenga, K., Melnikov, A.: Security Labels in Internet Email, draft-zeilenga-email-seclabel-05, IETF (2013)
15. ECMA: ECMA-376: Office Open XML File Formats, Part2: Open Packaging Conventions, 4th edn (2012)
16. ECMA: ECMA-262: ECMAScript Language Specification, 5.1 edn (2011)
17. Lunt, G., Oudkerk, S., Ross, A.: NATO Metadata Binding Service, NCIA, The Hague, Netherlands (2012)

A Framework for Privacy Protection and Usage Control of Personal Data in a Smart City Scenario

Gianmarco Baldini, Ioannis Kounelis, Igor Nai Fovino, and Ricardo Neisse

Joint Research Center (JRC)
Institute for the Protection and Security of the Citizen (IPSC)
Ispra, Italy
{gianmarco.baldini,ioannis.kounelis,igor.nai-fovino,
ricardo.neisse}@jrc.ec.europa.eu

Abstract. In this paper we address trust and privacy protection issues related to identity and personal data provided by citizens in a smart city environment. Our proposed solution combines identity management, trust negotiation, and usage control. We demonstrate our solution in a case study of a smart city during a crisis situation.

Keywords: Identity management, privacy protection, usage control, smart cities, trust negotiation.

1 Introduction

Digital identity is a concept that prevails in the domains of cyberspace, and it is defined as a set of data that uniquely describes a person or a thing and contains information about the subject's relationships to other entities The concept of digital identity has been extended recently with a sort of "inheritance principle": in smart home environments users configure their devices using their own credentials, giving these devices full rights to operate as if they are the users themselves; the same principle can be applied considering the more extended scenario of a *Smart City* where the identity is the enabler allowing to citizens and smart-objects to interacts. On one hand the digital pervasiveness of smart-objects raises several concerns related to the potential impact of cyber-threats on the citizen's daily life, on the other hand the presence of "on-line" smart devices might result extremely precious in case of emergency and crisis management.

Aim of this work is to propose a framework allowing to minimizes the privacy risks and increases the citizen control over their data and identity while allowing at the same time to rescue and crisis management forces to exploit the features of smart-cities and homes to timely deploy emergency plans and strategies.

2 Related Work

Yang et al. [1] show how IoT can support emergency support operations. In contrast to their work we go one step further and address privacy and security

E. Luiijf and P. Hartel (Eds.): CRITIS 2013, LNCS 8328, pp. 212–217, 2013.

issues that are of up most relevance for all entities in an IoT scenario. Du and Zhu [2] investigate the application of IoT to crisis management by presenting a layered architecture where various IoT technologies can be used. In their work it is underlined that security and privacy are an important aspect that must be addressed in an IoT system.

Vescoukis et al. [3] propose a flexible architecture for planning and decision support in environmental crisis management based on service oriented and geospatial technologies. Their framework is quite sophisticated but does not address issues of security of privacy nor does it provide trust capabilities.

A recent paper by Smari et al. [4] investigates aspects of trust and privacy in collaborative management systems used for crisis management. The paper presents an extended access control model based on attributes associated with objects and subjects to address trust and privacy issues.

3   Trusted Usage Framework

As stated in the introduction the proposed framework should enable end-users to have full control on the information in possession of their smart-devices while at the same time provide rescue forces with the capability of taking advantage of the pervasiveness of those systems in emergency cases. A similar framework should take in consideration three main concepts: (1) **Digital-Identity**, as to access the smart-devices would be needed to provide some sort of identity-proof; (2) **Trust**, as considering the potential invasiveness of emergency actions, a sort of process to establish the level of trust of a counterpart asking to a smart-device to provide information or to act in an unplanned way, is needed to define who is entitled to do what at every time; (3) **Usage Control**, to ensure that the data (or the right) obtained will be used only in the way defined by a certain policy. For example, to ensure that *all the data obtained during an emergency on a certain set of citizens is not misused*)

3.1   Identity

According to the standard ISO/IEC 24760 a digital identity is defined as "a set of attributes related to an entity", where *entity* refers to an individual, an organization, or a device. Attributes are properties of the entity (e.g. address, phone number etc.). Digital identities can be categorized according to the security level adopted in the registration and authentication phases (*Hard* and *Soft* electronic identity (e-id)). As in this paper we concentrate our attention on the Trust and Usage Control framework, we'll not enter in details related to the crypto-schema adopted here to generate the digital-identities. What we assume is that citizens are provided with a strong digital-identity (issued by governmental agencies) and that are able to generate, starting from these strong e-IDs a number of soft-identities.

3.2   Trust Negotiation

A Trust negotiation is an interactive process between two parties having the goal of establishing mutual trust to release a given resource or a part of it, considering the trust level achieved. In our case, a similar negotiation is needed to allow entities, such as smart-devices, rescue authorities, and end-users, to automatically identify the level of trust of the counterpart. After the level of trust is identified, they can decide if a certain request, either for information or action, should be granted or partially allowed. To our purposes we adopted the Trust-$\mathcal{X}$[5] schema as it appears to be to our knowledge the most suitable for our needs. In particular it was designed on the principle that two parties can establish trust directly without involving trusted third parties, other than credential issuers and it was specifically designed for a P2P environment.

3.3   Usage Control

Usage control extends access control with the concept of obligations, which specifies constrains on the use of data after access is granted. In our solution we apply an usage control framework [6] that supports the specification of policies using mechanisms according to an Event-Condition-Action (ECA) rule structure. These mechanisms have their *Action* part executed when an *Event* pattern is observed and the *Condition* expression evaluates to true.

From a usage control perspective, our mechanisms can be used to specify authorization and obligations without any changes. Authorizations are essentially mechanisms specifies by domain administrators to be enforced on their own domains. Obligations are mechanisms specified by domain administrators that are delegated to other domains when interactions that exchange sensitive data take place.

In contrast to existing frameworks for access and usage control our usage control framework is more expressive and can express complex authorizations and obligations. For example, using existing access control languages such as XACML [7] a policy stating that access should be denied to users after three unsuccessful logins can not be expressed because XACML does not support cardinality operators.

3.4   Framework General Overview

In this section we provide a a functional view of our Trusted Usage Framework (TUF) (see Fig. 1) using the building blocks described in the previous subsections. We identify two phases in the operation of the framework: a *setup phase* in which the owner of an hard e-id builds using a soft e-id generator a set of soft e-ids which will be left as inheritance to the smart-devices owned by the user, and an *operational phase* in which the smart-device is called to interact with the external world and provide information/services according to a set of policies.

More in details, this last phase is articulated as follows: (1) An external entity (EA) requests access to information or to execute an operation by the smart-device; the smart device (2) prior to provide what requested, engages with the

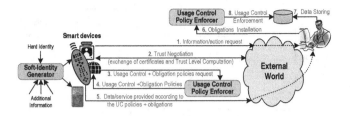

Fig. 1. Framework Functional Overview

external entity a trust negotiation. (3) A level of trust is associated to the external entity and the smart-device then interrogates the *Usage Control Policy Enforcer* (UCPE) asking for instructions on what to provide to the external party on the basis of the level of trust established. (4) The UCPE provides the corresponding disclosure/execution policy and a set of obligations and the smart device (5) executes what permitted and sends a set of obligations to the EA. (6) The EA enforces the obligations, stores the data received (7) and the EA's UCPE monitor the usage of the data obtained according to the new obligations received (8). It is important to notice that the information is provided to the requesting party only when the requester's UCPE would provide acknowledgement on the installation of the obligations.

4   Smart City Case Study

Using our framework, the smart city environment is used to support first time responders in the protection of citizens' life during a crisis situation without harming the citizens' privacy. A smart city environment is equipped with sensors and actuators owned by different entities and are not fully under control of the first time responders team. The citizens themselves may also own sensors at their smart homes that can provide important support during the crisis.

The crisis situation we address in our case study illustrate the application of our framework after an accidental IED (Improvised Explosive Device) explosion that disperses a highly toxic and persistent liquid (sulphur mustard) and starts a fire in a building. During the handling of the crisis *Public Safety Officers* (PSOs) must know the resources (e.g. water, energy) available in the area and have the capabilities to inform the responsible parties about their needs to handle the crisis. These resources or specific information (e.g. plans of building) may not be usually available to PSOs, who can be granted higher authority to access such resources and data in case of the crisis. In most cases, such information is of sensitive nature and it should not be accessed by unauthorized parties during and after the crisis. PSOs may also retrieve sensitive sensor information from smart homes in the area of the crisis and manage some aspects of the home.

We model our case study using an existing generic design language to represent the architecture of a distributed system across application domains and levels of abstraction called Interaction System Design Language (ISDL) [8]. In the

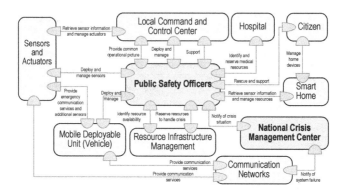

Fig. 2. Entities interactions

analysis of our case study we designed the model of the smart city (and the interactions among the Use Case's actors) using ISDL (Fig. 2).

Each interaction depicted requires a level of trust that is negotiated during the initialization phase of the interaction. The established level of trust after the negotiation authorizes the successful completion of the interaction, which possibly implies the execution of an operation and/or exchange of sensitive data. In order to govern the authorization to execute the operation or access to the sensitive data we apply the usage control module of our framework. Furthermore, we exchange with the interacting parties obligation policies that regulate how the data exchanged should be used. Trust levels, their corresponding authorization policies, and obligations must be specified for each interaction considering their impact and sensitivity.

As claimed before, the presented approach, together with the model in Fig. 2 would find a natural application in a crisis scenario. Let assume that a IED explosion in a building occurred in a crowded area of a "Smart City". In that case the TU framework would allow to the rescue forces to: (a) Check the available sensors in the area for known damages, risks, and dangers; (b) Reserve part of the city resources (e.g. energy, water, hospital and doctor availability etc.) to manage the crisis; (c) Access directly to reserved information as building plans, number of people in a certain home etc. ; (e) Provide direct support to the citizens guiding them through their mobile devices, or asking to them to contribute in filling the crisis knowledge base using as remote interface their mobile phones. The framework would ensure the rapid access to relevant information guaranteeing at the same time the preservation of privacy and usage rights, thanks to a set of well defined and strict policies.

5   Conclusion and Future Work

Smart-devices are becoming the repositories of a huge amount of information related to the personal life of the citizen and, in some case, they might have a critical role when called to perform actions impacting on the citizen's life. For that reason there is a strong need for mechanisms allowing to create a chain of trust and to regulate the possible actions that smart-devices can perform. In this paper we presented a framework that, by integrating the concepts of *identity inheritance*, *Trust Negotiation* and *Usage Control*, provides the citizen with a powerful mean to control and regulate the use that smart-devices can do of his personal information. Moreover, we presented a use case to show how a similar framework would be extremely useful to manage emergencies and crisis under a Smart-City context. For the future, we aim at deploying the framework on a real case scenario, to further demonstrate its feasibility and usefulness, and to deeply study cyber-security implications.

References

1. Yang, L., Yang, S., Plotnick, L.: How the internet of things technology enhances emergency response operations. Technological Forecasting and Social Change (2012)
2. Du, C., Zhu, S.: Research on urban public safety emergency management early warning system based on technologies for the internet of things. Procedia Engineering 45, 748–754 (2012); 2012 International Symposium on Safety Science and Technology
3. Vescoukis, V., Doulamis, N., Karagiorgou, S.: A service oriented architecture for decision support systems in environmental crisis management. Future Generation Computer Systems 28(3), 593–604 (2012)
4. Smari, W.W., Clemente, P., Lalande, J.F.: An extended attribute based access control model with trust and privacy: Application to a collaborative crisis management system. Future Generation Computer Systems (2013)
5. Braghin, S., Fovino, I., Trombetta, A.: Advanced trust negotiation in critical infrastructures. In: 2008 First International Conference on Infrastructure Systems and Services: Building Networks for a Brighter Future (INFRA), pp. 1–6 (2008)
6. Neisse, R., Pretschner, A., Giacomo, V.D.: A trustworthy usage control enforcement framework. In: Proceedings 6th International Conference on Availability, Reliability and Security, ARES (2011)
7. Rissanen, E.: Extensible access control markup language v3.0 (2010), http://docs.oasis-open.org
8. Dijkman, R.: Consistency in multi-viewpoint architectural design. PhD Thesis University of Twente (2006), https://doc.novay.nl

Author Index